Praise for *Your Defiant Teen*

"[This] comprehensive defiance-busting system helps parents define and assess the problem. . . . Without placing blame, the authors reveal that parents often unwittingly make a bad situation worse; the text gives solid tips on how to work toward a positive outcome and offers a variety of scenarios, demonstrating precisely how a parent's words and actions can be the source of a teen's compliant or defiant response. In the end, the authors offer a useful and detailed approach that respects the rights and expectations of parents and teens."—*Publishers Weekly*

"Extremely thorough and readable. . . . Much more detailed and parent-oriented than [others], this will be . . . much in demand. This book is written for parents seeking relief from the stress of living with an arrogant, aggressive, or noncompliant son or daughter. . . . Parents learn how to insist that their kids exhibit appropriate behavior for family life, school, and work."—*Library Journal*

"The transition from adolescence to adulthood can be tough as teens attempt to assert their independence. Now in an updated second edition, this is a very welcome, current resource that helps you guide your teen through difficult times. *Your Defiant Teen* has been—and will continue to be—the first book I recommend to parents struggling with challenging teens."—Sam Goldstein, PhD, coauthor of *Angry Children, Worried Parents*

"Here it is—a book that provides insights into your teen's behavior and a game plan for addressing it! This step-by-step guide can produce a stunning turnaround by helping you focus on the positive and strike that necessary balance between monitoring your teen and fostering independence."—Sharon K. Weiss, MEd, coauthor of *From Chaos to Calm: Effective Parenting of Challenging Children with ADHD and Other Behavioral Problems*

"Since the first edition of this book was published, growing evidence shows that the authors' program works. The second edition incorporates lessons learned from continuing research while maintaining the practical, warm, and supportive approach. Without placing blame, the authors help you understand your teen's behavior and explain 10 clear steps for creating positive change by improving the ways you interact."—Torrey A. Creed, PhD, Department of Psychiatry, University of Pennsylvania

Your Defiant Teen

For more information, visit Dr. Barkley's website:
www.russellbarkley.org

Your Defiant Teen

10 Steps to Resolve Conflict and Rebuild Your Relationship

SECOND EDITION

Russell A. Barkley, PhD
Arthur L. Robin, PhD

with Christine M. Benton

THE GUILFORD PRESS
New York   London

© 2014 The Guilford Press
A Division of Guilford Publications, Inc.
72 Spring Street, New York, NY 10012
www.guilford.com

Printed in the United States of America

This book is printed on acid-free paper.

Last digit is print number: 9 8 7 6 5 4 3 2

Library of Congress Cataloging-in-Publication Data

Barkley, Russell A., 1949–
    Your defiant teen : 10 steps to resolve conflict and rebuild your
    relationship / Russell A. Barkley and Arthur L. Robin with
    Christine M. Benton. — Second Edition.
        pages cm
    Includes bibliographical references and index.
    ISBN 978-1-4625-1166-2 (pbk. : alk. paper)
    ISBN 978-1-4625-1230-0 (hardcover : alk. paper)
    1. Problem youth—Behavior modification. 2. Oppositional defiant
disorder in adolescence. 3. Parent and teenager. 4. Child rearing.
I. Robin, Arthur L. II. Benton, Christine M. III. Title.
[DNLM: 1. Behavior therapy.]
HQ796.B2765 2014
649′.125—dc23
                                                                    2013042801

In memory of my twin brother,
Ronald F. Barkley (1949–2006),
and my nephew Ethan Barkley (1983–2013),
whose presence in my life is dearly missed

—R. A. B.

To my wife, Susan,
whose love and friendship inspire me daily

—A. L. R.

Contents

Purchasers may download and print selected practical tools
from this book at *www.guilford.com/barkley16-forms*

Acknowledgments

I would like to acknowledge the substantial contributions of my coauthors, Art Robin and Chris Benton, without whose assistance this joint product would have been impossible. I am also grateful to The Guilford Press "family" for once more supporting my publishing efforts, as it has over the past 33 years. Special thanks to Nina Hnatov and Anna Brackett for seeing this book successfully through the copyediting and production process. As always, I am grateful to my wife, Pat, and sons, Steve and Ken, for their support of my professional activities.

—RUSSELL A. BARKLEY, PhD

I wish to acknowledge a number of special individuals, without whose support and assistance this book could not have been written: my coauthors, Russ Barkley and Chris Benton, who made the writing of this book a fulfilling and fun experience; Dr. David Rosenberg, Chairman of the Child Psychiatry and Psychology Department at Children's Hospital of Michigan and the Psychiatry and Behavioral Neurosciences Department at Wayne State University, whose support made it possible for me to take the time to write the book; our editors at The Guilford Press; the many families with whom I have worked and from whom I am constantly learning new things about defiant behavior; and my wife, Susan, who provided unending support and love.

—Arthur L. Robin, PhD

Many thanks to Russ Barkley and Art Robin for their boundless knowledge, insight, patience, and humor. And to everyone at Guilford for their support and dedication to publishing, especially Bob Matloff, Seymour Weingarten, Kitty Moore, Marian Robinson, Anne Patota, Judith Grauman, Paul Gordon, and Anna Brackett.

—Christine M. Benton

Introduction

Slam.

That's the sound of teenage defiance.

You may be hearing it on a regular basis when your son storms out the door following yet another battle of wills. Or perhaps you imagine it every day as you wait in dread for your daughter to decide that walling herself off in hostile silence at home no longer puts enough distance between her and you. Either way, it's a frightening noise. It's hard enough to deal with your home being turned into a battleground. Agonizing over what might happen to a son or daughter you can no longer control can keep you up at night and break your heart.

This book is about how you can become a positive influence in your teenager's environment again rather than just part of the place your son or daughter chose to slam the door on. It's about how you can get your teen to follow the nonnegotiable rules for living in a civilized family—and how you can learn to negotiate the rest of the issues you have with your teenager. It's about shedding those entrenched beliefs about each other—"He's *purposely* baiting me!"; "You never let me do *anything* with my friends, as if I'm, like, *10*!"—that only end in no-win battles. It's about giving teenagers skills that will enable them to achieve successful adulthood and serve them well for a lifetime—about getting to the point where you might hear "So, how can we fix this?" instead of "I'm outta here!"

If you've picked up this book, you may already know that when every interaction with your teenager erupts into a fight, something is wrong.

You're probably no longer comforted by your own reassurances that your teenager is just going through a rebellious phase. If any of the following scenarios sound like what's going on in your family, it's time to take action to reverse a trend you're beginning to fear will never reverse itself.

Kevin is 15. Neighbors who were worried about what might be going on next door told his parents that their son was coming home at lunchtime a couple days a week with his girlfriend and never going back to school. Loud music, noises, and laughter coming from Kevin's bedroom window made them think that Kevin and his girlfriend were drinking and having sex. His grades were decent and his standardized test scores were off the charts, so his parents hoped he was just going through some phase. But when they found empty beer cans and used condoms in the trash, they realized they'd been downplaying their fears and finally confronted their son. A horrific argument broke out, during which Kevin screamed profanities at his parents.

Lauren's mother describes the 14-year-old as "completely changed" since elementary school, wistfully wondering where her sweet little girl went. Lauren hardly speaks to her these days except to make some snide comment about what she's wearing or to yell back at her when her mother's unsuccessful cajoling finally erupts into a shouted command. One night recently, when Lauren's mom got up in the middle of the night to go to the bathroom, she peeked in on her daughter as she always used to when she was small—only to find her on the Internet, talking with a strange man in another state. When she told Lauren to immediately turn off the computer, a huge argument resulted, replete with accusations and cursing. Lauren's father woke up and broke up the argument, taking away Lauren's computer/smartphone privileges for 3 months.

Gina is only 13, yet she is failing three of her five eighth-grade classes. When her mom asks her whether she has any homework, she claims she's already done it in school and just forgot to bring it home. Not so, said her teacher, so Mom grounded Gina on weekends, confining her to her room, where she was to make up missed assignments or study for tests. Gina sneaked on her smartphone and sent text messages to her friends instead of doing homework; her mother removed the phone, with Gina shouting and cursing. Now Gina just daydreams all weekend, getting little work done. Mother and daughter argue daily about school and homework.

Seventeen-year-old Mark skips school, comes home drunk on weekends, and doesn't try to hide the smell of marijuana smoke wafting from his room at night. When his parents confront him about all of these violations of their rules, he typically curses at them, threatens to hit them, and storms out, accusing his parents of "child abuse." His truancy is beginning to threaten his chances of getting a high school diploma. His mother says she can't force him to go to school by driving him there because he just runs away when she tells him to get in the car or leaves the school grounds after she drops him off. His father says he can't get involved in the morning or he'll be late for work.

These kids are not just suffering growing pains, and their parents are not "control freaks" prone to exaggeration. Mark's parents always knew they had a strong-willed son. When the curfew violations and "smart mouthing" started in eighth grade, they tried to cut him some slack to avoid "breaking his spirit" the way his father felt his parents had done to him. When they look back over the last few years, they realize that the infractions gradually grew in frequency and seriousness, but they have no idea when this tough guy who thumbs his nose at them and their rules first showed up. Lauren's mother says her daughter started clamming up around her and doing mostly what she felt like doing a few months ago, when she started high school. Kevin's parents have tried everything they can think of to get control of their very bright son—removing privileges, setting an early curfew, grounding him—but he's been finding a way around their restrictions for a long time, and half the time their demanding jobs leave them too exhausted to fight these days. Gina has attention-deficit/hyperactivity disorder (ADHD), and her parents had kept her on track by using time-outs, point systems, and medication since her diagnosis at age 9. But now she refuses to take her medication and doesn't seem to care half the time whether she loses screen time or earns points for a pizza party. During time-outs she sits silently and smirks.

Teenagers can become defiant for a number of reasons. It's worth exploring what may be going on if your child has made a sudden transformation and the behavior hasn't been going on for long. In Chapter 1, we'll tell you how to figure out whether there's a physical or other undisclosed factor at work. But regardless of the cause, the program in this book may be the solution you're looking for. Psychologists consider a teenager in need of help when one or more of these three conditions exist:

1. *The teen's behavior is much worse than it is for most kids of the same age.* How does the teen you're concerned about compare to other teenagers you've raised or other teens in your extended family or in the neighborhood? What reports do you get from other parents, teachers, and other adults in a position to supervise your son or daughter? We'll give you some questionnaires and checklists with which to assess your teenager in Chapter 1.

2. *The teen's behavior is making it hard for him or her to function as expected.* Like Kevin, your teenager might be quite intelligent but still unable to maintain good grades, positive friendships, or good family relationships. Maybe your teen doesn't seem to be able to take care of him- or herself or to follow rules typically expected of teenagers without constant adult supervision. Or, worse, maybe your teen's conduct is at risk of provoking serious consequences from others, such as being kicked out of school or being arrested for underage alcohol use.

3. *The teen's behavior is causing a lot of emotional distress or harm.* The distress is just as likely to be yours as it is the teen's. The point here is that if you and/or your defiant teenager are

suffering a lot of anxiety, depression, or chronic unhappiness as a result of the teen's behavior, some action is required.

What these three factors may add up to is a scenario like this: Your teenager seems to argue with everything you say, constantly breaks the rules, or lies to get around them. Maybe you regularly find yourself lying awake at night, alternating between states of terror and fury about your son's failure to get home by curfew—again. Perhaps you're watching your daughter's grades drop but get nowhere when you question the fact that she claims to have no homework—again. Maybe you're becoming aware that your teenager is breaking the rules at home and at school, and now you're starting to wonder whether your child is flirting with breaking the law too. Or maybe you're just tired of daily battles over what your teen is wearing, how the teen talks to you, the chores the teen is not doing, the mess the teen is leaving, and the kids your teen is spending his or her time with. Whether your problem is great or small, constant or periodic, this book can help. It can help you if defiance is entrenched or just beginning. It can help you whether you have an older teen or a preteen and you want to know how to stave off problems during adolescence.

The program you'll read about in this book consists of 10 steps that can restore a positive relationship between you and your teen and greatly reduce the conflict that pervades your home life. It can improve your teen's academic performance by changing the way homework and other school matters that you can control at home are handled. We can't promise that it will obliterate all signs of defiance in your teenager or even that it will work for all teens. But if you stick with it, you can expect your relationship with your teen to move in a more positive direction from now on.

If your teenager was defiant as a child and you have used the eight steps in *Your Defiant Child*, some of this program will be familiar to you. Some of the principles are the same, from the importance of paying positive attention to your son or daughter to the usefulness of reward systems. But, naturally, there are differences as well. After all, your son or daughter is no longer a child, can't be expected to respond like one, and should not be treated like one. *This program is not going to restore the type of control you may have had when your child was 7 or 8.* It will teach you how to take back the authority that is appropriate for you to retain over a teenager while recognizing and respecting the growth and maturity that your teen is seeking and experiencing. This means more negotiation and less "laying down the law." It means adding communication and problem-solving skills to the repertoire used in your interactions. The result of this program, ideally, will be that your teenager is no longer a tyrant controlling the environment in which your family lives. But, at the same time, your teen will be acquiring valuable skills to take along into adulthood.

We know this approach works for many families. Two of us (Dr. Barkley and Dr. Robin) are clinical psychologists who have devoted our careers to the clinical care of children and adolescents with defiant behavior and ADHD. Both of us are also highly experienced researchers. We've conducted numerous studies on these two disorders and tested various treatment programs for their effectiveness in addressing the individual and family problems these disorders are likely to pose. (More information on Dr. Barkley can be obtained at his website, *russellbarkley.org*.)

One of us (Dr. Barkley) specifically helped to develop the methods discussed here on behavior management of children and teens, including an emphasis on positive attending skills by parents; the use of privileges, point systems, and other organized incentive systems for encouraging appropriate prosocial behavior; and the incorporation of mild forms of discipline for dealing with defiant behavior. These treatment programs were based on those developed earlier by Constance Hanf, PhD, and were learned while training with her at the Oregon Health Sciences University in Portland. This work was later combined with Dr. Robin's program on problem-solving and communication training to study their effectiveness as a treatment package under two federally funded grants serving defiant teens and their families. Between us, we have more than 60 years of clinical and research experience addressing the problems of families with defiant children and teens. All the stories you'll find in this book are informed by those years of experience as well; they are fictional-ized composites of problems and solutions we have seen in action time and again. We sincerely hope you and your teenage son or daughter will benefit from all we've learned.

How to Use This Book

This book is divided into two parts. Part I helps you take a closer look at your teenager's defiance—what's really going on and what factors have been contributing to the conflicts you're experienc-ing. This understanding alone can help you all start to make changes that reduce defiance; at the very least they may increase your empathy for the teen who has become such a thorn in your side—and give you hope that things can get better at home.

What you learn about your teen, yourself, and the challenges you're dealing with that are causing conflict between you will serve you well when you start the program in Part II. There you'll find 10 steps that break down what right now probably seems like an impossible task: starting to take back control over your teen's behavior—and in a way that allows your teenager to mature and gradually gain the independence that all teens must strive for.

We strongly recommend that you read Part I before launch-ing into the program. The understanding you gain in Part I is groundwork that will increase your chances of success with the program. It will also introduce you to lots of families like yours so you'll remember that you're not alone in this struggle—and that there are creative ways of applying the lessons we've learned in our work.

If you decide to follow the program in Part II, you should plan on taking 3–4 months to get through it. In our work with parents, we usually allow 1–2 weeks per step so that the lessons and techniques of one step are firmly ingrained before the next one is added. You may be able to move more quickly; you'll be able to tell mainly by how comfortable you've become with using the new skills and changes in the general tenor of interactions at home. Whatever time you invest, remember what you stand to gain: you're not just getting a better relationship with your teen, you're shaping your son or daughter into an adult you can send off into the world with confidence and pride.

If you follow the program in Part II and find that you are not getting results after 4 months, we strongly recommend that you enlist the help of a qualified psychologist or other mental health professional trained to use this approach. The book then becomes the assigned reading that accompanies the family intervention in which you are participating. Often, a psychologist familiar with this approach can help you make changes that were difficult to make on your own, even though the general approach is the same.

You and Your Defiant Teen

1

What Defiance Is—and What You Should Do about It

Seventeen-year-old Mark (mentioned in the Introduction) usually doesn't show up at home on weekdays until dinnertime, if then. So when he made a rare appearance at 3:00 one Friday, his mother, Sandy, looked at him suspiciously when he entered the kitchen, pointedly looked at her watch, and said sarcastically, "To what do I owe *this* honor?"

Mark just sneered and opened the refrigerator.

As she watched him pawing through the food on the shelves, Sandy became more and more irritated. She didn't want to start a fight. It had already been a long week. But she couldn't keep her silence.

"Mark, did you actually go to school today? Doesn't the last class end at 3:00?"

"Relax, Ma. My last class was canceled. Besides, what the hell do *you* care? You haven't asked me about school since, like, Christmas."

"Watch your mouth, young man," Sandy snapped. "If you miss much more school, you're not even going to graduate!"

"Oh, yeah, like that matters." Mark grabbed sandwich fixings from the refrigerator and plopped down at the kitchen table, where he started making three huge sandwiches.

"What do you need all that food for?" his mother demanded. "You get lunch money every week."

"Yeah, well, I spent it on cigarettes," Mark shot back, then leaned back in his chair and aimed an insolent grin at his mother. "Besides, I'm gonna be out for a while; I'm taking this with me."

Sandy spun around from the sink. "You're not going anywhere till you mow the lawn, like I asked you last Saturday—and the Saturday before, and the Saturday before that."

"It's Friday, and I'm going out. You want the grass cut so bad, *you* do it! All you ever do is sit around here anyway."

"Don't you talk to me that way! And don't you even think about leaving here without cutting the grass!"

"OK, I won't think about it," Mark said slyly. Then he stood up, went back to the refrigerator, grabbed a six-pack of beer, and walked out the front door so fast he didn't hear his mother yelling: "You get back here, Mark! Don't expect to waltz back in here whenever you feel like showing up! Everybody has to pitch in around here, you know!" Mark was thinking about his plans for the weekend and had already tuned his mother out.

This scene or one a lot like it has been replayed in this household dozens of times over the last year. When Mark started to act as if his parents' rules were negligible and their requests optional, his parents said nothing, hoping the phase would pass. When it didn't, they tried threats and removal of privileges. Mark just laughed at them. Now he comes and goes as he pleases and treats them with more and more disdain. Periodically he erupts into cursing and threats of his own. Frankly, both of his parents are a little bit afraid of him.

How We Define *Defiance*

Pull this interaction apart, and you'll have before you all the elements by which we define *defiance:*

1. *Failure to comply with an adult's request within a reasonable time.* Believe it or not, a mere minute or so is considered a

reasonable time within which to comply with an adult's request—that's about the same window in which you'd expect an adult to do something you've asked, and it's fair to expect a teen to do the same. Yes, if a teen is already busy with another project, then a longer time to comply is reasonable, but in those cases the teen should at least acknowledge the request and an intention to comply with it within a minute or so. Mark not only didn't mow the lawn when his mother asked him, he's totally ignored her request for 3 weeks!

2. *Failure to keep doing what has been requested until the task is finished.* Maybe this seems like it goes without saying. But many teenagers start out doing what they're asked to do and then don't follow through. They pay lip service—they do half the job and then switch to something they want to do, they do a sloppy job, or they drag out the task for so long that it doesn't get done when you need it done. Mark, obviously, never even got started. Of course in some circumstances it's clear that compliance with an adult instruction is not expected immediately. But in those cases it's up to you to state explicitly when compliance should begin.

3. *Failure to follow previously taught rules of conduct.* Mark has racked up quite a score on this one: His parents expect him to attend school; let them know where he is; come home when expected; speak to them respectfully and listen attentively; and spend the money they give him as they intended, not for cigarettes and beer. He defies them on every count.

Although we'll use the term *defiance* throughout this book, it's important to understand that we mean both *noncompliance* (passively not doing what is asked or expected or not completing it) and more active *verbal or physical resistance* such as Mark's arguing, swearing, challenging, and threatening. It may very well be the latter that has brought you to this book, although 14-year-old Lauren (mentioned in the Introduction) has driven her mother to seek help just by quietly breaking all the rules and generally making herself scarce.

Why You Need to Know More about Your Teen's Defiance

If your teen resembles Mark or Lauren or the other two adolescents depicted in the Introduction, you already know enough to justify trying the straightforward steps in Part II. You may *not* know enough, however, to get everything you possibly can from the program. First you need to know whether this self-help program is really what you need and whether it's *all* you need.

Is Your Teen's Defiance a Behavior or a Trait?

If we asked you to tell us what you mean by "defiance," you'd probably be quick to define it as resistance, opposition, and disobedience—complete disregard for whatever you request, demand, or instruct your teenager to do. You may even liken it to Groucho Marx's refrain in the movie *Horsefeathers*: "Whatever it is, I'm against it!"

Of course you might look at it that way only on good days, when you can summon up a sense of humor about the issue. On most days your teenager's defiance is no laughing matter. Dealing with someone who always seems to want to resist or to fight, and constantly displays contempt or aversion, wears you down and beats you up. You want to "get this kid in line" and get your lives back to normal.

The trouble is, your lives may never get back to normal if you view the problem as something your teen *is* instead of something he or she *does*. As you can see from our definition of defiance, it's measured by specific acts. Yet when those acts add up to what feels like endless grief for you, defiance in a teen can begin to seem like a personality trait instead of a behavior. Personality traits generally can't be changed very much, but behavior can be changed. If you view your teenager as just *being* defiant, you're sort of stuck with the condition, aren't you? It's this perspective that leads to finger-pointing of the "You *always* . . ." and "Why can't you *ever* . . . ?" variety. It puts you at loggerheads and keeps you there.

Yet if you look closely at the way your teenager acts, you'll probably see that she isn't defiant as "constantly" as you may feel; she may not be defiant everywhere, with everyone, all the time, and in exactly the same way. Some kids are so defiant at home that their parents can't believe they don't act the same way at school—but they don't. Others are much more defiant with certain people than with everyone else or when faced with certain demands. Defiance is often demonstrated to different degrees, but it all begins to run together and seem like one big rebellion to parents who are expecting it. When you become aware of these nuances, you gain information about what goes wrong and what goes right—and consequently where to address the problem first and how to capitalize on the positives.

Remember, behavior can be changed. Looking more closely at your teen's defiance will reveal the cracks in the behavior and help you see where you can wiggle your way in and make a difference.

Is It Just Normal Adolescent Behavior or More Serious Problems?

Your lives may also never get back to normal if you put the emphasis on "back." Taking a closer look at the history of your teen's defiance and training a magnifying glass on the current behavior will help you see how easy it can be to confuse normal adolescent striving for autonomy with out-of-control rebellion. We'll get into this important topic more in the chapters that follow, but, for now, try to keep in mind that there *is* a line. It's just that it gets pretty blurry in the heated battle of wills, and we all take a little time to adjust to these new creatures who are so eager to be shed of our supervision and care. If you can begin to see the difference between "normal" assertions of growing independence—the way kids typically behave when they hit the teen years—and how what we call "defiance" departs from that pattern, you won't make the mistake of trying to "correct" behavior that is just fine as it is (as trying as it can be).

Remember What You Stand to Gain

When your patience has been pushed so far past its limits that you don't remember what calm feels like, it's hard not to view defiance as a one-way street. Your teenager defies you (the cause), and conflict erupts (the effect). Look more closely, though, and you'll be reminded that defiance is not just an action; it's a *reaction*—to the person being defied or to a situation deemed intolerable. Technically, it's an *interaction*. Your teen cannot defy your instruction if no instruction is given or break a rule if one has not been laid down previously and you do not react with anger or frustration at everything your teen does. Defiance doesn't occur in a vacuum or when a person is alone. "It takes two to tango," as they say. This may be hard to believe considering that teens often express defiance through their absence. You tell your 15-year-old to do the dishes and then hit the books, and instead he hits the pavement—running. You've set a weeknight curfew of 10:00 P.M., and your daughter responds to your edict by staying out till midnight. Whether the teen is present or not, every act of defiance is a response to something you or some other authority figure has said. Defiance makes the interaction a conflict. It pits you and your teen against each other; it pulls you farther and farther apart over time. When you look closely at your teen's defiance, you'll see the damage it's doing to the parent–child relationship. We hope this realization will motivate you to keep at the program even when it's tough because you have so much to gain. And we hope you'll remember that, if you're part of the interactions where defiance occurs, it means you have a lot of power to make a difference. Fairly simple changes in your behavior may lead to big changes in your teen's behavior.

In the Introduction we said that if you answered "Yes" to any of the following questions, you probably need to address your teen's defiance.

1. Is your teen's defiant behavior much worse than it is for most other adolescents?

2. Is your teen's defiant behavior making it hard for him or her to function as expected, or does it risk eliciting serious consequences from others?

3. Is your teen's defiant behavior causing a lot of emotional distress or harm?

The rest of this chapter will help you examine the nature of your teen's defiant behavior so you know how to answer these questions. On page 24 you'll have a chance to enter all the information you've gathered on a Decision-Making Worksheet to help you determine whether you need help, and, if so, whether self-help is likely to be enough or you need professional help.

What Does *Your* Teen's Defiance Look Like?

Defiance takes all kinds of forms in teenagers. Just to get an overview of what you've been dealing with, check off the behaviors in the Defiant Behaviors list on page 18 that you've been noticing recently. Feel free to copy the list for later use or download it from *www.guilford.com/barkley16-forms.*

Notice the four categories of defiant behavior: Verbal (**V**), Physical (**P**), Aggressive (**A**), and Passive Noncompliance (**PN**). How many behaviors in each category did you check off? Keep this in mind as we proceed through the rest of the book. We'll be suggesting different techniques to deal with different categories of defiant behavior. In Chapter 15 you'll learn to use communication skills to deal with verbal defiance. In Chapters 10–12 you'll learn to use contracts, point systems, and punishments to deal with physical and aggressive defiance. In Chapter 14 you'll learn to use problem solving to deal with passive defiance as well as elements of the other types of defiance. If you checked off any of the last five symptoms in the Aggressive category, be sure to read the section "Do You Need Professional Help?" later in this chapter.

Defiant Behaviors

Verbal

☐ Yells
☐ Whines
☐ Complains
☐ Screams
☐ Insults
☐ Swears
☐ Lies
☐ Argues
☐ Humiliates/annoys
☐ Teases
☐ Cries
☐ Sasses or talks back

Aggressive

☐ Physically resists requests
  or instructions
☐ Throws objects
☐ Destroys property intentionally
☐ Physically fights with others
☐ Carries or uses weapons
☐ Breaks into other people's homes
  or businesses
☐ Is cruel to others
☐ Is cruel to animals
☐ Lacks guilt or remorse or seems to
  have no conscience

Physical

☐ Defies
☐ Throws tantrums
☐ Disrupts others' activities
☐ Steals
☐ Runs away

Passive Noncompliance

☐ Ignores requests
☐ Fails to complete routine chores
☐ Fails to complete school homework
☐ Ignores self-care tasks

Other: _____

Is Your Teen's Defiance Much Worse Than Defiance in Other Teens?

Is your teen's defiant behavior much worse than it is for most other teens? To answer this question, we need a standard for other teens to which you can compare your teen. First, circle the word below that represents how frequently your teen exhibits the following three behaviors:

Fails to comply with an adult's request within a reasonable time

never   sometimes   often   very often

Fails to keep doing what has been requested until the task is finished

never   sometimes   often   very often

Fails to follow previously taught rules of conduct

never   sometimes   often   very often

Second, fill out the Conflict Behavior Questionnaire for Parents, developed by Dr. Robin. Feel free to copy the questionnaire or download it from *www.guilford.com/barkley16-forms* for later uses. Save your frequency ratings above and your scores on the Conflict Behavior Questionnaire for Parents to use in the Decision-Making Worksheet that appears later in this chapter.

Is Your Teen's Behavior Creating Impairment?

Is your teen's defiant behavior making it hard for him or her to function as expected at home, in school, or in the community? To help you answer this question, we have listed the major settings where defiant behavior may be a problem. Consider all the oppositional behaviors that you rated *sometimes, often,* or *very often* on the previous checklist. Taking all these behaviors into account, circle the ratings on the Impairment Rating Form on page 22 that represent how much these behaviors interfere with your teen's ability to function in each life activity. Feel free to copy or download the form from *www.guilford.com/barkley16-forms* for later uses.

Even if you circled *often* or *very often* only once, your teenager's defiant behavior is interfering significantly with his or her ability to function in a major life activity. As with your frequency ratings, keep your results handy so you can use them in the Decision-Making Worksheet.

Conflict Behavior Questionnaire for Parents

The following is another way to measure your teenager's defiance. If you wish, fill out this questionnaire and compare the results you get with those from the rating forms earlier in the chapter. Essentially consistent results should reinforce the decision you've made about what action to take.

This form is also an excellent way to see whether your teen's problematic behavior occurs more with you or another parent or caregiver (such as a grandparent who plays a parenting role). As you'll see later in this book, when the teen's behavior (or perceptions of the behavior) differs significantly between parents, or is perceived differently by the two, you may have to take extra measures to fend off a "divide-and-conquer" strategy and to stay on the same page when working through the program.

If more than one adult plays a significant parenting role with the teen, all of these adults should complete this form.

I am the child's ____ mother ____ father (check one).

Think back over the last 2 weeks at home. The statements below have to do with you and your teen. Read the statement and circle True or False for each statement. Answer for yourself, without talking it over with anyone.

True	False	1. My teen is easy to get along with.
True	False	2. My teen is well behaved in our discussions.
True	False	3. My teen is receptive to criticism.
True	False	4. For the most part, my teen likes to talk to me.
True	False	5. We almost never seem to agree.
True	False	6. My teen usually listens to what I tell him/her.
True	False	7. At least three times a week, we get angry at each other.
True	False	8. My teen says I have no consideration of his/her feelings.
True	False	9. My teen and I compromise during arguments.
True	False	10. My teen often doesn't do what I ask.
True	False	11. The talks we have are frustrating.
True	False	12. My teen often seems angry to me.
True	False	13. My teen acts impatient when I talk.
True	False	14. In general, I don't think we get along very well.

True   False   15. My teen almost never understands my side of an argument.

True   False   16. My teen and I have big arguments about little things.

True   False   17. My teen is defensive when I talk to him/her.

True   False   18. My teen thinks my opinions don't count.

True   False   19. We argue a lot about rules.

True   False   20. My teen tells me he/she thinks I am unfair.

Scoring and Interpreting Your Results

1. Add one point for each of the following items answered TRUE: 5, 7, 8, 10, 11, 12, 13, 14, 15, 16, 17, 18, 19, 20.

2. Add one point for each of the following items answered FALSE: 1, 2, 3, 4, 6, 9.

3. Add all of the points together.

There are two ways to interpret the Conflict Behavior Questionnaire for Parents Summary Score:

1. Compare your score to the mean scores that we obtained in our research for families in conflict and families without conflict. See which mean your score is closer to:

    Mothers: Mean score for families in conflict = 12.4 (standard deviation = 5.0)

    Mean score for families without excessive conflict = 2.4 (standard deviation = 2.8)

    Fathers: Mean score for families in conflict = 10.5 (standard deviation = 5.0)

    Mean score for families without excessive conflict = 3.2 (standard deviation = 3.0)

2. Use the following cutoffs for high scores:

    Mothers: Any score above 8 is definitely in the problem range (higher than in 98% of families without excessive conflict). Any score of 6-8 is probably in the problem range (higher than in 84–93% of those families).

    Fathers: Any score above 10 is definitely in the problem range. Any score of 7–10 is probably in the problem range.

=========== **Impairment Rating Form** ===========

In home life with the family	rarely	sometimes	often	very often
In social interactions with peers	rarely	sometimes	often	very often
In school	rarely	sometimes	often	very often
In community activities	rarely	sometimes	often	very often
In sports, clubs, or other activities	rarely	sometimes	often	very often
In learning to take care of him/herself	rarely	sometimes	often	very often
In play, leisure, or recreational activities	rarely	sometimes	often	very often
In handling daily chores or other responsibilities	rarely	sometimes	often	very often

From *Your Defiant Teen* (2nd ed.). Copyright 2014 by The Guilford Press.

Is Your Teenager's Behavior Causing a Lot of Emotional Distress?

Emotional distress comes in many different forms. Maybe your teenager's defiant behavior is making you or others in your family feel angry, frustrated, upset, depressed, and/or hopeless. This is a difficult experience to measure because each person experiences emotional distress differently, so your ratings in the Emotional Distress Rating Form below are bound to be inexact, which is fine. Just try to rate the overall degree of emotional distress you and other family members experience on a typical day because your teen engages in the defiant behaviors that you've reported on our earlier rating scales. Feel free to copy or download the form from *www.guilford.com/barkley16-forms* for later uses.

Emotional Distress Rating Form

1. Emotional distress that I experience	none	very little	moderate	a lot	very much
2. Emotional distress that my spouse experiences	none	very little	moderate	a lot	very much
3. Emotional distress that my other children experience	none	very little	moderate	a lot	very much

From *Your Defiant Teen* (2nd ed.). Copyright 2014 by The Guilford Press.

If one or more of the people in your family are experiencing at least moderate degrees of emotional distress because of your teen's oppositional behavior, you need to think seriously about trying the program outlined in this book or seeing a therapist.

Setting a Course of Action

Now you have some measurements to help you see where your teen's defiant behavior has brought you. Use them to fill out the Decision-Making Worksheet on page 24 to help you figure out what to do about the problem. Our recommendations are general guidelines based on our clinical experience, not on research data. Feel free to copy or download the form from *www.guilford. com/barkley16-forms* for later uses.

Do You Need Professional Help?

The Decision-Making Worksheet gives you a rough idea of whether you need self-help or professional help. If you have any doubts, read this book and try our suggestions first; if they don't seem to help after you make a decent effort, find a mental health professional. We have included information on how to find a qualified professional in Appendix B at the back of this book.

Decision-Making Worksheet

1. How many of the three behaviors on page 19 did you rate *often or very often?* _____

2. Did either parent score the Conflict Behavior Questionnaire in the problem range? _____ Yes _____ No

3. On the Impairment Rating Form (p. 22), did you circle *often or very often* for impairment in one or more settings? _____ Yes _____ No

4. Did you rate at least one of the three items on the Emotional Distress Rating Form (p. 23) as *moderate, a lot*, or *very much*? _____ Yes _____ No

Here's how to interpret your answers to each question above:

Were your answers like these?

    1. 2–3   2. Yes (especially a Yes for both parents)   3. Yes   4. Yes

If so, consider using this self-help book and consulting a mental health professional to help you deal with your teen's defiant behavior.

Were your answers like these?

    1. 1 or more   2. Yes   3. Yes   4. Yes

If so, this book *may* be enough to help you deal with your teen's oppositional behavior.

Were your answers like these?

    1. 1 or more   2. Yes or No   3. No   4. No

If so, this book will probably be enough to help you with your teen's defiant behavior.

Were your answers like these?

    1. 0–1   2, 3, and 4. No to any one of these

If so, you probably will find this book sufficient.

Were your answers like these?

    1. 0   2, 3, and 4. No to any one or all of these

Your teen is probably within the normal range of defiant behavior. You may find the advice in this book helpful, but you probably don't need professional help.

In broad strokes, your teen's defiance may require professional help even if it's not quite that severe but has been going on for so long that you can't begin to imagine disentangling it. If it's a more recent development but is causing your child or you such huge problems (e.g., refusing to go to school, complete withdrawal from family activities or mealtimes, persistent sadness or depression, an abrupt change in your teen's personality) that school and home life are totally disrupted, you also might need professional intervention, at least to get you on the right track.

But you can also look a little more closely at the specific behaviors of your teen: During the last year, has your son or daughter started physical fights or used a weapon, bullied others, demonstrated physical cruelty (to animals or people), or committed crimes such as assault or burglary? Has your teen run away from home and been truant? If you answer Yes to any of these questions (roughly corresponding to the last five symptoms in the Aggressive category in the Defiant Behaviors checklist, page 18), you're dealing with a problem that is more than you can handle without expert help; seek a professional evaluation. Your teenager may have conduct disorder, discussed in Chapter 4. If you find yourself having any doubts about the severity of your child's problems, talk to others who have had a chance to observe and interact with your son or daughter: teachers, coaches, friends' parents.

Is There More to the Story?

It's not unusual for parents completing the rating forms in this chapter to realize that things may not be as awful as they thought. Stepping back and looking at your teen's behavior objectively could reveal that the daughter who's driving you crazy isn't impaired by her actions or attitudes, meaning you need to figure out whether something else is going on that's causing her to behave differently. Or maybe you'll find that the son who is causing such tension between the two of you isn't really headed for the life of crime that has become your worst fear. Marsha's daughter, Julie, had started at a new high school following her parents' move 6 months earlier, but no one noticed that she wasn't adapting well until she started acting out at home. The "defiance" exhibited by Darrell's 13-year-old, Jake, has been pretty innocuous—like "purposely" leaving his clothes all over the house or having to be reminded three times to take out the garbage or to walk the dog. But Darrell can't see that his son's developmental needs are different today than they were just a few months ago and expects his son to act like the acquiescent kid he was before puberty.

Marsha may get something worthwhile from the program in this book even though her daughter is mainly reacting to a tough transition in her life. At the very least, learning to pay more positive attention to her daughter—instead of always focusing on her moodiness—may offer her the support that serves as a suit of armor for some kids when they go out into a harsh world. But giving her incentives to be more civil in her interactions with family members and others and showing her respect by engaging in problem solving the way two adults would might also help her daughter develop the confidence to deal with the changes in her life. On the other hand, Marsha might consider whether her daughter is suffering from symptoms of depression and talk to Julie's doctor, if not to a mental health professional.

Darrell can use Part I of this book to start examining his expectations regarding his son and adjusting them to jibe with Jake's developmental changes. The behavior management techniques at the beginning of our program will help Darrell keep his responses (and his requests) to his son reasonable. Once he's found that he can enforce nonnegotiable household rules effectively, he and Jake can learn to communicate better and start negotiating the, well, negotiables—a right that all maturing kids should get as long as they show they can handle the responsibility of additional freedom. Meanwhile, the rest of Part I of this book will help both Marsha and Darrell figure out in detail what's going on with their teens' behavior so they know how to make the best use of the program in Part II.

Are You Ready to Take Action?

There's no doubt about it: Change is hard and lasting change is even tougher to make. You may have no doubt that you want to reap the benefits of a change in your teen's defiant behavior, but it can be a challenge to get there, and it's easy to get discouraged when the path proves to be anything but a straight line. The fact is, we all need to go through a series of stages to implement any significant change in our lives. There's always a period of time when we have a problem but aren't quite ready to see it that way. You may have gone through several months, or even longer, of battling with your teen before reaching the point where you realized that this might not be a phase and that you want to do something about the conflict that's taken over your family. It's probably at that point that you picked up this book. Reading these words is your way of preparing to start doing what it takes to make the changes you and your teenager need to make. Reading the rest of Part I is a terrific, and critically necessary, start. But once you dive into the program, it's important to understand that you need to do your best to stick with it. As you'll learn at the beginning of Part II, consistency is one of the hallmark principles behind successful behavior change. Your chances of hanging in there will increase if you keep in mind that you may take one step forward and two steps back sometimes—and you'll probably take a lot of sideways steps too. The path toward less conflict between you and your teen can look much more like a zigzag than a straight line. Don't be discouraged if you move back and forth for a while; just keep at it.

Taking Action

- Observe your teen's current behavior and think carefully about his or her behavior in the recent past, then fill out the rating forms in this chapter. Pay attention to what the Conflict Behavior Questionnaire for Parents tells you about how conflict with your teen may differ between parents.

- Based on your answers, decide whether your teenager is truly defiant and whether this book might help.
- Determine whether you might need professional help in addition to this book. If so, find a qualified clinician to consult for an evaluation and possible treatment.
- Figure out where you are in the "stages of change":

  1. Do you feel defiance is a problem for you, your teen, and your family? If not, set this book aside for a while, but continue observing your teen's behavior and the interactions between you. If the problem doesn't resolve on its own within a few more weeks, come back to this chapter and complete the checklists again. If the problem really is the same or is worse, read the rest of this book.

  2. If you do believe defiance is a problem you need to address, finish reading this book before deciding whether to tackle the program on your own or with professional help.

  3. If you're ready to take action, pay careful attention to your reading of Part I; you're in the thick of the "preparation" stage.

     Your next stage will be "action"—working through the 10 steps in the program. Once you've learned all the skills and techniques, you'll be in the "maintenance" phase—keeping what you've learned in practice. Occasionally you may slip into "relapse," but that's perfectly normal—and reversible. Just return to Part II and see where you can take a refresher course; we'll offer plenty of troubleshooting tips with each step that can pull you out of these slips and get you back on track.

How Defiance Develops

It's been a rough day for 14-year-old Jenna and her mother, Marla. Jenna's been in a bad mood all day, giving her mother "lip" and "attitude" every time Marla makes a request. Nerves are frayed and tempers are short. Now it's 9:00 P.M. and, as usual, Jenna has not started her homework and is wasting time texting her friends.

"Jenna!" Marla yelled up the stairs to her daughter. "Stop texting your friends and start doing your homework right now!"

Marla heard her daughter's door open. "Just a minute!"

Marla waited expectantly for a minute and then tried again. "*Jenna!*"

"I said 'Just a minute,' Mom!"

Marla shook her head, took a deep breath, and then gave it one more try: "I've been asking you to do this all evening, and now it's getting late and you're wasting time. It's *your* grades, you know, and you are failing math."

Jenna stuck her head out of her bedroom door, put her hand over her smartphone, and yelled back, "I *said* I'd do it in a minute! I'm busy!"

Infuriated by her daughter's nasty tone and reminded that she has also been warning her daughter about her astronomical cellphone bills, Marla stomped up the stairs and banged on her daughter's door.

"*What?*" her daughter yelled.

"*What? What?* You *know* what. Get out here this minute, young lady!"

"Just a *minute*," Jenna hissed through the door.

Furious now, Marla banged on the door again. Jenna ignored her.

Finally, seething and feeling totally helpless, Marla screeched, "We'll deal with this later, Jenna. You're in *big* trouble." Marla charged back down the stairs, sank into a kitchen chair with a glass of wine, and felt tears welling up in her eyes. So this is what it feels like to be tyrannized by a 14-year-old, she thought. Exhausted and discouraged from these daily and repeated confrontations with Jenna, she thought back to when Jenna was 10 and she was so proud that she had a child old enough and eager to be a help around the house. What had happened since those days?

Upstairs, Jenna was saying to her friend, "So, tell me what happened with Jason . . ."

Score: Marla, 0; Jenna, 1—or maybe 100, if you count all the other times this week that a similar scene has unfolded in the Burton household.

Defiance Develops over Time

Defiance doesn't develop overnight. More often than not, it's a behavior that has blossomed over time, sometimes over several years, from a pattern of interactions that at first seemed like parenting business as usual. Maybe your 9-year-old son seemed to love to test your authority and so "made you" ask him three times to complete the most basic of chores, like picking up dirty clothes that had been thrown about his bedroom as if a tornado recently hit his room. Or your fourth-grade daughter constantly "talked back" to you, and you described her to friends as "much snippier" than your other kids. You found yourself yelling a lot whenever you had to tell her to do anything, anticipating her predictable resistance, sometimes even when you were just asking her for information, such as about whether she had soccer practice the next day or she liked the lunch you packed for her that day.

As time went on, your interactions with your growing child seemed to get more and more unpleasant when there was even a hint that you wanted something from the child that he or she might not find acceptable. By adolescence, you might have racked up a history of thousands of hostile exchanges, and your teenager had now solidified a repertoire of defiant behavior and an attitude toward you—and possibly other adults—that was disrespectful at best, belligerent to say the least, and openly defiant and confrontational at worst.*

Most defiant teens end up that way because they've learned there's something in it for them. For your teen, maybe it was simply the ability to get you off her back. Or perhaps she knew if she put off complying she'd be able to socialize just a few minutes longer. Sometimes the initial benefit is just getting your attention. When parents are distracted and overwhelmed by other demands on them, as so many of us are, it's hard to pay the kind of attention to kids that instills positive social behavior. So their kids get it with negative behavior. When the parents reward the behavior with attention, naturally the child is going to use this strategy again—and again. If the child feels the parent's attention is slipping away, the obvious response is to up the ante and advance to even more negative behavior. This is one way teenagers become chronically defiant.

Another way, and one more likely to increase defiant behavior, is when parents find a child's disobedience intolerable and simply cave in to his or her demands. Let's say you ask your son to take out the garbage. He ignores you. Now you yell at him to do it. He ignores you again. You walk over to him and pull him up from the floor where he's ensconced in front of his computer and order him again to take out the garbage. He yells at you. You yell back at him. He shouts, "You *never* leave me alone when I'm watching a show!" and runs up to his room, slamming the door

---

*By the way, if your teenager's defiance really has popped up all of a sudden, you should consult a doctor to make sure there is no medical cause and possibly a psychologist to determine whether some emotionally traumatic event that you're unaware of, such as bullying at school, sexual abuse, or the onset of drug abuse, has precipitated a radical change in behavior.

behind him. You then take out the garbage yourself if only to get it done and maybe instill peace in the household.

As with Jenna, your son has accomplished what he wanted: to delay or entirely avoid doing the chore you assigned him. His yelling at you and running away got him what he wanted. The odds are extremely high that he then tried it again the next time he wanted to avoid doing what you asked. This pattern may have put down roots a few years ago. Now your son is a foot taller than you, he has a driver's license, and he is more likely to sneer at you contemptuously than smile during any encounter. After years of trying all different types of discipline, along with cajoling and rewarding, maybe you just let him do what he wants—which he does. Or perhaps your conflicts just keep escalating.

One day when her daughter was 13, after an argument that got so loud that 5-year-old Tyler was sobbing and the 7-year-old twins were sitting nearby with their hands over their ears, Marla suddenly stopped herself in horror when she found herself charging toward her daughter with her hand raised. Jenna had emitted a string of obscenities aimed at her mother that Marla had never even imagined coming from her daughter. Maybe it was Jenna's sudden look of real fear that got to her, but she stopped herself before actually hitting her daughter. Both mother and daughter collapsed in sobs, and Marla begged her daughter's forgiveness, vowing never to raise a hand to her again. Jenna went off to bed— without doing the dishes that had been the bone of contention to begin with—and the two spent the next week dejectedly dragging themselves around the house, generally avoiding being in the same room.*

Coercion Is the Name of the Game

We call this kind of behavior pattern *coercion*. It is the use of negative, aggressive, hostile, or otherwise threatening words or

---

*If the level of conflict between you and your teenager has reached these proportions, we strongly advise that you see a therapist. Violence is never acceptable, and if either you or your teen has carried out threats of physical harm or erupted into physical violence in any way, it's a sign that you probably need more than the self-help offered by this book.

behavior to get others to do what you want. Jenna got out of doing her homework by instigating a screaming match. Marla got Jenna to stop screaming obscenities by threatening to hit her. Both used hostile emotions, raised voices, insulting or abusive language, and even physical force to achieve their goals. The problem, obviously, is that Jenna's behavior has been reinforced: it got her out of doing the dishes and capitulating to her mother's demands. She's going to use the tactic again, consciously or not. Marla's behavior ended the angry exchange, but only for now— and at what cost?

If you're reading this book, you'd probably say that all you really want is for your teenager to start doing what you want, at least some of the time, at least when it's important. But you may be out of ideas for how to get there. You've reached a state often known as *learned helplessness*. This occurs when none of your coping behavior seems to work and you are intellectually clueless as to what to do next and too emotionally drained to even bother trying to solve the problem. What you've learned that makes you feel so powerless is that every exchange with your teen proves again that you can't force him or her to do what you need done. You've learned that whatever you do, things seem to get worse. Here's a way to look at the coercive pattern of behavior between the two of you that may help you see how each exchange contributes to the feeling of learned helplessness:

Request → OK
                or
       →   No
             ↓
    Request! →   OK
                    or
          →   No!!
                 ↓
      Request!! →   OK
                       or
             →   No!!!
                    ↓
          Force or give up

The number of times you repeat your request and the intensity with which you try to force your teen to do what you want has increased over time as your strategy has remained unchanged. So has how emphatic your teen's "No!" has gotten. In many cases the pattern becomes so predictable that the middle steps, or even the first one, are skipped altogether. Some parents find themselves jumping right to coming on like gangbusters the minute they approach their teen. They're braced for resistance and so resort to "defensive offense." Their teens are usually ready too and may leap to the most extreme behavior even though what's at stake may be something as small as whether homework is going to be done before or after dinner.

When you've reached this point, you may feel completely trapped, but there is a way out. The way to reverse this cycle of coercive behavior is to stop giving in but also to stop resorting to anger, empty threats, or force. Clearly, this is easier said than done. But that is where the program in this book comes in. It will help you increase your teenager's compliance by giving you something else to do in the face of defiance. You'll *un*learn helplessness step by step.

The Four Factors That Contribute to Defiance

Meanwhile, though, you can take heart in the fact that you came to this state of affairs through a winding path that misleads a lot of us. Coercion becomes the fallback position and defiance gets entrenched not because you're a bad parent or your teenager is a bad kid. Instead it's a product of four intertwined factors:

- The teenager's characteristics
- The parent(s)' characteristics
- Stress
- Parenting style

Your Teenager's Characteristics

Certain inborn characteristics like personality and temperament can set the stage for defiant behavior in a teen. Some teens are just more easily frustrated by events, anger faster, and may be more irritable, impulsive, inattentive, poorly self-controlled, and just plain emotional than others as part of the normal variation in human personality traits. On top of those, there are developmental characteristics that come with the terrain of teenhood: the need to become more independent, to develop an identity separate from parents, and to prepare to leave the nest. Some behavioral upheaval is inevitable as a result of these strivings. In addition, some teens come with other inherent challenges, whether they are physical disabilities or psychological impairments like attention-deficit/hyperactivity disorder (ADHD), bipolar disorder, depression, and other disorders that affect thinking, emotions, and behavior. All of these traits in a teenager will contribute substantially to the likelihood that a teen can become defiant. Why? Because all of them contain problems with emotion regulation. Anger is as much an emotion as fear or depression, and some disorders neurobiologically predispose teens to have far less emotional regulation ability than normal. Such disorders result in some teens being far more likely to exhibit defiant behavior than others. Other forms of psychological treatment, including medications, may be needed to help address a neurobiological predisposition to being so emotionally unregulated.

Your Characteristics

Just as your teenager has inborn personality characteristics, you do too. You also may be dealing with physical limitations that increase stress or alter your typical reactions to the challenges that maturing teens present. Let's say you suffer ongoing pain from a back injury or you've been dealing with chronic anxiety—you're not going to have as much patience or energy for dealing with an impulsive, temperamental, or defiant teen as someone without these additional pressures. Then there's the question of "fit." Maybe you're extremely neat and organized. If you have a teenager who's exactly the opposite, you're starting every day with the stage set for a clash. And like your teen, you can also be prone to psychological disorders such as anxiety, depression, and ADHD, any of which can contribute to your conflicts with others for the same reasons as noted above for the same disorders in your teen. Again, where such disorders are present in the parent, other forms of psychological treatment and medications may be needed to help parents better regulate their emotions.

You may also have certain deeply ingrained beliefs about your teen that color your every reaction to the teen's behavior. You may believe that if your daughter doesn't stick to the straight and narrow path as defined sharply by you, she will end up pregnant, drug addicted, and in jail. You may also have come to believe that your teen's entire mission in life is to make you miserable, that your son is "worthless" or your daughter "hopeless." If you hold such beliefs, you're going to have a hard time making the kinds of changes in your family that will begin to eliminate defiance. Psychologists call these exaggerated beliefs *cognitive distortions*. When we subscribe to them, they have a way of exaggerating our emotional responses and steering us away from constructive actions.

Stress

There's stress all around us, and it bears on everyone. If you've recently experienced a significant loss, such as a death in the family, or you're struggling with legal or financial problems, marital conflict, or job pressures, this too will sap your patience and reduce your tolerance for even minor misbehavior. The stress may leave you quicker to punish, leading to increased conflict. Or you might react to stress by becoming withdrawn, distracted, less consistent in implementing household rules. This could be a temporary state that rectifies itself as the stress is resolved, but teens allowed to "get away with murder" for a period of time are likely to balk when the rules are enforced again. This may be what is causing your teenager to be defiant right now.

And let's not forget that teens are under a lot of stress as well, and not just from the obvious hazards of adolescence: academic pressures, struggles with authority at school, being bullied or harassed, losing a job, boyfriend–girlfriend problems, or just trying to fit in with a desired peer group. So-called good stress—for example, excitement over being asked to a dance, anticipating summer vacation, getting a driver's license—also impacts behavior. Just ask any teacher what it's like to manage a class right before Christmas vacation, whether it's fourth grade or eleventh grade.

You may already be thinking about how these factors could have contributed to your teen's defiance. But one thing you should realize—no matter what your personal "profile"—is that, generally speaking, these three factors are not easy to change permanently. Personality and temperament are fairly fixed. Disorders like ADHD and bipolar disorder can be treated but, at least to date, not cured. No one has found a cure for stress or a way to prevent it from entering our lives altogether. There is only one factor over which we have a fair amount of power:

Parenting Style

By "parenting style," we mean the way you respond to your teen's behavior. Even right now, you have the power to start considering alternative ways to react to your teenager. Think about this: You don't really need to make all the requests of your teen that you may be currently making. The simple decision to stop asking your son or daughter to do a certain chore or to go to bed by a certain time or to wear a certain type of clothes to school for the time being reduces the number of potential conflicts between you. If you think this is just another way of giving in, remember that right now your requests are being denied anyway. You can get into a battle with your son over taking the garbage out and end up doing it yourself, or you can just do it yourself. Not forever, but maybe just for today. It takes thought, skill, and practice to reverse defiance by ensuring that your teen either complies or suffers a negative consequence for not complying, and that's what we'll work on in the program in Part II. At this moment, however, you may not have what you need to turn things around. So for just the next day or two, when you're about to ask your teenager to do something or make a demand that a rule be followed or that an expectation be met, ask yourself these questions: Do I have the energy to follow through? Do I have a consequence planned? Should I make a smaller request so I can handle the situation more easily? If not, it's best not to make the request at all if it can be avoided—at least for now.

Parenting style is the principal target of the program in Part II of this book not because where defiance is concerned *it's all your fault*—but because it's where you have the most control. Even though your teenager is still a child in many ways, and therefore you would hope to have a significant effect in molding him or her to become a happy, healthy adult, none of us can really change another person. What we can change is the way *we* act—and, to some extent, the way *we* think and feel. Changing your parenting style by acquiring the skills taught in Part II won't completely eliminate the effect of the other three factors, but it will act as a buffer to mitigate their impact—as a sieve through which teen characteristics, parent characteristics, and stress must be filtered before the teen's behavior emerges.

If your teenager was noncompliant as a child, especially if that behavior was part of a pattern caused by ADHD, you may already be familiar with how this change in parenting style works through a strategy called *behavior management*.* Through behavior management you are trained to anticipate problematic behavior from a child, such as noncompliance or defiance, and set consequences for that behavior. When you prepare for bad behavior and you also impose consistent negative consequences, you have a lot of control over a child's behavior. Just as important, behavior management involves anticipating problem settings with your teen and trying to change them in some way, ahead of the actual

---

*See *Your Defiant Child* (2nd ed.) by Russell A. Barkley and Christine M. Benton (New York: Guilford Press, 2013).

problem, in hopes of warding off the trouble entirely. Giving commands or requests in a more effective manner, changing the timing of these requests, giving a mild "heads-up" warning a few minutes before making them so your teen is forewarned that a request is coming, or simply breaking the request or chore into simpler steps done one at a time are all means of behavior management.

Specifically for Teens: Beyond Behavior Management

Behavior management forms a large part of the basis of the program in this book. But you'll find some additional strategies and skills here, formulated to address adolescents in particular—because of the developmental realities affecting families with teenagers and the magnitude of change that has had a chance to occur over the years since childhood. Specifically:

- *Problem-solving and communication skills.* You already know you can't just dictate to teenagers. In acknowledgment of your teen's striving for independence, you have to find new ways to collaboratively solve problems and mutually respectful ways to communicate.

- *Reshaping unhelpful beliefs.* As we said above, faulty beliefs and expectations about each other and the dynamics between parents and adolescents are the tinder that can set off parent–teen conflagrations or the wind that can fan the flames of burgeoning defiance. As your son or daughter matures, it becomes more important than ever to examine and consider supplanting beliefs that may be contributing to conflict between you.

- *Understanding your family's structure.* Once your child has reached adolescence, time has allowed a number of patterns to form in the way your family operates, some of them very conducive to defiance and parent–teen conflict. How "tight" do you expect you and your teen to be? In response to a teenager's changing level of maturity, appropriate levels of parental monitor-ing and guidance need to change. Not recognizing that shift can certainly cause a teen to rebel. What about you and your child's other parent (if there is one)? Are you united in your efforts to shepherd your teen, including discipline, or is your teen a master at "divide and conquer"? Do you rule with an "iron fist" or know when to negotiate? Would you call your parenting style "permis-sive" or "indulgent"? Have you ever found yourself abdicating your role out of sheer frustration? Many parents of highly defiant teenagers yield to this temptation.

All of these considerations demonstrate how tortuous the path to defiance can be. That path hasn't been forged by your child alone but has been carved out by inborn characteristics of both your teen and you, stressors over which you may have little control, the psychological and physical changes that come with adolescence, the various relationships that have formed in your family over the years, and the way you as parents deal with all of this. This is why we think it's more accurate to say that the *family*, not the *individual teen*, has a defiance problem. You will spear-head the efforts to reverse the defiance that is currently ruling your household, but in doing so you'll be taking into account all of these factors affecting your family.

Defiance as Part of the Family's Development

Marla couldn't help looking at her daughter's defiance as if it were something that took root in her daughter and now had a life of its own. Defiance often looks that way from the outside. But it was really much more complicated. Sure, Jenna had always been a bit of a hothead, a little oversensitive. She'd had her parents all to herself for 6 years before the twins were born, and for the first couple of years the sibling rivalry had been a lot rougher than she'd ever anticipated. But Jenna had adjusted, at least till Tyler came along 3 years ago. Marla had really needed her help then, but Jenna had been all caught up in the business of being 11-going-on-16, and Marla had just left her headstrong oldest to her own devices a lot of the time. Things had been fine, at least until Jenna entered seventh grade, when Marla had really tried to crack down, seeing her daughter drifting off into her social life and suddenly getting very nervous about what she was up to.

Marla had no idea how she'd lost touch with Jenna or why her daughter seemed so hostile to her all the time. She knew young teenage girls could be volatile and were eager to assert their independence from their parents, but Jenna's constant antagonism was far more extreme than she'd seen in her older sister's kids or the older kids of her friends. If this kept up, where would Jenna end up? What would happen to them as mother and daughter?

When Jenna had been 8 or 9, it was all Marla could do to keep her two rambunctious 2-year-old sons from destroying the house—and each other. When Jenna wanted attention, Marla often had to put her off until the time was right, which was sometimes never. Jenna went through a phase when she started throwing temper tantrums that rivaled those of her younger brothers. To keep the peace, Marla would occasionally give in to whatever her daughter was demanding, as many harried parents do. Then she'd try to make it up to her daughter by spending time with her after the little boys were finally in bed, at which point she was often too exhausted to show a lot of enthusiasm for playing a board game with Jenna. Marla's husband, Greg, realized his wife was at her breaking point and stepped in to take over a lot more of the household duties, and peace reigned in the house for a couple of years. Jenna became a loving sister who was proud of occasionally being asked to babysit while her mother ran to the convenience store for milk.

Then baby Tyler came along and the chaos returned. Marla decided Jenna deserved to be treated like the maturing girl that she was and often just let her make her own decisions. By the time Tyler was 3 and the twins were 8, things started to settle down again, and Marla wanted to spend time with her teenage daughter. This was what she had been looking forward to for years: the chance to go shopping together, the chance to talk about her daughter's dreams and fears and hopes. But every time she asked Jenna if she wanted to go out to lunch or get their hair cut or go to the gym and work out together, Jenna said she had something else to do. She was always texting, and when her mother tried to show an interest in her life and asked who was texting her back, Jenna said, "Oh, you wouldn't know her."

When the answer evolved first to "It's none of your business, Mom," and then to "Stay out of my life, Mom. Why are you so interested *now*?," Marla got worried. When her daughter started to break curfew and she was sure she'd smelled cigarette smoke on her a couple of days when she got home from school, Marla started to crack down, demanding to know who her daughter's friends were, making her curfew earlier, and pounding her with questions about her homework and her grades. Jenna reacted with increasing disdain, their daily interactions escalated into louder and louder battles, and most of the time Marla ended up crushed, with her daughter behind her locked bedroom door and Marla doing whatever chore she had demanded that her daughter finally get to.

Over the last few years, Jenna had learned a terrific strategy to get her mother off her back. All she had to do to get what she wanted or to avoid doing what her mother wanted was to act tougher and tougher, more and more outrageous. At a certain point, her mother would give in—because she was paralyzed by the shock she felt at her daughter's behavior, because she was just too tired to have the same battle "again," because it wasn't "worth it," because the job needed to get done by someone, and so on. If you asked Jenna why she was doing what she was doing, she'd say "I don't know" or "It's my mother's fault, the way she treats me like a kid." But she doesn't really know. She hasn't formed a secret plan to drive her mother crazy; she doesn't consciously think, *Well, let's see, last time I called Mom mean; this time I'll call her an ass, and that'll stop her in her tracks*. All she knows is that if she pushes hard enough, her mother yields. All Marla knows is that nothing she tries works to get her daughter to comply. What's really happening is that by giving in, Marla is unwittingly rewarding the very behavior that she wants to stop.

*We are our teenagers' greatest plaything.**

Fortunately, it doesn't have to be that way. In the next four short chapters, we'll help you take a closer look at your teenager and yourself so that you can get a more complete picture of what's at work in your resident teen's defiant behavior. Armed with that knowledge, you'll be prepared to start to make a difference. For now, though, spend a few days just observing the coercive behavior pattern at work in your house.

Taking Action

- Each day for the next few days, as you continue to read this book, make a point to observe your interactions with your teen. When you have a conflict, jot it down on a piece of paper: for example, "Fought about how Tina was dressed for school" or "Danny didn't do any of his homework tonight."

- When you're not in the heat of "battle"—but not so much later that you'll have forgotten details—try to write down a description of the exchange using the model on page 33: Record your request, your teen's response as either compliance or noncompliance, subsequent requests as they happened, and how the conflict escalated between you. Do this for as many conflicts as you can stand to record, being sure to note how the interaction ended.

- At the end of this exercise (after a few days or a week, however much time has passed), take a look at the recorded exchanges. What's the same about them? What's different? Do you see any patterns? Do these patterns jibe with what you recorded on the checklists in Chapter 1? If not, what would you change?

- For now, try not to ascribe any motives or blame to your teenager. But think about your role: What do you see in each encounter that you did or did not do that could have contributed to the escalating defiance? Can you think of anything you could have done differently?

---

*With thanks to Howard Glasser, who said in *Transforming the Difficult Child* (Tucson, AZ: Nurtured Heart, 1999), "We are by far our child's favorite 'toy.'"

What Does Adolescence Have to Do with It?

Your 14-year-old son has left the cat litter uncleaned for 6 days running, despite numerous reminders that this is his daily responsibility.

Is he being defiant?

Your 13-year-old son runs out of the house on weekends before you can remind him that Saturday morning he babysits for his little sister while you do the weekly shopping and Sunday he attends church services with the family.

Defiance?

Your 12-year-old daughter leaves a mess behind her wherever she goes. She teases her younger brother mercilessly, talks back constantly, and sometimes even swears at you.

Is this behavior defiance?

Your 15-year-old daughter has missed curfew three times in the last 2 weeks.

Is she defying you?

If your first instinct is to answer "Yes" to these questions, stop and think about why. Because a boy who fails to do a chore despite repeated requests is clearly being disobedient? Because a 13-year-old is mature enough to know full well what is expected of him? Because a daughter who is creating havoc in the house is showing total disrespect for everyone else who lives there? Because curfew violations represent flagrant rule breaking?

All of these are good reasons to call the preceding behaviors defiance. The problem is, they may not tell the whole story. How would you answer the questions if you considered the following details?

Steven, the boy who has stopped cleaning the cat litter, can't think of much besides girls and whether they'll ever pay him any attention. A lot of the other guys his age have already sprouted up, and even the ones who used to be his friends make fun of him for being a "wimp," which is the way he's starting to view himself. He's started lifting weights in an attempt to bulk up and look "more buff," but that's after soccer practice and homework, and it energizes him so much that he surfs the Net till midnight, finally falls into bed exhausted, then stumbles around in a fog when his alarm clock wakes him up at 6:30. When his mom reminds him about the cat box after school, he always says "In a minute," and means it, but then gets distracted by rehashing the "look" a girl gave him or how a guy trashed him at lunch or just spaces out. When his mother "bugs him" again and again about the chore, he feels like she's treating him "like a baby" and deliberately puts it off.

Nick bolts out of the house on weekend mornings without giving babysitting or church a thought. He leaps out of bed and runs directly to the park to get in on the first round of pickup basketball with the other eighth-grade guys. He's determined to make the freshman team next year and wants to have a group to hang with when he starts high school. He figures his parents understand how important this is to him.

Macy, the 12-year-old girl who has become a trial to live with, is going through puberty. Her parents brushed that off as a possible cause of her behavior changes because her older sister never acted like that. Macy has no idea how to handle how she feels.

Lina has missed curfew by a few minutes on several occasions, by half an hour a couple of times, and by a whole hour once. Her explanation was that she was working on a group project that's worth 40% of her history grade for this semester. Her parents don't know the classmate at whose house the group meets, and she hasn't answered her cellphone when she's been at least 30 minutes late, explaining afterward that it doesn't ring in her friend's basement family room. Her parents have never had to deal with this issue before so they keep threatening to ground her "the next time this happens."

It's hard to define a problem, much less solve it, unless you understand the context in which it's occurring. In the case of teenage behavior problems, the context is always adolescent development. And that means *change*. Of course you know that adolescence brings change. But it's easy to lose sight of the evolving needs and desires that could be driving your teen's behavior when you're seeing red. Also, the motives underlying your adolescent's actions may not be self-evident, especially when the teen doesn't understand them him- or herself. The goal of this chapter is to help you take a closer look at the full context in which your teenager's behavior is occurring—not so you can excuse it all as just part of adolescence but so you can formulate the most effective response to unacceptable behavior. Understanding and remembering the facts of teenage development can help you:

1. *Get past the dead end of labeling your teen's behavior—and your teen.* We'd never learn anything without the brain's capacity to categorize new information for later retrieval and use. Unfortunately, that capacity steers us wrong in some cases. If your teen's noncompliant or disrespectful behavior has started to become a pattern, anything that could be classified as "defiance" will be. Because Nick has skipped out on babysitting and church repeatedly, which angers his father, Dad now assumes that Nick is insolently shirking his responsibilities and is in danger of losing his religion and his moral grounding with it. Because she has given him plenty of reminders and plenty of chances to clean the cat litter, Steven's mother assumes he's being a big baby and just abdicating this responsibility.

Repetition in cases like these may instantly trigger the "Oh, no, not again" response. You are then on alert, already angry, already anticipating that this encounter will go the way others have. Not surprisingly, this automatic response may quickly produce the same knee-jerk action you've taken before—even if it hasn't solved the problem. Steven's mother just keeps yelling at him to clean the cat litter, upping the volume and frequency of her demands and getting nowhere; Steven digs in his heels. Nick's father keeps pulling in the reins, adding chores designed to keep Nick at home with his family and interrupting with "No excuses!" when Nick tries to explain why he hasn't been around. Now Nick resents his parents' lack of understanding and shuffles around at home in a sullen cloud.

Over a shockingly short period of time, this pattern becomes so entrenched that all of your encounters with your teenager are shrouded in a negative, conflict-ridden attitude. The brain is a very efficient learner and a very reluctant *un*learner. But unlearning those negative expectations about your teen is exactly what you'll have to do if you expect to make positive change. After all, how easy do you think it will be to work openly toward change if you firmly believe your teenager will *never* stop trying to thwart you?

2. *Get down to the business of finding a better way to tackle the problem.* Adolescence isn't an excuse for bad behavior, but it certainly can trigger defiance or feed it. If Steven's mother knew what was going on in his mind, she might be able to come up with incentives that would be far more effective than ratcheting up the nagging. If Nick's parents understood his motives, they might have been able to adjust schedules so that everyone's needs were met. Macy could have gotten help for her emotional and physical discomfort, which might have made it easier for her to comply with rules about mutual respect at home.

Lina is a perfect example of how complex the task of dealing with defiance can be. At first her parents tried the "Next time there will be consequences" approach. After a few more "next times" Dad blew up and grounded Lina for a month while Mom stood by and muttered, "Don't you think that's a little harsh?" After a long fight, everyone went to bed exhausted and dejected. The next day Mom and Dad called Lina downstairs and granted her full amnesty. For a couple of weeks they bounced from over-looking the curfew violations to overreacting to them to impos-ing reasonable consequences and then losing their resolve. Lina's parents are torn. They don't really know why their daughter is breaking a longtime rule. They don't know how seriously they should take these infractions. They need to ask themselves and their daughter a lot of questions to find a solution they can stick to. They might start by figuring out where the facts of adolescent development are driving their daughter's behavior.

The Undeniable Facts of Teenage Development

The general fact that adolescent change makes teenagers act a little crazy may seem like such a cliché that you shove it into the back of your mind. It's too obvious to shed any light on your prob-lem. Knowing more specifically why and how this happens, how-ever, *can* help solve your problem. Acknowledging and respond-ing appropriately to your teen's developmental needs can reduce defiance and conflict. Ignoring or fighting these needs can actu-ally encourage defiance. You ignore them at your own peril.

Fact 1: Your teenager's primary developmental task is to become independent of you. This need is not only primary but primal. It drives virtually everything a growing teenager does because it's nothing less than a self-preservation instinct. Kids who don't achieve independence from their parents don't stand much of a chance of being fit enough to survive as adults.

If you can remember that this striving is a *need, even a require-ment for long-term survival*, you might not jump to the conclusion that every apparent act of defiance is your teen's attempt to get your goat. No teen should be so gullible and easily influenced as to do everything an adult, even a parent, tells him or her to do. While it might make your life a lot easier in the short run if your teen did so, you can surely see that in the longer term this would be disastrous. Your teen could not survive to become an independent, self-directed person if he or she were unthinkingly obedient all the time. Could breaking a rule, testing your limits, or claiming a privilege you don't grant at your teen's age be his way of screaming that he needs to start establishing his independence? We're not saying this should make the rule-breaking and other defiant behavior acceptable to you. That's for you to decide. You need to determine what's really important to you and whether it should remain so in the grand scheme of things.

- Has your teen been adamant about shedding your influence in a particular area of life? Clothing? Hairstyle? Musical taste? These can be fairly obvious attempts to separate from parents. Do you find them easy to deal with, deal breakers, or something in between?
- Is your teen insisting on more privacy, personally and socially? You may find doors closed, phone conversations hushed, friends unnamed. How much can you allow your teen a private life without viewing it as a dangerous relaxing of the reins?
- If you think back to recent days and weeks, were there times when you unthinkingly forced your teen to do something your way just because that's the way it's always been done or just because you really do think your way is better? With the clarity of hindsight, would you now consider it a big, important issue or "small stuff"? Would you do anything differently?

Maybe you could grin and bear blue hair for a while if it means your teen will obey curfew gladly? Or you can't tolerate blue hair, but you can extend your teen's curfew a little in recognition of the fact that she just turned 16? The point is that if you remind yourself that your teen *needs* to assert a certain measure of independence, you might exercise your creativity in finding ways to let her do that outside the areas you consider inviolate.

In Chapter 14 you'll have a chance to take a systematic look at the particular issues that have caused conflict between you and your teen, which may help you figure out where you want to compromise or negotiate and where you want to stand firm. For now you can start looking at various areas of interactions to see if you can spot where striving for independence may be leading to defiance. It's not always easy to see, especially when a teen is trying to meet the need in several ways at once.

Nick is trying to assert his independence from his family by exercising what he sees as his right to act on his priorities on weekend mornings. But he's also exercising teenagers' self-bestowed right not to explain themselves. He tells himself his parents will or should understand what he's doing and why. He may very well be afraid to test their reaction. It will be up to Mom and Dad to ferret out what's going on in their son's mind and then to decide what is acceptable and how to put a stop to what is not, without unduly frustrating their son's primal need to inch toward independence.

Lina's parents know they're dealing with an issue involving independence seeking. The problem is they don't know how to grant their child a certain amount of autonomy without giving her enough rope to hang herself. Are there ways they could fulfill Lina's need for growing independence while still protecting her safety? Can they help preserve their daughter's pride while demanding honesty and consideration from her? They'll have to if they want to avoid feeding the conflict that's brewing over who has control over this 15-year-old girl. A certain amount of conflict is natural when your child pushes away from you to become independent. Whether that conflict begets a pattern of defiance depends on how well you hold on to the idea that the striving is right and necessary and on how skillfully you resolve early conflicts. The program in Part II offers lots of help.

Fact 2: As teenagers individuate from their parents, they discover who they are and what they stand for—that is, *they* define their identity. This fact is intimately intertwined with Fact 1. It's normal for teenagers in the process of self-discovery and defining their identity to reject their parents' ideas, opinions, and values in favor of their friends' ideas, opinions, and values. Your teenager is not some blank slate on which you get to write so as to determine all the teen's preferences, goals, wants, and overall identity as you desire them all to be. Instead, your teen is a mosaic (genetically and otherwise)—a unique combination of traits, talents, personality, and interests of your entire family, past and present. Even when you know that, though, it's easy to feel hurt when Junior no longer wants to be seen as a chip off the old block. When Junior tries to assert his own preferences, do you assume he's doing it just to defy you? Sure, it may be hard to believe that *anyone* actually prefers to have blue rather than brown hair. And maybe Junior doesn't like it so much that he'll want to keep it. But the fact that he wants to try it out could just be his way of saying it's his hair, not that he thinks *your* personal style is awful.

Fact 3: Searching for their identity makes teenagers feel fragile inside, but they don't want to appear weak, especially to their peers but even to their parents. Another connection, with both Fact 1 and Fact 2. Your teenager needs to feel independent, and he needs to feel he's unique, not just an appendage of you and the rest of the family. He may suddenly seem to have an excessive amount of pride, particularly with regard to his striving for independence and uniqueness. He may seem ready to fight to the death over matters like the right to wear a certain shirt to school or to come in 15 minutes later on Saturday night, not because what he wears today is so critical or because another 15 minutes is going to make the difference between having a miserable time and having fun on Saturday. It's a matter of pride. When teens, especially younger ones, feel they are being treated like children, defiance may very well be their reaction.

Complying, especially once a conflict is under way, may feel like failure, and your teen may be unwilling to suffer the attendant loss of face. Keep this in mind when you sense that an argument has become self-perpetuating, its point no longer central. Can you find a way for your teen to give in gracefully, without appearing weak, stupid, or childish and without suffering humiliation?

If your child has a disorder, such as ADHD, or any common chronic illness, his need to appear omnipotent to his friends may lead him to reject any association with that disorder, including treatment. This, in and of itself, can certainly create an additional layer of conflict. It can also mean you will encounter some resistance to the teen's participation in the program in this book. If that's the case, see Chapter 7 for help.

Fact 4: The conflict that occurs when your child pushes away from you and toward independence is most common at ages 12–14. You might expect it to be otherwise—that the biggest conflicts will occur when the "big" milestones are reached: eligibility for a driver's license, after-school jobs, college or technical school, and more and more independence. This is why so many of us are caught off guard when the boy or girl who just yesterday was a sweet little kid starts testing boundaries and trying to grow up "too fast." Are you resisting seeing your son's maturation because he still looks like a kid? Or, in contrast, are you expecting too much mature logic and common sense from your daughter because she looks older than her years? It's not just your son's voice that's periodically cracking and more erratic as it vacillates from that of a child to that of a young adult; it's also his bid for independence.

Fact 5: Your teen's mental time horizon is *very* different from your own. As children mature into adults, an invisible but incredibly important mental faculty is emerging and expanding—the ability to contemplate their future—their foresight. It helps to think of this as an expanding time horizon or window, the period over which they are contemplating their future and so making their decisions about that future. This capacity varies considerably from childhood to adulthood and even then across different people. (Economists call it our time preference.) It also helps to know that people do not act to prepare for the future until an event has entered this personal window on time or crossed *their* time horizon.

Preschoolers have no horizon; they live in the now and contemplate no future at all. So they act in response only to the now, making them entirely reactive and not proactive in their behavior. They are time blind. The here and now is all that counts. You can talk about tomorrow or next week all you like, but they don't know what you mean and don't care.

By early elementary school, children are developing a sense of the future. They start thinking and even talking about what has happened in the recent past and what they may want or need to do in the near future, except that future is a mere 6–12 hours. But some of their words and actions will start to be focused on this near future. This is why you learn of the art supplies they need for school tomorrow only when you tuck them in the night before.

Despite its brevity, their window on time, or time horizon, is opening. By late childhood, this time horizon expands to a day or two. They start thinking about and making some plans on Thursday or Friday about what they may want to be doing the next day or two. By adolescence, this time horizon expands further to probably 3 or 4 days. By late adolescence to adulthood, this has expanded to 1 or 2 weeks. And by age 30, it is 1–3 months—the typical time period over which the average adult contemplates and directs decisions and behavior. The specific time intervals here are not important; it's the concept that is critical and the fact that the window on time is expanding with age.

Just as important, teens are thinking about, making decisions about, and acting toward *their* time horizon—not yours! Your teen is thinking about a future far closer in time than you are. He or she is looking ahead a day or two and couldn't care less about anything further away than that time period. In contrast, you are looking ahead several weeks and even months. No wonder you encounter conflict. You think your teen shares your time horizon but just doesn't care about it. Naturally you believe your teen should be contemplating the same time span into the future as you, and when he or she doesn't do so, you can become incredibly frustrated. The unavoidable fact is that the two time horizons are not even close to each other. So you are harping about summer reading assignments in June, weeks ahead of their due date, while this is entirely off your teen's "radar screen," which is probably just this weekend. Left to their own, most teens wouldn't start summer reading assignments until a few days before they were due in the new school year.

By keeping this great difference in time perspective in mind, you can more easily see why your teen may be thinking, deciding, and acting as the teen does—and why the two of you end up in conflict so often. The only future that matters to teens is their shorter-term future, as they perceive it to be. It is as if all they care about is what their friends are doing or who has posted what on their favorite social media site, while you are thinking about what projects they have due this month and even what colleges they should be applying to next year. Each person's priorities here are vastly different. You are not only not on the same page; you are not on the same planet timewise.

To work with teens, who have a grossly different time horizon from your own, you must break that longer-term future into pieces (small steps) so that it fits within *their* time horizon and not torture or harass them so that theirs will fit yours. It can't and it won't. Your teen is always far more nearsighted to the future than you are. To get teens to cooperate, you must think the way they do. You must help them structure this near-term future to accomplish a smaller goal (subgoal) so that it makes a small step toward the longer-term future and larger goal about which you are so concerned.

If you have an older teen who is causing more conflict than during early adolescence, one of two factors is likely at work:

1. As with 17-year-old Mark, introduced at the beginning of this book, defiance began in early adolescence or possibly even before but was not addressed. It has now grown to proportions that clearly warrant professional help. (See Appendix B at the back of this book for guidelines for getting a therapist's assistance.)

    Or

2. Your teenager is maturing more slowly than the average or is dealing with other problems that are contributing to defiant behavior. See the box below.

If Your Teenager Has ADHD or ODD . . .

Teenagers with ADHD are going through the same drastic changes in body and mind as other teenagers. However, their minds are behind their bodies in development in certain ways, particularly regarding self-control and judgments about the future and its consequences for their actions. They have the same desires for independence, peer affiliation, and sexuality as their peers, but they may be less mature, less able to anticipate the delayed consequences of their proposals or actions, more impulsive and disorganized, and less ready for independence. This means they may cause the most conflict not between the ages of 12 and 14, as with other kids, but when a few years older. Their lack of maturity creates a dilemma for parents and must be kept in mind as they deal with their problems. The same may be true for a teenager who has been diagnosed with oppositional defiant disorder (ODD) or has at least shown signs of defiant behavior for a significant period of months to years.

Fact 6: Teenagers typically give their mothers a more difficult time than their fathers during this process. It's not that mothers are doing anything wrong, intentionally or otherwise; this is a product of basic differences in human nature between men and women. Take physical size and muscular strength. On average, fathers are larger, taller, stronger, and have deeper voices that are interpreted as more authoritative. Teens naturally recognize which parent is more likely to give them grief and the difference in level of harm they may bring upon themselves if they try testing that parent's rules or instructions. Fathers also talk less, are less patient, and are quicker to punish on average than are mothers, who are more likely to talk, reason, build consensus, negotiate, or just verbally harangue than they are to impose a real consequence—a fact that most children recognize from a very early age. This too may result in mothers' limits being tested more often than fathers' limits because teens know they just might succeed, at least partially, at their limit testing or social coercion.

This limit testing is especially likely to occur between sons and mothers and particularly when fathers have been absent from the home for a few days on business trips. Remember that males are more likely than females to establish social relationships as hierarchies of power assertiveness and even physical strength. So when Dad—the alpha male, so to speak—is away, his son is more likely than his daughter to try to move into that "top dog" position. Yet that is hardly the complete story. Daughters can be testy with mothers at this age as well. Daughters, like many women, establish social relationships and hierarchies less as a function of power assertiveness and more as a process of consensus building and social-reputational influences. Disagreements are therefore more likely to have to do with such social images, social relations, and reputational disputes than would be the case with a son. The bottom line is that you need to recognize that both boys and girls are testing social relations to determine their current place within the family and the larger social milieu. During some periods they do so on a near daily basis. Understanding this can go a long way in helping you face such challenges with patience.

This power differential between mothers and fathers can cause problems on a number of levels. If you're the mother of a defiant teen, you may feel like you're entirely to blame for the problem if your teen is more cooperative with his father. This perspective engenders guilt and self-blame that can weaken your self-confidence and drain you of the energy you need to tackle the problem. You may end up demoralized and exhausted. If there are two parents in the house, can the two of you find ways to give Mom additional time for herself, to relax and regroup? Exhausted parents are ill-prepared to learn new skills like those in Part II.

If you're the defiant teen's father, you'll have to resist any temptation to agree with your child's view that Mom is somehow to blame. Read the rest of this book and you'll see that this is unlikely to be the case. Your teen may, in fact, be taking advantage of the better relationship he has with you to try the "divide-and-conquer" strategy to get what he wants when his mother denies it to him. If you're aware of this possibility, you can take extra steps to form a united front, to minimize the chance of conflict between parents, and to stay firm in your reaction to any defiance from your teen.

Fact 7: Friends begin to play a bigger role in the teen's life, sometimes supplanting parents. Just as your teenager may begin to rely more on friends' opinions and values than yours, he or she will want to spend as much time as possible with friends and as little time as possible with you. Developing the capacity for closer peer relationships and intimacy with peers is a critical developmental task of adolescence. Teenagers need to prepare themselves for the intimate partnerships, workplace collaborations, and community alliances that define adulthood. They start by practicing on their teenage friends. Again, can you put aside any hurt feelings over rejection and allow your son or daughter to grow into this larger social world of relationships with others, especially those of the teen's own age, while the teen pursues this important task? It's yet another tough balancing act—in fact, one of the toughest. Maybe you can endure your teen running off to be with friends the minute the school day is over or the weekend begins. But when it's to be with someone who exhibits values and a style that seem diametrically opposed to your own, and you think your teenager acts like someone you don't recognize when around this friend, and you're starting to consider this kid a "bad influence," you may put up barriers that your teen considers unfair—and that may in fact *be* unfair. And so the flame for conflict is lit.

Shifting Gears

Teenagers are not children. That may seem like stating the obvious, but the fact is that when kids have been living in our house all along, it's hard to see how much they are changing now that they are in adolescence, especially because everyone experiences these changes a little differently, at a different pace and cadence.

The point is that we can't rest on our assumptions or just glide along when defiant behavior arises or increases in adolescence. We need to get a grip on how developmental changes might be involved and make a conscious decision to shift gears. We may need to relax our control in some areas and to increase it in others. Maybe we have to talk more to our teens—while expecting them to talk less to us. We need to keep them safe and maintain harmony in the home without quashing their biological need to start establishing an identity separate from that of their parents. We need to understand our own mixed feelings about our kids growing up. And we need to *negotiate* more than *dictate* the terms and conditions around their behavior than with younger children. The penalty for failing to attend to these shifts could very well be not just an occasional blowup but a growing pattern of defiance and increasing conflict at a time when our kids need us more than ever—and in a different way than ever before.

Where do the undeniable facts of adolescent development leave us? With a few simple guidelines that will become easier to apply once you've read the rest of this book:

• *Develop reasonable expectations.* Your teen is in a state of flux, less mature than you expect at one moment, more at the next.

• *Pick your battles wisely.* Too much control will always be felt as a denial of your teenager's need to become independent and will be resisted, often leading to warfare when peace talks were more than possible.

• *Let them think what you want them to do was their idea.* When you give teenagers clear reasons for your rules, they make such sense that they'll feel they would have reached the same conclusions. Naturally this won't be foolproof, but they are much more likely to do what you wish if they could have come up with the idea on their own.

• *Give choices or options, not ultimatums.* Permitting teens to choose from among a menu, even a limited one, of behavioral choices is more likely to enlist their cooperation than simply dictating the terms and restricting them to one path of action. Whether it concerns clothing, friends, curfew hours, allowance, music, or whatever, offering reasonable ranges of acceptable options rather than stipulating a one-sided, case-closed, and restricted solution on your terms will go a long way to limiting opposition.

• *Catch them being good.* This is a solid principle for parenting kids of any age. But now it's more important than ever, because conflict *will* occur and you need to reinforce the fact that you notice what they do that you approve of and appreciate.

• *Start thinking in terms of problem solving.* If you're reading this book, you obviously already know that what you've been doing to try to enforce your rules and elicit compliance from your teen isn't working. That may be because you're trying tactics designed for younger kids. Or it may be because you're so often at odds with your teenager that neither of you is really very open to cooperation. Either way, the strategy that will work best is the one that adults rely on effectively: problem solving. You come to an agreement on the issues at hand, brainstorm possible solutions, and then decide which ones you'll try and what you'll do if they don't work. It's a process that instills mutual respect and removes the emotional barbs from hot-button encounters. And it's a procedure that you can adapt as you progress toward your teenager's adulthood.

The Negotiable and the Nonnegotiable

The beauty of problem solving is that it doesn't mean you have to pronounce your teenager an adult with privileges equal to your own. It's a way of acknowledging that you're shifting gears from you as solo pilot of your child's life to you more as shepherd and mentor. You can and must still set some rules and be able to enforce them. It's just that there now must also be some negotiables. The challenge is to figure out which matters are negotiable and which are not. A clear understanding of the difference is a start toward minimizing defiance and conflict.

Consider the nonnegotiables to be the bottom-line rules for living in a civilized household—the value-based things without which you don't have a functioning family. They are usually a short list—no more than six to 10 items—and they are things that you are willing to go to the mat to uphold. Examples often include "No drugs or alcohol," "No violence," "Treat people with respect and decency," and "Respect privacy." Everything else is negotiable. It often helps to view nonnegotiable and negotiable issues as pairs. A basic rule for family life may be nonnegotiable, but the conditions surrounding the implementation of the rule are often negotiable.

Let's look again at two of the teenagers introduced at the beginning of this chapter, keeping the idea of pairs in mind. That Nick would attend church was nonnegotiable; whether he attended it every week was negotiable. The family negotiated an agreement that every other week Nick would babysit for his sister on Saturday in return for permission to go out with his friends on Sunday instead of attending church. That Nick would contribute to the family by doing chores was nonnegotiable; the selection of chores and when to do them was negotiable. Nick and his parents worked out an agreement that he would help clean the house and mow the lawn in return for an allowance.

In Lina's case, her parents wanted to show that they trusted their daughter. They knew that some amount of mutual trust would help them keep their daughter safe, which was their main priority. Being able to permit her a certain amount of space from her parents would also earn her trust in them. They told Lina that being home by curfew or calling within 15 minutes if she was going to be late was nonnegotiable. So was being able to reach her by phone, so they insisted that she give them a land-line number for the house she would be in whenever she was with friends. This also ensured that they knew where she was. Negotiable were things they used to insist on: that they talk to the parents of her friends to make sure an adult was present when the teenagers were there; that they meet her friends before she be allowed to go out at night with them; that she check in with her parents in the middle of the evening. They reserved the right to insist on those conditions in individual cases where it seemed wise but promised to listen to reason and not demand these conditions every time Lina went to a friend's house in the evening.

Lina's parents found it fairly easy to identify the negotiables and the nonnegotiables. What was much harder for them was agreeing on consequences for breaking the nonnegotiable rules and then following through. We'll get into how they were able to do that in Chapters 9–12. What's important to understand for now is that you, as parents, must be the ones to decide what is negotiable and what is not. No one else can tell you where to draw that line. Some parents might have insisted on stricter rules for Lina, and some might have been comfortable with looser ones. Some parents find blue hair and punk clothing an easy way to let their teenagers find their own identity; others find such things intolerable—a nonnegotiable. We won't tell you what is "right" and "wrong" for you. We'll merely help you define it for yourself so that your teenager can push toward independence without pushing you away so hard that the gap gets difficult to close.

Taking Action

- Make a list of your nonnegotiable rules. Keep the list to six to 10 items. Following the examples in this chapter, list negotiable issues that follow from each nonnegotiable rule. Record the number of times that your teenager violates each nonnegotiable rule for 1 week.
- For the next few days, record conflicts that arise between you and your teenager, as we suggested you do at the end of Chapter 2. (Or you can just use the ones you recorded after Chapter 2 if you remember the details clearly enough.) But this time look at these interactions through the lens of adolescent development and see whether you can answer these questions:

  1. Could your teenager have been trying to assert his independence in this exchange? In what way?
  2. Were your expectations reasonable? Were you treating your teenager as if she were less or more mature than she is?

3. Was this a wise battle to pick, or, if you had it to do over again, would you have tried harder to avoid this one?

4. Were the rules or your expectations clear? Should the request have seemed reasonable and logical to your teen? Why or why not?

5. Was there anything in this exchange that you could have focused on that was positive behavior from your teenager?

6. Did you adjust your time horizon down to that of your teen (1–3 days) or were you insisting that he or she begin preparing for something that lies a week or more ahead? Could you have broken down that task into smaller, shorter-term steps and just focused on that first step for now?

7. How could a problem-solving approach have changed the outcome?

Is It Just Your Teen's Personality?

The facts of adolescent development form an important backdrop for understanding teenage defiance, but to see the whole picture you need to learn something about the personality traits—and any signs of diagnosable disorders—that come together uniquely in your teenager.

Are Some Teens Just Defiant by Nature?

Not really. Defiance is an attitude, an emotion, *and* a behavior, all of which are shaped by other influences, both external and internal. But some kids are born with characteristics that make them more likely to become defiant. We call the collection of these characteristics *temperament*, and they are the inborn traits that guide how each of us approaches the world—in essence, they help to shape our eventual personalities.

The terms *temperament* and *personality* are often used interchangeably, but there is a difference between them. A person's temperament is fairly stable, meaning it doesn't change much with growth and development or learning. We're born with a certain temperament and it stays with us.

Your personality (and your teen's) is made up of the combination of your inborn temperament and your life experiences. As we'll see in the next couple of chapters, life experiences can combine with certain temperamental characteristics to create a tendency toward defiance. Theoretically, that tendency could become so ingrained as to be considered part of a teen's personality. Whether personality becomes fully formed at some point is a question often debated by psychologists. But since our work has shown that defiance *can* be changed, it's simply counterproductive, and usually inaccurate, to view it as part of your teenager's permanent personality.

Instead, it can be instructive to look at how inborn personality traits (temperament) may have predisposed your teenager to defiance. You've probably heard of many different ways of categorizing personality, among the most recent of which is the "Big Five" (extraversion, agreeableness, conscientiousness, neuroticism, and openness to experience), which were arrived at and largely agreed on as core traits by psychologists of the late 20th century. Any such scheme may help you understand your teenager's personality, but when we speak of temperament per se, we're usually talking about nine dimensions identified by Alexander Thomas, Stella Chess, and associates in the mid-20th century, albeit in slightly different words than the originators used:

1. Activity level
2. Regularity
3. Openness to new people and experiences
4. Adaptability
5. Intensity
6. Mood
7. Persistence and attentiveness
8. Distractibility
9. Sensitivity to sensory input

On the basis of ratings in each of these dimensions, these scientists classified kids (particularly babies, for whom the system was designed) as having one of three types of temperament:

"easy," "difficult," or "slow to warm up." Teens (or adults or younger kids) we might call "strong willed" would probably be said to have a difficult temperament; those we'd call "happy-go-lucky" have an easy temperament; being slow to warm up could be viewed in various ways—these are the kids who are sort of difficult at first but then become easier over time.

It's probably not too difficult to guess that a teen who always would have fallen into the "difficult" category might be more inclined to become defiant than others. These kids don't adapt easily or well to new situations. They may have negative, intense reactions to a variety of events and people. Resistance in the form of defiance is one way that these reactions might take shape behaviorally. As it turns out, research has shown that teens who have the following temperament traits are prone to defiant behavior:

- Highly emotional (corresponds essentially to negative mood [6] and high intensity [5] above)
- Frequently irritable (corresponds to the same dimensions)
- Difficulty regulating their habits (corresponds to low regularity, or low rhythmicity [2])
- Highly active (corresponds to high activity level [1])

Teens who are comparatively more inattentive and impulsive are also more likely to develop defiant behavior. These are hallmark symptoms of ADHD and are discussed later in this chapter. For now, think about where your teenager falls along the continuums of emotionality, irritability, ability to regulate habits, and activity level. Let's go back to three of the kids we introduced at the beginning of this book as examples.

When Mark's parents thought back over his childhood, they were reminded that their son had always been a "free spirit," as they used to call him when he was young and his inability to stick to a routine or complete a task seemed more charming. Whenever they tried to force him to get to bed at a reasonable hour or do his homework right after dinner, he would start snapping at them. The harder they pushed, the louder he snapped back.

Eventually he would take out his aggravation in some physical activity. They would dejectedly retreat downstairs to the living room, where they'd hear their son bouncing a tennis ball off the wall of his room till he ran out of steam. Or he'd jump on his skateboard and zoom off to the skate park, failing, naturally, to come home after the half-hour time limit his father called out in the direction of Mark's retreating back.

Lauren definitely was, as her mother recalls, a sweet girl when younger. But she was always prone to "overreacting," said Jan. There were times when her mom caught herself spending the entire trip home from work plotting how she would break disappointing news to her little girl, such as that they wouldn't be able to go to the movies that night because of the files Jan was carting home. Or she would go to great lengths to prepare her daughter for a change that most kids would take in stride, such as *not* having pancakes for Saturday breakfast. Mac, Lauren's father, had always told Jan she should stop coddling their daughter so Lauren would "toughen up." Instead, as Lauren got older, Jan started avoiding her except when she was sure their interactions would be peaceful.

Kevin's parents would really like to say that he was always "precocious," but the truth was that even though he was smart and funny, and a lot of the teachers couldn't help liking him, most people had viewed him as "a handful" from toddlerhood. He was the kid who always took the dare, always tested the rules. He often left destruction in his wake, even if it was of the minor kind: broken toys, mud tracked through a friend's house, the freezer door left open so all the food melted.

If you'd describe your teen in his preadolescence years as moody, volatile, disorganized, spacey, touchy, unpredictable, antsy, tireless, hot-headed, theatrical, unreliable, scattered, or the like, the stage may already have been set for your son or daughter to become defiant. We have no scientific evidence that the other dimensions of temperament may predispose kids to defiance, but it's not hard to see that they could. Kids who aren't open to new experiences, who have trouble with transitions or breaks in routine, who give up when a task doesn't come easily to them, who are easily distracted or impulsive, or who are unusually bothered by loud noises, bright light, scratchy clothing, or "funny-smelling" food are not going to glide smoothly through most childhood activities and events. When they need to enter a new setting, change their schedule, finish an assignment, listen to the teacher, put up with a change in weather, wear the clothes that happen to be clean, or eat the snack served by a friend's mother, they may be inclined to react in one way: with resistance. If the circumstances don't permit accommodation of the child's preferences, the next step may very well be defiance.

Does any of this sound familiar?

Could Another Problem Be Causing Your Teenager's Defiance?

Certain psychiatric disorders, including ADHD, as mentioned earlier, can set the stage for defiance in children and, over time, teenagers. If your son or daughter has already been diagnosed with one of these illnesses, you may have a good feel for how the symptoms can spur conflict. A child who suffers from social phobia, for example, may resist school and extracurricular group activities, setting the stage for parent–child push and pull. A teen who suffers from bipolar disorder is highly likely to end up in conflicts with parents during the manic episodes that spawn grandiose ideas and high-risk behaviors. These are just a couple of examples of how conflicts that look like defiance can arise in the midst of another disorder. It's beyond the scope of this book to help you determine whether your teen might have one of these other disorders. The program in Part II of this book is not intended to address behavioral problems associated with these disorders. See the box on page 68 for a list of warning signs that indicate you should seriously consider having your teenager evaluated for an anxiety or mood disorder, which needs to be addressed particularly if the problem has gone on for at least 6 months.

Warning Signs
of Another Diagnosable Problem

- If the conflicts between you and your teenager center around the teen's avoidance of a specific object or situation (such as a spider or seeing blood), and this avoidance is interfering with normal activities and causing the teen lots of distress, consider an evaluation for specific phobia.

- If your teen consistently tries to avoid school, friends, family gatherings, or anyplace else where the teen might be embarrassed or humiliated, or where his or her performance may be found wanting, and the avoidance is interfering significantly with his or her life and the fear is causing much distress, consider an evaluation for social phobia.

- If conflicts between you center on your teen's excessive, constant worries and anxiety over a number of events or activities, such as work, school performance, and sports, which are interfering with the teen's life and causing much stress and distress, consider an evaluation for generalized anxiety disorder.

- If your teen has been excessively irritable, sad, or agitated; feels hopeless and has difficulty concentrating; and/or has had problems with appetite or sleep, and these problems have gone on every day for at least 2 weeks, consider an evaluation for depression.

- If your teen has, for at least 1 week, been giddy, overly happy, or ecstatic; expansive or grandiose; or irritable—and also needed little sleep, talked a lot more than usual, was relentlessly persistent at certain tasks, and/or had racing thoughts but had been flitting from one subject to another—consider an evaluation for bipolar disorder (a very difficult disorder to diagnose but one that is usually diagnosed on the basis of mania, that is, symptoms like the ones listed here).

- If your teen has for many years "just not gotten it" socially—missing important social cues and having difficulty knowing how to relate appropriately to peers—and if your teen seems obsessed by one theme that has taken over his or her entire life (everything is video games, a particular sport, computers, etc.), consider an evaluation for autism spectrum disorder, a form of pervasive developmental disorder characterized by severe social problems and restricted interests.

Attention-Deficit/Hyperactivity Disorder

We mentioned above that inattentiveness, impulsivity, and over-activity—the hallmark symptoms of ADHD—are also closely associated with defiant behavior. If your teen was inattentive, impulsive, or hyperactive as a baby or toddler, you and your child's health care practitioners could easily have chalked it up to temperament. But when these tendencies persist as the child grows, they are more and more likely to feed conflict between you and your son or daughter. Why? Because another central feature of ADHD that is not often discussed in descriptions of it is poor emotion regulation. Children with ADHD are as impulsive in showing their emotions as they are in their thoughts and actions. This means they are displaying more immediate, raw, and primary emotions when others would be inhibiting them, moderating them, and making them more appropriate for the situation. Essentially, ADHD is a disorder of self-control, and so it makes perfect sense that those with the disorder would have trouble regulating their emotions as others are able to do.

Remember the coercive pattern of behavior described and diagrammed in Chapter 2? When a child can't sustain attention, acts impulsively, and can't sit still—characteristically, not just occasionally—parents (and teachers) are likely to end up issuing more commands, to supervise more closely, and to be more critical, creating disproportionately more negative than positive interactions with the child. The more severe the ADHD symptoms, the more likely that the child will have negative emotional reactions to parents' "hovering" or "demands." And the child will express that frustration, impatience, and even hostility far more quickly in these situations than will others. If, in turn, those reactions open an escape hatch from further demands (the teen coerces the parent and the parent caves in), the teen will naturally up the ante and react this way more often and for longer durations.

We know from plenty of research over the years that lack of impulse control, in particular, creates more conflict between teens and parents.

Remember Gina, one of the teenagers introduced at the beginning of this book? At age 13 her academic performance was so low that it threatened to affect her entire future. Meanwhile, Gina and her mother were at such odds over Gina's failure to catch up on missed assignments and turn around her performance that Gina missed out on a lot of the parental shepherding and support that are essential to thriving in early adolescence. With a consistent medication regimen, the program in this book repaired the mother–daughter bond and helped Gina stick to what she needed to do to succeed in school and elsewhere. We'll show you how Gina's parents helped her get back on track using the tools and skills in this book, with a little help from the therapist who diagnosed Gina's ADHD several years earlier.

Conduct Disorder

There is one other disorder that you should know the signs of, because if your teenager qualifies for this diagnosis, you will definitely need professional help. The program in Part II may be of some assistance—or at least the tenets of the program—*but self-help will not be successful and could actually do more harm than good.*

A teenager who exhibits defiance in ways that are particularly aggressive, destructive, possibly violent, and/or illegal may very well have *conduct disorder*, a serious problem that must be addressed as soon as possible to prevent the teen from heading for an adulthood marked by antisocial, possibly criminal, behavior. Over the last year, has your teen been getting into fights, running away from home, skipping school frequently, stealing, bullying others, vandalizing property, or using physical force to get what he or she wants, whether that's money, someone else's property, sexual activity, or something else?

Mark, the 17-year-old we met in the Introduction, shows at least some signs of conduct disorder. He is regularly truant, and he regularly threatens and tries to bully his parents. He comes in so late at night on weekends that he might as well be gone overnight. Mark's problem is too severe for self-help. He can, however, benefit from the program in this book. We'll show you how he and his family worked with a therapist using the same steps you'll be following in Part II.

Are Personality and Pathology Destiny?

Yes and no. As we said earlier in the chapter, temperament is generally stable. A child born "difficult" will retain the same tendencies toward irritability, moodiness, disorganization, or unpredictability for life. But that doesn't mean that these traits have to cause the same problems they may be causing in your teen right now. Being aware of their influence on your teen's behavior can help you know what to try to "fix" (the behavior) and what to try to "get around" (the inborn traits) so that the behavior is easier to change. Part II is filled with examples of how you can use your new insights into your teenager's personality to craft the most effective possible program to help your family overcome defiance.

As for pathology, a lot depends on the problem and its severity. If your teen gets the best possible treatment for ADHD, for example, the symptoms that feed defiance will be lessened, possibly even neutralized. Realistically, though, you should be prepared to continue to deal with some degree of symptoms. Disorders like ADHD, anxiety, depression, and bipolar disorder cannot be cured, at least not at this time. But they can certainly be improved tremendously with appropriate care—and with them their contribution to defiance. And some disorders, like ADHD and bipolar disorder, actually do usually get less severe (or pose fewer challenges) in adulthood (see the Resources for sources of additional information).

Is Stress Contributing to Your Teen's Defiance?

We don't have to tell you that stress is a fact of life. But adults often forget that stress comes from sources other than the adult problems and responsibilities that we usually associate it with. Even the youngest teens (and younger kids, for that matter) are exposed to external pressures, whether it's getting a failing grade, being disciplined at school, being bullied, or being rejected by peers. These are examples of what we call "bad" stress, and the family environment might bring additional forms of this kind of stress as well (see the following chapter). But there is also "good" stress, the kind usually associated with excitement and anticipation, as mentioned in Chapter 2. Stress of either kind can make a teen behave more impulsively or erratically. This may mean defying parents in ways that aren't in keeping with the teen's temperament. Or it might just have a negative effect on the parents, who react by clamping down or otherwise provoking conflict themselves. Is your teen subject to stress from sources you haven't considered?

One type of stress that often gets intertwined with defiance in teenagers is dealing with a chronic illness. Consider diabetes. Thirteen-year-old Faith has juvenile-onset diabetes, which requires her to check her blood sugar five times a day and take insulin shots three times a day. She has to calculate the amount of insulin based on what she plans to eat, and she has to make sure not to eat too many carbohydrates. If she fails to follow this regimen, her blood sugar may get dangerously high; she could get sick and end up in the hospital.

Faith hates diabetes. She feels like a prisoner to diabetes. She can't go anywhere without checking her blood and taking her insulin. She can't eat like her friends; she feels different from them. She feels that it is terribly unfair that she got diabetes. She rebels against following her medical regimen by "forgetting" to check her blood sugar about half the time and sneaking foods that she shouldn't eat. She doesn't tell her mother when her blood sugar is high. Her mother nags Faith about her diabetes care. They argue frequently about blood checks and diet. Faith has had three admissions to the hospital for uncontrolled diabetes this past year. Diabetes is clearly a stressor that has set the stage for defiant behavior in Faith and parent–teen conflict. Similar challenges arise for teenagers with other chronic illnesses.

Taking Action

- Of the characteristics that have been associated with defiance, check off those you've seen in your teenager. If you can, relist them in descending order by how much conflict they've caused or how long your teen has demonstrated them.

☐ Highly emotional

☐ Frequently irritable

☐ Difficulty regulating habits

☐ Highly active

☐ Impulsive

☐ Inattentive

Hold on to this list. You're going to use it again.

- Now think about what types of stress your teenager may be under—pressures at school, in the social arena, at home? Does your teenager have a psychiatric disorder like ADHD or a chronic physical illness?

- Now *stop* thinking about the negative aspects of your teenager's temperament. It's time to identify—and appreciate—your teenager's psychological and social strengths. Fill in whatever you can below.

My teenager is good at these hobbies, sports, and recreational activities:

_____

_____

My teenager does well at these subjects in school and these extracurricular intellectual interests:

_____

_____

My teenager is a good friend in these ways:

_____

_____

My teenager is a good sibling (cousin, grandchild, etc.) in these ways:

_____

_____

As an adult, my teenager would probably make a good (fill in occupation, profession, vocation, avocation):

_____

_____

If I needed it, I could count on my teenager to:

_____

_____

- Consider one personality trait that you have identified in your teenager that you think contributes to defiance and write down one thing you could have done differently in a recent conflict to neutralize the escalating effect of that trait on the conflict.

_____

_____

_____

_____

5

Where Do You Come In?

"I can't believe two people can look so much alike and be so different!"

"Of course you're constantly butting heads—you're *exactly* alike!"

Sound familiar? It takes two to engage in any conflict. So it makes sense to look at how personalities intersect in parent–teen clashes. In this chapter, we ask you (both of you, if your teen has two parents) to take a few minutes to consider your own temperament and your personal circumstances objectively, just as you did for your teenager in the last two chapters. The goal is not to point the finger at yourself or your teen's other parent for causing the problems between you. No one wins the "blame game." It's a contest that can end only in guilt, hurt feelings, and even more family conflict. The goal is to identify some important keys to success with the program in Part II. It's kind of like figuring out how your pack-rat tendencies have produced an overflowing basement so you know how to clean out the room and keep the clutter down in the future—or knowing the circumstances that lead you to eat foods you'd rather avoid so you can reach a health goal that's eluded you.

How You Could Be Contributing to Your Teen's Defiance

Leon's family often refers to him as "Albert" because of the half-completed "inventions" he leaves all over the house and his Einsteinian propensity for wearing mismatched socks. They're keeping a running tally of the times he's forgotten to pick the kids up from school or a soccer game.

Enrique says his constant worry about the kids and their activities is just normal parental vigilance. But the older they get, the more his kids chafe at his protective measures.

Latoya has always been moody. Sometimes she stays in bed till noon, even if it means taking a "personal day" away from work. The kids tiptoe around the house on those days so they don't get yelled at to "Be quiet!" Crystal, the oldest, just makes herself scarce.

Each of these parents is struggling with a defiant teen. Christian, Leon's 15-year-old son, just doesn't listen to his father when he gets exasperated because Christian hasn't done some chore or another. He knows Dad won't follow through on making him do the chore or the threatened punishment. Leon then gets infuriated at his son's "insolence" but has a hard time settling on a plan to deal with it.

Enrique's son, Joaquin, has started to take the easy way out from under his father's magnifying glass and just lies about what he's doing. Enrique senses that he's losing control of his son and keeps trying to clamp down harder, which leads to a verbal battle virtually every time Joaquin exits the house.

Latoya has always counted on Crystal to take charge when she's having one of her bad days. Lately she's awakened to find the little kids playing by themselves with Crystal nowhere in sight. Each time, she's withdrawn one of her oldest child's privileges, but Crystal just shrugs off these punishments with a sullen "Whatever." This new problem just makes Latoya feel even more exhausted.

Leon, Enrique, and Latoya aren't "causing" their teenagers to behave defiantly, and neither are you. But you may be unwittingly contributing to your teen's defiance on a couple of levels:

1. *By the way you act in any single encounter with your teen.* Would you say you have a short fuse? Do you tend to blurt things out without thinking? Do you find yourself easily feeling defensive? Do you often feel tongue-tied or generally inarticulate? These are just a few obvious ways that your reflexive reactions can inadvertently spark or feed conflict. There are many more complicated, subtle ways that this can happen as well. Parents who have never felt like very effective disciplinarians sometimes overreact to assert their authority. Or we unconsciously bring our work stress home and take out the hostilities we feel toward an unfair boss on an "unfair" teenager. Or a tendency toward moodiness or impulsivity can make any encounter unpredictable and uncontrolled. In such cases it doesn't take time for a pattern of coercion to build. Each interaction with the teenager holds great potential for erupting into conflict.

Leon is a generally affable guy, but when he feels frustrated, he blurts out whatever pops into his head, and he and Christian end up bickering for reasons that escape the rest of the family. Enrique grasps for a way to keep Joaquin at home and under control and will start shouting even when he's not feeling angry just in the hope of being heard.

Moody and depressed, Latoya inappropriately expects Crystal to take over her parental duties. Then she lashes out at Crystal for trying to be a teen, not a parent. When our problems cause us to "parentify" our teens, defiant behavior is a natural reaction. Our teenagers want to be who they are right now—teens, not adults.

2. *By the pattern of your behavior over time.* Are you consistent from one encounter with your teen to the next? Do you follow through on what you say you'll do as a consequence for misbehavior or noncompliance? Do you assume every time your teen talks

to you that the encounter will end in a blowup, as has happened so often in the past? As we explained in Chapter 2, a pattern of coercive behavior usually builds over time when parents don't have the tools or strategies to take a new, more productive tack with their teens.

Leon always has good intentions, but he has trouble sticking with the program (any program, if truth be told). Occasionally he'd put aside his absentminded-professor style and attempt to be a tough taskmaster, but Christian was unimpressed and still did what he wanted. Over time, Christian's mother, Brenda, pointed out that Leon was allowing their son to grow up with no boundaries or adult guidance. So Leon started trying to get tough more often. Unfortunately, these efforts weren't any more effective just because they were more frequent. Christian figured out that he could distract his parents from dealing with his behavior by feeding disagreements between them—then he could go about doing whatever he wanted while Mom and Dad continued to duke it out.

Also keep in mind the old adage that kids do what we *do*, not what we say. So even if you've set very strict rules for your teen's behavior, she may very well interpret your tendency to break those rules with others as tacit permission for her to ignore the rules too. Shawna's parents often ended up screaming at her to stop wheedling and whining every time they insisted she do her homework before getting on the Internet, and they couldn't understand why she kept up this tactic that never—well, almost never—worked. Yet that's what she saw her mother do every time Mom and Dad disagreed on decisions large and small—she whined and nagged and cajoled until finally her father gave in or stomped off, only to give in later. These are just two examples of how the coercive pattern of interactions is established by parental participation as well as the teen's.

Your own characteristics, especially in combination with your teen's characteristics, plus the stresses you're dealing with and your day-to-day parenting style, can all influence whether and how you contribute to your teen's defiance, in individual encounters and over time. One of the first things to consider is whether you and your teen both have characteristics that are known to contribute to defiance.

Sometimes the Apple Doesn't Fall Far from the Tree—and Sometimes It Does

Relatives are always telling Christian how much he resembles his father and Crystal how much she reminds them of her mother. Conventional wisdom tells us that when two people possess the same "difficult" trait—say hypersensitivity, overemotionality, or stubbornness—they are even more likely to clash than when only one of them has such traits. The research into defiance in kids and teens tends to agree. Studies have shown that difficult teens who are easily frustrated, who are quick to get angry or emote, and who have poor self-control often have parents with similar attributes due to shared genetics regarding those traits. So the reason you and your teen clash so often may be because the apple *doesn't* fall far from the tree.

This may be particularly true if you have an older teen. As your teen matures, you have less and less control over his or her environment, meaning environmental issues are less and less likely to be the cause of conflicts. Likewise, developmental issues diminish as you and your teen get further and further into adolescence and everyone adjusts to the teen's new stage of life. Therefore, if your conflicts continue (or increase) into older adolescence, there's a pretty good chance that shared personality traits are playing a significant role.

Does this mean you should just throw up your hands, considering that personality is essentially static? Not at all. It just means that learning strategies for playing up your personal strengths and getting around any "difficult" traits is even more important because nothing else may make a difference.

How do people usually compare you to your defiant teen? What words do they use to describe you both? High-strung? Quick-tempered? Mercurial? Do they say you don't like change or aren't very adaptable? It's hard to see ourselves clearly, but you can ask for input from a relative you trust not to relish the opportunity to criticize you. Or simply do a mental review of the ways people have described your personality over the years. Try to be open to the possibility that your defiant teen might have inherited a difficult temperament from you or her other parent. And keep in mind that if your teen has what could be called a "difficult" temperament, the chance of conflict between you is high; when you have the same tendencies, the odds grow exponentially.

Do You and Your Defiant Teen Both Have ADHD?

Through our genes we can pass on not just personality characteristics but also risks for various disorders that affect behavior. Research evidence concerning the genetic basis for ADHD, mood disorders, anxiety disorders, and many others is now substantial and continues to mount. As you learned in Chapter 4, the hallmark symptoms of ADHD are a formula for defiance in kids and teenagers. Christian was evaluated for ADHD in fourth grade, when his grades fell and he seemed constantly distracted. The practitioner who evaluated him determined that he didn't fully qualify for the diagnosis, and he wasn't treated, though Christian was lucky enough to have a savvy teacher adept at behavior management strategies that often help kids with ADHD stay on track. With this help, Christian's academic performance and classroom behavior improved somewhat. But now his defiant behavior at home is beginning to affect his academic performance and behavior at school again. Christian's mother compared her son to the descriptions of ADHD in Chapter 4 and decided to have her son evaluated again. Christian was diagnosed with relatively mild ADHD. At Brenda's urging, Leon was scheduled for an evaluation to see if he too had ADHD. The results conclusively said that he did. With treatment for the disorder plus the use of some of the strategies in this book, Leon's conflict with his son gradually began to subside.

It's important to determine whether you or your teen's other parent might have ADHD if your teenager has been diagnosed or exhibits the signs of the disorder. There seems to be at least a 40–50% chance that one of the two parents of a defiant adolescent with ADHD will have adult ADHD (approximately 15–20% of mothers and 25–30% of fathers). Adults with ADHD are also more likely to have problems with anxiety, depression, personality disorders, alcohol use and abuse, and marital difficulties; to change employment and residence more often; and to have less education and lower socioeconomic status than adults without ADHD. As we'll explore later in this chapter, these additional problems only increase the risk of defiance in a teenage son or daughter and the chance of conflict. In fact, when a parent has ADHD, the probability that the teen with ADHD will also have ODD increases markedly. There's also evidence that having ADHD can interfere with one's ability to undertake the training in this book, though that interference lessens when the ADHD is treated.

But even without all the other ancillary problems that may accompany ADHD, it's easy to see how impulsiveness, inattentiveness, and/or hyperactivity on the part of both parent and teen can blow tranquillity out of the water, in the same way that both having "difficult" temperaments can.

When Christian asked his father if he could go hang out at a friend's house, Leon at first mumbled "Fine," and Christian started to run out of the room. But Brenda blocked her son's exit, saying, "Wait a minute. It's a school night. Have you done your homework?"

Christian answered, "I'll do it later. I'll be home in plenty of time."

Brenda replied, "No, you won't, because you're not going out. Right, Leon? Isn't that what we agreed?"

"Oh, I think it's OK for him to go, Brenda. He deserves some fun. . . ."

"Leon, we can't keep changing the rules."

"Don't be such a jerk, Mom," interjected Christian. "Dad said it's OK."

"Hold on, Christian," Leon jumped in. "You can't call your mother names like that! Now you apologize and then march up to your room and get going on that homework!"

"But, Dad—"

"And come to think of it, you're grounded! You *never* do your homework when you're supposed to!"

"Hey, that's not fair! You're always changing your mind about everything! You said I could go until *she*"—Christian pointed sharply at his mother—"messed everything up."

Leon leaped from his chair and grabbed the hand his son was using to point accusingly at his mother, whirled him around, and gave him a not-so-gentle shove toward the stairs. Christian spun back toward Leon for a second, then gave him a defiant glare and ran out the front door.

This kind of conflict could certainly occur outside of ADHD, but it's also a good example of the turmoil caused when interactions are influenced by ADHD symptoms on the part of both teen and parent. Leon didn't want to wrench himself away from the game he was watching on TV to play the parental role, and he didn't really recall the rules he and Brenda had agreed on for school-night activities anyway. Christian was lured away from his homework by the prospect of something more fun to do. Without Brenda's intercession, Christian probably would have gone to his friend's house and never done his homework. But even with her pulling her husband and son back to terra firma, the encounter blew up. Leon couldn't control his impulsive anger prompted by his son's insolence toward his mother. Christian couldn't control his indignation at being denied what he wanted to do and being humiliated by his father. Even though their respective ADHD symptoms are now being treated, this father and son need tools that will keep their interactions well structured over time if they are to avoid increasing clashes.

What about Other Psychological Problems?

Other emotional and behavioral disorders may also contribute to conflict in your family and defiance in your teen. Latoya has been battling depression for years. Research points to maternal depression as a particularly strong risk factor for defiance in kids. If you're depressed, you may not be able to mount the energy and fortitude to be a consistent authority figure, especially if your teen has defiance-increasing characteristics (see Chapter 4). Latoya certainly can't, and matters have been even worse because of the tendency mentioned in Chapter 3 for young teens (Crystal just turned 13) to give their mothers a harder time than they give their fathers.

The last thing Latoya wants is to harm her children. Trying to deal with her depression without bringing in "outsiders" has been one way she has attempted to protect them (in this case, from the stigma of mental illness). But Crystal's growing defiance *is* harming the teen, and it's having a negative effect on Latoya and her other kids as well.

Let's say you too suffer from mood swings—nothing so severe that you've sought treatment, but you've always been described by others as highly emotional and unpredictable. Like Latoya, you may suddenly feel so down that you just can't deal with the demands of daily life. Your teenager disobeys you in some way, and you don't have the energy to call him on it. His mind registers that he's gotten away with something—and that if he can do it once, he may be able to do it again. Which he does.

Similarly, Enrique may be suffering a mild form of anxiety. Ever since his wife died when Joaquin was only 9, he has felt it was his obligation to exercise every bit of care the kids' mother would have, in addition to doing his paternal duties. The pressure of trying to be both "Superdad" and "Supermom" while keeping up with a demanding job leaves him exhausted, yet he can't sleep at night. He lies awake envisioning all the bad things that could happen to his kids if he lets his guard down and how he would be dishonoring his wife's memory if he relaxed his vigilance one iota. Now that Joaquin is getting away from home whenever he can, Enrique's imagination only runs wilder.

If you've been wrestling with mood swings, like Latoya, or with excessive anxiety, like Enrique, and you're now wrestling with a defiant teen as well, now is the time to seek professional counsel. Appendix B at the back of this book has guidelines for finding someone who can help you.

Is the Fit between You a Good One?

The concept of "goodness of fit" originally came from the field of child development: The better the child's fit with the environment and especially the child's caregiver (usually the parent), the better his or her chances of growing up healthy and happy. Because parents are such a big part of children's environment, the fit between parents' personalities and their children's personalities was naturally explored. What makes a good fit is complex. Some similarities between parents and kids are fortuitous, others challenging—like the characteristics and disorders that some parents and teens share because the kids came by them genetically. Some differences cause thunderous clashes, where others just keep things interesting and lively. We won't be able to generalize constructively but simply try to get you thinking about your own relationship with your teen.

One way to explore the parent–teen fit is to examine which issues tend to cause conflict. You can take a quick look now at the Issues Checklist on pages 264–265 to see whether any hot buttons jump off the page at you. If so, jot those down and then see if you can find a common thread. Do they all have to do with a particular personality difference or similarity? Is there some other connection among them?

Even a single difference or similarity that causes disagreements between you and your teen can mushroom into ongoing conflict. Like many teens, Nora doesn't pay much attention to neatness in her room or in the rest of the house. When Nora ignores Gail's repeated requests to clean up her room and Gail says she can't stand to look at it, Nora replies, "Well, just close the door." For years she has been calling her mother a "neat freak." Her father, Brandon, tends to agree. But Gail takes Nora's response as a sign of total disrespect for *her* feelings, *her* house, and *her* life. Feeling totally powerless to change her daughter's act, she ends up trying to punish or control her daughter in other ways, though she's not always aware that that's what she's doing. After a morning of tripping over clothing, then finding a load of her daughter's laundry sitting in the washer that she needs to use, Gail finds herself telling Nora that no, she can't have the car to drive to her friend's house, and, furthermore, she needs Nora to babysit for her little sister while she does some errands. On other occasions like this, she would have gladly rescheduled her errands and taken her younger daughter along to accommodate her teenager. Being thwarted riles Nora up, and she lashes out at her mother with a volley of accusations about her motives, most of which are accurate. This brings Gail's ire to the surface, and she grounds her daughter for her attitude.

Was Gail right to expect Nora to keep her room neat? Possibly. Was she right to expect her daughter not to leave chaos in her wake throughout the house? Probably. But these are boundaries that each family has to set for itself, a topic we'll return to later in this book. For now, the important point is to think about how far differences like neat parent/sloppy teen have pushed you into conflict and whether those differences are based on fixed personality traits or something more mutable. Just giving a little more thought to this than you ordinarily would might head off a skirmish or two of the variety that Gail and Nora just had. At the very least it's likely to motivate you to learn the skills to sidestep conflicts like it in the future.

The example of Gail and Nora is just one of many that can mark a poor fit between parent and teen. A slow, deliberate parent may spark such impatience in a quick teen that no chore or other task goes smoothly. An open-minded, expansive parent may get easily frustrated with an overcautious teen. A politically or socially liberal teen may push the buttons of a conservative parent (or vice versa) over and over until hardly any conversational topics are "safe." A fearful parent, like Enrique, may suffocate an adventurous teen, like Joaquin, to the point where the teen bolts whenever possible.

Think about where you and your teen diverge and where you come together peacefully. Some problem areas may involve mere habits or preferences, while others are more ingrained. Objectively seeing characteristics you've found undesirable in your teen can help you realize that these traits and tendencies aren't "bad" in and of themselves; rather, they simply contrast with your own.

It's the difference between you and your teen that may be causing the problem, not your child's personality on its own.

A poor fit in temperament between a parent and a teenager is especially likely if your teen was adopted. After all, you had no way to know your child's temperament before adopting him or her as an infant. There's also a reasonable chance that an adopted child had impulsive parents who didn't plan to have a child, increasing the genetic loading for impulsive behavior and difficult temperament in the child. If your adopted teen is displaying a great deal of defiant behavior, you may be doubting your decision to adopt and even wondering whether you should give up the teen. These are perfectly normal thoughts in such a situation. Try to be patient and follow the suggestions in this book; they are just as likely to work with adopted teens as with biological offspring.

What Kinds of Stress Are Affecting You and Your Family?

From the preceding chapter, you know what kinds of stress your teenager is under and how stress might be contributing to a defiant attitude or behavior. But you're undoubtedly suffering some stress too (outside the stress of dealing with defiance from your son or daughter!). Who isn't?

Social, Financial, and Marital Problems

We know from research and from counseling numerous families that external stressors like financial problems, social adversity, and occupational pressure contribute to defiance in teens. So does marital status. Statistically speaking, single mothers have been shown to be the most likely to have aggressive teens, followed by mothers living with male partners but unmarried. Married couples are the least likely to have aggressive teens. Socially isolated mothers also have a greater tendency to have aggressive teens. Marital discord too has frequently been linked to defiance, though the mechanisms that contribute to this are still being debated. Similar stressors may apply to single fathers, but research has not been completed in this area.

Parents dealing with social or economic disadvantage or adversity often tend to be irritable for obvious reasons, which in turn can make them inconsistent or indiscriminate in managing their teenagers. Being indiscriminate in managing teens can both cultivate and sustain defiance.

Jim lets the emotions of the moment determine how he reacts to his son, Tyson. That's how his own father treated Jim when he was growing up, and he figures he survived, so why should he waste any time trying to psychoanalyze himself? Tyson idolized his dad when he was little, so he just crept away when his father unexpectedly barked at him. Now he's beginning to resent not having any idea what to expect from his father, so he often goads him into a fight—he figures it's inevitable anyway.

Jim takes his son's aggression as an indication that his worst fears are being realized: even his own son looks down on him for never finishing high school and hardly knowing how to read. The loss of his son's admiration is more than he can tolerate, so he fights back the only way he knows how. With each encounter, he yells a bit louder and threatens to hit his son, which just proves to Tyson that he can't depend on his father to act rationally—ever. So Tyson ups his defiance too. Tyson's mother is just waiting in terror for the day when their arguments turn into fistfights.

The problem with social and family stressors is that they both exacerbate defiance and are exacerbated by it, in a vicious, ever-widening circle. Keith and Sadie have had a tumultuous marriage punctuated by several separations. In their constant arguments their son, Liam, has often been a pawn, with both trying to get him on their side, each egging him on to defy the other out of revenge. By the time he was 14, Liam did pretty much exactly what he wanted, paying little attention to either of them. His behavior problems eventually extended beyond the home, and his scrapes at school and elsewhere put more stress on the parents individually, which they then blamed on each other, often erupting into yet another door-slamming fight.

Health Problems

Another source of stress that you and your teen may be dealing with is illness, disability, or injury. To put it simply, being in pain can sap the strength, energy, and creativity you can apply to interacting with a teenager, causing you at the very least to let go of your resolve to parent consistently. As we'll see, consistency is the hallmark of effective management of teen behavior, especially teenage defiance.

What's Your Parenting Style?

The whole idea of "parenting style" might seem foreign to you. Many of us simply do whatever feels right or seems to work at the moment, or maybe we simply raise our kids the way our parents raised us or the way we've seen someone else parent. Others of us have given a lot of thought to how we interact with our kids. Maybe we've read a lot of books or we just want to do things differently than our parents did. We may have very strong opinions about how to deal with various aspects of parenting—yet still not have a thorough grasp of how our style of parenting might or might not contribute to the development or reinforcement of defiant behavior in a teen.

Lou and Janet love their kids unconditionally, just like the rest of us. But their approach to parenting might best be described as "impromptu." Sometimes they resort to the way their respective parents handled an issue (usually causing conflict between them because they were raised in quite different manners). Other times they randomly apply some tip one or the other saw on a morning talk show or read in a magazine at the dentist's office. Their kids never know what to expect. They come down hard on Gary, their oldest, most of the time, asserting in a way that even they don't really believe, that he needs to set a good example for the younger kids. Their youngest, Maureen, is given whatever she wants most of the time—as long as she screams for it loudly enough to drown out the TV her dad is trying to watch. Middle child Eric is sometimes treated like an "older child" and other times like the "baby of the family." At any given time, the kids know that Janet is likely to be irritable when they don't do what she wants and Lou is likely to try to look the other way when misbehavior occurs. When they really want their parents' attention, they get it by acting out. When they want to get out of doing a chore or their homework, they ratchet up their protests rapidly to end their parents' "nagging." Now that Gary is 14 his parents are dismayed that he talks to them sarcastically and seems to have no compunction about shouting at them as if they were all equals. Eric is less aggressive but never seems to get his chores done; they think he's just "a space cadet." Maureen just keeps throwing tantrums.

Consistency versus Inconsistency

Lou and Janet severely punish negative behavior sometimes and ignore it at other times. The kids have no idea where the boundaries are, so they keep pushing them. They also harbor a deep sense of injustice because it hardly escapes their notice that each of them is treated differently—yet their demands to be treated fairly are ignored. In fact, parent–child conflicts usually end with Lou and Janet getting lost in their favorite argument over whose parents took the right approach to disciplining children. When inconsistency reigns, kids have no idea what to expect from their parents and therefore tend to refuse to cooperate.

Equanimity versus Irritability

Janet has always been subject to mood swings. The stress of being surrounded by loud, defiant kids doesn't help her. She's often irritable as a result, and this puts the kids on edge too. Lou is calmer but abdicates his responsibility as a parent as often as he can get away with. The kids have no model for equanimity and therefore conjure up all the histrionics they can muster when they want something from their parents or want to avoid a request. The longer this state of affairs continues, the angrier Janet tends to feel.

She's beginning to wonder how bad a parent she might be now that she doesn't really enjoy her kids' company much.

Reinforcement of Bad versus Good Behavior

Lou and Janet are often overwhelmed and exhausted, so they sometimes just try not to interact with their kids at all. They never catch them being good; they just feel so relieved that there are no problems for the moment that they ignore the kids, almost superstitiously afraid that if they breach the calm, it will explode into another scene. Their kids have discovered that if they really want to get out of a chore or other parent-imposed task, all they have to do is go right to the explosion that ended the encounter the last time around. Lou and Janet's giving up on enforcing the completion of the chore just reinforces their kids' negative behavior. Lou and Janet aren't particularly guilty of overuse of punishment, but many parents of defiant teens (and kids) are. They're so quick to exact punishment for any infraction that the teens figure they might as well take their chances on pulling out all the stops because the consequences will be the same.

Right-Side-Up versus Upside-Down Family Hierarchy

Families naturally have a hierarchy or "pecking order" with parents in charge of children, even adolescents. We'll discuss this point further in the next chapter. But for now it's important to note that Lou and Janet have no hierarchy. They place themselves at the same level of power as their children, failing to take charge. Throughout adolescence parents should gradually grant their teen increased freedom, elevating their power status in the hierarchy step by step. Lou and Janet act in a seemingly random way toward their children. In the absence of a clear hierarchy, defiant behavior flourishes.

All of these forms of behavior increase defiance. So do certain overall parenting styles. Psychologists sometimes categorize parents as being authoritative, authoritarian, indulgent, or neglectful. *Authoritarian parents* tend toward the "Because I said so!" response to any questioning of their authority. They're not necessarily consistent, and they don't teach their children good behavior by example: they just dictate. *Indulgent parents* want to be friends with their kids and want their kids to have as much of what they want as possible, so they may not set very firm rules and may be viewed as overly permissive. *Neglectful parents* take permissiveness one step further: they just don't pay attention. *Authoritative parents* are consistent, fair, predictable, and firm yet open to reasonable negotiation. Because they both set rules that may be questioned by their teens, the authoritarian and authoritative parenting styles create more conflict with teens than the indulgent or neglectful parenting styles. But kids raised by neglectful parents are the least well adjusted, whereas those of indulgent and authoritarian parents are mixed. Kids of authoritative parents, who tend to reason and negotiate with their teens, tend to be the most well adjusted of all. It seems that authoritative parents can accept the fact that their rules may be questioned and even broken but know how to respond in ways that don't lead to their teenagers becoming defiant or hostile as they grow into adulthood.

So, What Can You Do to Reverse Your Teen's Defiance?

The answer may be obvious. We know that personality and temperament are unlikely to change, whether it's yours or your teen's. We know that you can take some actions to lessen stress, but you can't eliminate all of it, possibly not even most of it. What's left? Parenting style. That's where we'll aim our efforts in the rest of this book.

Taking Action

- Check off which of the following characteristics you believe you possess, based on an honest self-assessment and any conversations you've had with others who know you well. If you can, relist them in descending order by how much conflict you think they've caused with your teen.

☐ Highly emotional
☐ Frequently irritable
☐ Difficulty regulating habits
☐ Highly active
☐ Impulsive
☐ Inattentive

Now compare your list with the one you worked up for your teen at the end of Chapter 4. Where are the similarities? If the lists are accurate, you should be able to see how these traits played a role in some of the conflicts between you. Keep these revelations in mind. They'll help you set priorities for which types of problems you decide to tackle first in Part II.

- When your teen is disruptive or defiant, what steps are you likely to take to deal with the problem?
- If these methods don't work and the problem behavior continues, what are you likely to do then to cope with your child's misbehavior?
- What do your answers to the two preceding questions tell you about your parenting style? To what extent would your parenting style fit the definitions of authoritative, authoritarian, indulgent, or neglectful?

6

How to Find a Way Out

Maria and Joe say they "have no idea what's happened to Mike." Their 14-year-old son used to be so reliable; now he's either sullen or argumentative.

They used to be able to count on Mike to take care of his little brother and sister after school until Maria got home from her part-time job and then supervise their homework while she rushed to start dinner preparations. When Joe got home, he'd check their homework and then play with them for a while before dinner so Mike could get his own homework done. But when Joe entered seventh grade, he grew 3 inches and became the star forward of his middle school basketball team, and, his mother joked, "his head no longer fit through the front door." Suddenly girls were texting him all the time and Maria started having to ask him repeatedly to put the phone down and help the little kids with their math or spelling. Then Mike's friends started coming home after school with him to "shoot some hoops" and keep up their game. A couple of times they headed off to the playground and Maria came home to find her 7- and 8-year-olds alone in the house. When she railed at her son for leaving them, he yelled back that he was only a block away and they could come find him if they needed him for anything. Maria took away Mike's cellphone for a week. Two days later Joe gave it back to him, saying basketball could get him into college.

"I can't believe you gave it back to him without talking to me!" Maria shouted. "How do you expect him to do what I ask when you cancel the punishments I give him?"

"If you'd quit your job and stay home, we wouldn't have to rely on Mike to watch the little kids in the first place," Joe retaliated.

"We need the money, and you know it!" Maria yelled back.

"Oh, yeah, bring up the fact that I don't make enough money—*again*. Another cheap shot from you. Big surprise!"

"We're talking about *Mike* here."

"Oh, really? I thought we were talking about me and all my shortcomings."

Around and around they went. Meanwhile, Mike closed himself up in his room with his smartphone and forgot to do his own homework that night.

The next day Maria was still fuming. She called Mike from work when he got home from school every half hour "just to check" on him, and when he started to reply sarcastically that he was right where he was supposed to be, like a good little kid, she snapped, "Don't you talk to me like that, young man. You apologize right this minute." Mike hung up on her. When she called back, he didn't answer. When he did answer the second time she called, he said he was in the bathroom and didn't hear the phone; Maria swore to herself that she could hear the sneer in his voice. Then she hung up on *him*.

When Maria got home, she demanded to see not only the kids' homework but Mike's. Mike said, "Hey, that's not fair! I haven't even had time to get to my own work since I'm so busy being Mr. Babysitter. And I don't even get to see my friends after school like everyone else!"

"If you were more efficient, *Mr.* WiseGuy, you'd get it all done, and then maybe you'd have time to see your friends too."

"You'd just find some excuse to keep me here anyway," Mike yelled.

"No, I wouldn't. I'd probably be sick of hearing you complain by then!"

"Yes, you would! You always treat me like I'm a slave around here, and when I'm not doing stuff for you, you act like I'm some sort of baby!"

"No, I don't! I just expect you to act your age, and when you don't, I treat you that way."

The argument continued until Joe got home from work.

The minute he walked through the door, Maria announced, "Well, your son is at it again," before Joe could even ask how her day had been.

"What do you mean?" Joe asked.

Before she could answer, Mike ran out from the kitchen, where he was making himself a snack. "Dad, I didn't do *anything* wrong. You gotta make her stop treating me like a baby! None of the other guys have to stay home and hang around with little kids. I have a *life*."

"You know he's right, Maria—"

"*Don't* start ganging up on me like that again. Who's the adult here?" Maria interrupted.

"Well, you tell me, honey," Joe said sarcastically. "Do you think you could calm down long enough to tell me what's going on?"

"She'll just make it sound like I'm some kind of gangster, Dad! She never listens to me at all!"

"Well, son, she doesn't listen to me that much either," Joe replied with a laugh.

Maria glared at her husband and her son and stomped out of the room. Mike said, "I'm going to go meet the guys, OK, Dad?"

"Yeah, you better get out of here before Mom comes up with something for you to do," Joe said to his son with a wink and a joking nudge.

Maria came back out of the kitchen, looked around to find her son gone, and complained sarcastically, "Great job, honey. Now who's going to help Tina and Tommy with their homework, get dinner ready, and start the laundry?"

"Mike can help out when he gets back. Relax."

"*Relax?!* And when do you think he'll then do *his* homework? You are *unbelievable*. I can't figure out which one of you is the 14-year-old."

Maria and Joe thought they had their family routine all figured out. Like most of us, they're dealing with lots of stress regarding money, time, and parenting obligations. They were proud that they could depend on their oldest child to help out. It never occurred to them that he'd become *less* reliable as he entered adolescence, rather than more reliable. But the fact is, Mike's character isn't changing. He hasn't become a less reliable person by nature. If Maria and Joe could step back and think about the facts of teenage development laid out in Chapter 3, they'd realize that their son is trying to send them some very loud messages: he needs some freedom and independence and he also needs to shift his allegiances a little bit away from his family and toward his friends. He doesn't want to follow the dictates of his parents; he needs them to understand his changing needs and to be willing to bend with them.

Because Mike is inclined to give his mom a harder time than his dad—in part because she's the "adversary" he's dealing with most of the time and in part because of human nature as described in Chapter 3—Mom is starting to feel oppressed, isolated, and exhausted. She hates feeling like the "bad guy" all the time, but she believes *someone* has to shoulder the adult responsibilities. Mike senses the edge he has in allying himself with his dad and has started to take advantage of the fact that his dad loves the idea of being close to his teenage-son-the-athlete. Joe thinks Maria is too harsh with Mike and that *someone* has to lighten things up or they'll drive him away for good. Both are terrified that this recent behavior is a sign that their wonderful son is hell-bent for a life ruined by laziness, disrespect for authority, and maybe even dangers like alcohol and drugs.

Meanwhile, their communication skills are being challenged to the hilt—and shown to be sorely lacking. Maria and Joe easily slide into shooting darts at each other whenever they have even a minor parenting disagreement. And they're no better when it comes to talking to their son. Maria—and sometimes Joe too—can't remain calm enough to talk about what they really need or to find out what their son needs. All three are so busy storming out of the room or hanging up on each other that their discussions never even get close to the point where they could begin to shift gears based on everyone's shifting needs. Mike is getting more and more angry and resentful. Maria starts yelling at the first sign of defiance from Mike, and Mike quickly opts for an exit, either hanging up on his mother or leaving the room, because he knows that gets him out of whatever it was she wanted him to do, in addition to sparing him from being screamed at.

Mike talks to his friends a lot about his "hopeless" parents who won't let him do *anything* and yet expect him to act like the parent of his younger siblings. He's starting to avoid his mother, and he secretly thinks his father is a pushover because all he has to do is act "all buddy-buddy" with him and Dad lets him get away with whatever he wants. Maria and Joe sense that they're losing all control over their son and don't know what to do except tighten the vise, which has the exact opposite effect from the one they're seeking.

The scenario just described illustrates the negative communication, side taking, coercion, and unrealistic, rigid beliefs that can sow the seeds of teenage defiance and then nurture its growth when parents are trying instead to eliminate it. Relationships like the one among Maria, Joe, and Mike, in which Joe ends up in the middle, throw the appropriate pecking order into disarray and make it impossible for parents to put up a firm, united front when a teenager starts to test the limits of parental authority. They dilute a couple's confidence in their authority, leading them to adopt distorted, calamitous beliefs about their teenager and making it hard for them to empathize with their teen's developmental needs. There are, fortunately, ways to change these elements of interpersonal and parenting style that can help parents find the appropriate level of control to exercise with an increasingly independent teen and that can reverse defiance and reestablish a loving, empathetic relationship.

You can learn to shed unrealistic and exaggerated beliefs, adopt better communication skills, practice effective problem solving, and reestablish a pecking order that works. You can use everything you've learned about your teen and yourself in the last three chapters to inform family routines, discipline, and all your interactions with your son or daughter, innocuous or defiant. The steps in Part II will show you how in detail. But first, take a closer look at the problems that create parent–teen conflict, as demonstrated so clearly by Maria, Joe, and Mike.

Your Family's Structure: An Effective Pecking Order or a House of Cards?

Who's in charge at your house? Conventional wisdom says that it should be you, along with your child's other parent in a two-parent family. Research says so too. It doesn't take a scientific genius to know that teenagers aren't ready to make all the adult decisions that the person at the top of the pecking order in a family needs to make. When they're allowed more power than they should have—which means more power than you have—all hell breaks loose. And this is exactly what happens in many families where defiance reigns. Maria and Joe made 14-year-old Mike feel as if he was a coparent by making him too responsible for his younger siblings, an error that many parents make when there is a big age gap between the oldest child and younger children. Mike resented the responsibility, but also decided if he was going to have it he should have the attendant privileges (i.e., freedom) as well. Unfortunately, his parents didn't guess that he was operating according to that logic.

From a practical businesslike perspective, it seems perfectly sensible to spread out the responsibilities so that the household runs smoothly. It seemed perfectly logical to his parents to delegate more and more responsibility to Mike as he got older and could handle it. The trouble is, families aren't businesses, where similar principles do make perfect sense. And Mike isn't an up-and-coming employee who is proving his worth by accumulating adult accomplishments on the job. He's entering adolescence, a phase that often involves taking two steps forward and one step backward. He needs his family to offer a structure that will support his forward progress, just as much by accepting the backward steps as by encouraging the forward ones.

The pecking order in Mike's family has been shifted. As in a house of cards, when one part of the foundation is dislodged just a little, the whole edifice can come tumbling down. Expecting too much of Mike has triggered a series of events by which his parents are now relaxing the monitoring that their teenage son needs to stay out of trouble. Understand, though, that too much monitoring, like the overvigilance that Maria and Joe occasionally exercise in response to defiance in their son, may be just as harmful. Hovering oppressively over a teenager will always be seen by the teen as an invasion of privacy, and that too can fuel parent–teen conflict.

Mike needs his parents to be involved in his life, but not just to monitor his behavior. A warm, caring relationship with his parents will help him take the necessary teenage test flights out of the nest. With an appropriately close relationship, he'll know he has a safe haven to return to when he encounters parts of the outside world that he's not quite ready for. Being *too* close with his parents will stifle his need to make those forays into independence. Not being close enough will make him feel alienated from the world in general and stunt the growth of his self-confidence. It's not enough that Mike is becoming his father's buddy. Joe needs to do his part to uphold the pecking order and support the family structure. In playing his role, he can help reestablish the closeness with Maria that Mike needs.

Maria and Joe need to form a united front at the top of the pecking order, or they will face growing problems with discipline and their son may become increasingly defiant. When one parent sides with the teen against the other parent, as Joe did with Mike against Maria, their authority in discipline and other matters is diluted—not surprisingly, by about half. Likewise, when two family members put a third in the middle of conflicts, and the one in the middle vacillates between allegiances, family structure gets shaky, as it did when Joe came home from work and immediately was put in the middle of an ongoing argument between Mike and Maria, where he supported one and then the other. What Mike sees in cases like this is a family structure that can be jiggled to suit his purposes as they arise.

Maria and Joe's problems with family structure are mostly recent, being more a product of failing to recognize their son's new developmental needs than a longtime structural flaw. But many families have structural problems from the start. When the vagaries of adolescence enter the mix, the tremors that have been weakening the family foundation for a long time become damaging earthquakes. Parenting styles contribute to the architectural design of a family, so it's often helpful to use what you learned in Chapter 5 to understand your own parenting style. Stepfamilies also are more vulnerable to structural problems. The mother of a teenage son, for example, who has remarried may frequently find herself in the middle of conflicts between her new spouse and her son. Or the boy's natural father puts the teenager in the middle of his conflicts with his ex-wife. Many families that feel helpless to overcome such long-standing conflicts benefit from family therapy.

Beliefs and Expectations: Realistic or Exaggerated?

Everyone harbors certain core beliefs and bottom-line expectations. Beliefs and expectations about parenting and family life are habits of mind that come from our life experiences and from our families of origin. If you ever find yourself surprised by your own knee-jerk reactions to your teen—possibly because even you know your response is illogical or out of proportion to the situation—there's a pretty good chance that some unquestioned core belief is operating below the surface. These beliefs definitely influence our behavior toward our teens. Especially if you adhere to them rigidly, even in the face of conflicting evidence to the contrary, they can hamper your ability to solve problems and resolve conflicts involving your teenager.

Cal, for example, believes that if his son fails to do his chores, he'll grow up to be a worthless, aimless, unemployed "welfare case." When the two clash over those chores, Cal has a lot of trouble remaining calm and even considering negotiating a mutually acceptable compromise—even though when asked outside of these conflicts he readily agrees that there could be acceptable alternatives.

Of course teens have their own unrealistic expectations. Fifteen-year-old Jackson believes that teens should have total freedom and that being expected to do chores will ruin his adolescence. He can't compromise either.

Cal acquired his extreme beliefs from his own father, who insisted, "for his own good," that Cal spend most of his free time helping out around the house so that he'd "learn to pull his own weight." Jackson hangs out with his friends as much as possible to escape his father's tyranny. Together the high school freshmen pump each other up with bravado about their right to be free and not enslaved by parents who "don't really give a damn about us anyway."

Maria and Joe both grew up in big families where the oldest kids always had to take care of the youngest, so they've never questioned expecting this of Mike. Maria spends a lot of her time alone fuming silently about how *she* would never have talked to *her* parents the way Mike talks to her, but she's run out of ideas for getting him to show her the respect she deserves, so she's resorted to giving him a taste of his own medicine, such as hanging up on him when they're on the phone. Joe was the oldest in a family that wholeheartedly embraced the tenet that "boys will be boys" and gave him pretty free rein as a teen because he had to "learn to be a man."

Neither parent was all that conscious of how much these beliefs governed their parenting, but with trouble brewing between them and Mike, they find themselves clinging to these deeply rooted ideas as if they're lifelines. Yet it is these beliefs, to some extent, that are standing in their way of backing off from conflicts to solve problems rationally and to communicate effectively with their son (and, for that matter, each other). We'll discuss extreme beliefs and unrealistic expectations in more depth in Chapter 16, but for now it's important to understand the impact they have on our ability to resolve conflicts without feeding teen defiance.

How Are Your Communication and Problem-Solving Skills?

If solving problems—specifically, the problems caused by your teenager's defiance—is the end you're trying to reach, then skillful communication is the means. Both you and your teen need to be able to express your feelings and opinions assertively but inoffensively, to listen attentively, and to understand the messages you're receiving accurately. Accusations, denials, threats, commands, excessive interruptions, sarcasm, and poor eye contact are all negative communication habits. So is hanging up on someone, rolling your eyes, or conveying disdain and frustration through other body language. All of these negative types of communication are fueled by negative, extreme beliefs and expectations of one another.

Maria and Joe are both relatively articulate, and they certainly love Mike. But Maria feels so desperate to cut off her son's argumentative responses and reassert her authority—before he goes down the path to ruin—that she has started to use conversation-stopping means of communicating. She's hoping that the "conversation" will thus end and her son will comply with her wishes. But it doesn't work that way. The conversation does end, but usually with door slamming, escape, and more defiance from Mike. In Chapter 15 we'll help you start to learn to communicate with your teen in the same way you may already communicate with coworkers and other peers.

The goal is not "caving," giving in, or giving up. It's problem solving, a process by which one or more people follow a set of steps to reach a mutually agreeable solution. It's a necessary part, even if a new part, of parenting your child who is now a teen, because dictating to teens just doesn't work. As we said at the beginning of this book, they are generally old enough now to vote with their feet and use other means to easily circumvent your rules. Besides, dictating to them doesn't prepare them for handling conflicts in the adult world—something you definitely want to accomplish before they depart from the nest. Negative communication methods like accusations, threats, and dictatorial commands are also likely to enrage your teen such that you all get detoured away from problem solving and get stuck in the "No, I didn't"/"Yes, you did" groove. Chapter 14 will help you learn the procedure for effective problem solving so you can nip conflicts in the bud.

Nine Principles for Reversing or Preventing Teen Defiance

You should now have a pretty good grasp of all the ingredients that can lead to defiance in a teenager. You also should have an inkling of which of these behaviors and characteristics are at work in your family. Where does that leave us? With the following set of principles for counteracting defiance in your teenager. Some of these may sound like what you're already doing—and it hasn't worked. Others may sound like lofty goals of the easier-said-than-done variety. In both cases, the program in Part II can help. Each of these principles is fully explained and illustrated in action in at least one chapter in Part II. You'll be able to see where you may have misinterpreted some of these principles in trying to translate them from the abstract realm into daily practice. And we give you plenty of accessible, realistic ways to adopt a principle that right now may seem pretty ambitious.

1. *Focus on the positive.* If your immediate reaction to this principle was "*What* positive?" you have some idea of how far your relationship with your teen has strayed from one that can

lead to effective problem solving and conflict resolution. Without reestablishing the positive they see in their son, Maria and Joe won't be able to negotiate mutually acceptable solutions that will sidestep conflict and neutralize defiance. And neither will you. You'll learn to focus on the positives—yes, your teenager still has them, and so does your relationship with the teen—in Chapter 8. You also need to help your teenager develop her gifts and talents—be they musical, artistic, athletic, computer-oriented, or even video game–oriented.

2. *Strive for good communication.* As mentioned earlier, good communication lays the groundwork for effective problem solving. It also reminds all of you of your positive feelings for one another, which can go a long way toward heading off conflict in and of itself. Because communication is part of every interaction, you'll really be learning to hone your communication skills throughout Part II, but particularly in Chapters 9 and 15.

3. *Use positive and negative consequences wisely.* Consequences are among the most powerful means for influencing anyone's behavior, and your teenager is no exception. The key is to consistently reward positive behavior with positive consequences and to address negative behavior with negative consequences. Always use positive consequences first. Only if they are insufficient to change the behavior should you introduce punishments or negative consequences. In families with a defiant teen, this is where parents have invariably gone awry. Teaching the effective use of rewards and punishments is the goal of Chapters 10–12.

4. *Establish bottom-line rules for living in your home and enforce these rules consistently.* Every family has certain inviolable rules, based on core values and standards that you, the parents, want to pass on to your children. Yet when you're so caught up in the struggle to wrestle control back from your teen, you can end up fighting over things that really don't matter to you just because you want to win *somewhere.* On the other hand, many families with defiant teens lead their lives in a kind of roiling chaos, where rules come and go and violations are sometimes met with an iron fist, other times with a wave of the hand. You already started

writing up your list of negotiables and nonnegotiables in Chapter 3. You'll keep reviewing and revising them as necessary throughout Part II and learn how to deal with each group in Chapters 10–12 and also Chapter 14.

5. *Involve your teen in negotiating solutions to all issues that are not bottom-line nonnegotiables.* Hang up your scepter and get out your gavel. The days of dictating to your child are over almost the minute she or he enters adolescence. Outside those bottom-line rules, negotiation is now the name of the game, and it's a game that everyone wins: you all get what you need and want, and your teenager learns indispensable ways to navigate the waters of the adult world. Negotiating skills are addressed particularly in Chapter 14.

6. *Maintain adequate structure and supervision.* It's a moving target, we know. What was appropriate supervision and structure yesterday may not be today—or tomorrow. What to do to maintain the flexible, adaptable vigilance that thwarts defiance is discussed in our chapters on contingency management and problem solving: Chapters 10–12 and Chapter 14. Examples of how parents have adopted the skills for use in the structure and supervision issues that constantly come up with teens can be found throughout Part II.

7. *Facilitate appropriate independence seeking.* This is another tricky tightrope. You want to reduce or eliminate your teen's defiance, but that doesn't mean you can try to turn back the clock and act like the parent of a 6-year-old again. Knowing that independence seeking is *necessary* to your teen's health will help you look carefully at how to exercise enough control without taking *too* much, as described in Chapters 14–16. Gradually grant your teenager more freedoms in return for his or her demonstrations of responsibility.

8. *Make sure your beliefs and expectations are reasonable.* Defiance both springs from and feeds some extreme negative beliefs and expectations. If you're having a hard time letting go of the idea that your offspring owes you strict and total obedience even though he's now 15, it's not surprising that you're butting heads.

And if you've been battling defiance for some time, you may now believe that your teen is headed for total ruin, an attitude that can become a self-fulfilling prophecy if your teen feels he's "damned if he does and damned if he doesn't." On the other side of the fence, conflict is often fed by defiant teens' belief that all parental rules are unfair and that their lives will be ruined by these unjust restrictions. We'll get you thinking about your own extreme beliefs as we go along, but in Chapter 16 we'll zero in on the unconstructive thoughts that may be keeping defiance in place.

9. *Respect family structure.* Siding with your teen against his or her stepparent or putting your teen in the middle of long-standing arguments between you and your spouse shakes the foundations that keep families on an even keel. Likewise, abdicating your parental role to your own parent (or someone else if you're a single parent and depend on the help of other relatives) leaves holes in the family structure that can keep your relationship with your teen sound. We'll show you with illustrations throughout Part II how a shaky family hierarchy perpetuates defiance.

Taking Action

- You now have a pretty complete picture of your teen's defiant behavior as an interaction of multiple factors—the teen's personality and temperament, your personality and temperament, family background factors such as marital discord, financial problems, or stress from work—all superimposed on your teen's rapid development and desire for independence and a separate identity from you, his or her parents. All of these factors conspire to affect your teen's behavior toward you and yours toward your teen. Refer to your previous notes from time to time about these specific issues in your own family and with your own teen from the exercises in earlier chapters to remind yourself of how things may have gotten this bad and what factors require some attention. If you like, make a list of parenting-style factors (from this chapter and Chapter 5) that you'd like to change.

- The nine principles for reversing or preventing teen defiance underlie the entire approach of our proven program, so try to take them to heart and consider them the foundation of the work you're about to undertake. Make a copy of the principles to keep where you can access it quickly. When you have no idea what to do with your "over-the-top" defiant teen, stare at the list of principles and do *something* based on the list rather than impulse. If nothing else, the time spent staring at the list will give you a chance to calm down a bit and act more rationally.

- Review the last week of interaction with your teen, analyzing "the pecking order" or hierarchy in your family structure. Make a list of any examples where you and your spouse disagreed and one of you sided with the teen against the other. Make a list of any examples where two family members put the third in the middle and the third family member had to choose sides. Just being aware of how often and in what ways family structure is compromised can help you keep any cracks from widening.

10 Steps to a Better Relationship with Your Teen— and a Better Future *for* Your Teen

7

Getting Ready

If you read Part I of this book, you've acquired a lot of information about your teen's defiant behavior. If you haven't yet read Part I, please do so before starting this program. The instructions in the next 10 chapters are based on a wealth of research and clinical experience with families. We know these steps reduce conflict between many teens and their parents when followed as written. But we can't address all the unique differences between families. This is where the knowledge you've gathered about your own family's dynamics comes to the fore. When you know where the "hot buttons" are or why "Plan A" hasn't worked in the past, where your personality clashes with your teen's, or how your teen's need for independence is manifesting itself, you'll be much more likely to adapt the program fruitfully and come up with "Plan B" or "Plan C" as needed.

The program is divided roughly into two sections, the first on behavior management and the second on communication and problem solving. Part I of this book presented the inescapable truth that the best chance any parent has of resolving adolescent defiance lies in changing his or her own parenting style. So we're going to put you back in control, reestablishing the appropriate hierarchy at home by helping you change the way you interact with your teen so that he or she behaves differently in response.

This is not some sneaky way of saying you're to blame for your teenager's defiance. As we hope you've seen by now, family interactions are reciprocal. You may have come to this book believing that your teen's behavior problems are entirely your fault or entirely your child's fault. Nothing is that black and white in any relationship. We don't really know exactly what drives the complex interaction patterns in families. What we do know is that they go both ways: your behavior is in part a function of your teen's behavior toward you, your teen's characteristics, and all of your past experience with that child, and your teen's behavior is in part a function of the way you treat him or her, your own characteristics, and your teen's history of experience with you. Trying to assign blame is therefore not only impossible but unconstructive. The fact that we're going to teach *you* ways to change your behavior when it's your teen's behavior that seems problematic is simply a matter of practical convenience. You're here, you're reading this book, and you're motivated to do something to change what has become an untenable situation. You're older, wiser, and already inclined to be open to a solution. So we'll start with you; your teen will follow.

Besides the reciprocity of family interactions, the behavior management training that kicks off the program is based on a few other principles that you'll learn more about in Step 2:

• *Becoming proactive.* Most parents (and people generally) don't give too much thought to how they structure a social situation from the start, such as homework or shopping time with a teen. They simply march right into the thick of the situation, and only if it goes awry are they likely to react with consequences, and often negative ones. That's being reactive. It's like playing football with only a defensive team. In this program, you'll learn to also be proactive—playing football with your offensive team as well. "Being proactive" means thinking about a situation before you enter it and trying to structure it so that positive behavior from your teen is more likely to occur. When you do this, negative behavior is automatically less likely to occur because your teen can't do both at once. Let's say you want your teen to do his homework—always a bone of contention between you. Being proactive might mean asking your teen if there's anything he might need from you tonight to help with the assignment, telling your teen just before he starts the evening's homework that you'll check in with him every 20 minutes to see if he needs help and how he's doing, letting him know you'll review the work against his assignment sheet to be sure it's complete, promising an incentive or reward when the work is done, and ensuring that there's a place in the teen's room that's conducive to doing homework (a relatively uncluttered desk, a clock, a pen and pencil container, a calculator, clean paper, and other supplies handy).

We want you to start thinking ahead about what situations are potentially problematic so that you can figure out a way to head off conflict. How many times have you braced yourself for a fight when you had to make what you knew would be an unwelcome request of your teen? Or found yourself shouting "I *knew* you'd try to get around the rules like this!"? In the past when you've anticipated resistance from your teenager, you've probably tried to preempt it by coming down hard on your teen from the start. Now you may realize this only promoted the conflict instead of nipping it in the bud.

• *Consequences, consequences, consequences.* The repetition of that word is no accident. One of the most important ways to reestablish your authority with a wayward teenager is to start imposing consequences for behavior *consistently.* You probably feel you already do this: When your teen talks back or acts out, you react (boy, do you react!). But do you react exactly the same way for the same exact infraction every time? Probably not. It's a trap most parents fall into. When we indulgently let a 9-year-old slide on her chores every once in a while, it doesn't necessarily cause trouble. But when all the other ingredients that can brew defiance are also present, you have the recipe for an explosion. OK, this is the reactive part of your strategy and it's an important one too, but it can lose its effectiveness without the proactive part of your strategy being in place as well. In the first few steps of the program you'll learn how to create a good offense and a good defense in your interactions with your teen and also how to stick to your guns—even when you don't feel like making a "federal case" out of anything, even when you've already done it 12 times today. Sounds pretty good, doesn't it? Not so fast.

• *Rewards before punishments.* We have to start with the positive. Where defiance reigns, punishment often sets the tone, and you can end up forgetting to recognize, respect, approve, praise, show appreciation for, or otherwise reinforce the positive behavior of your teen. If you're quipping to yourself that there is none, that's a good sign in and of itself that you've let one of your most powerful tools fall by the wayside, rusting with disuse. Ironically, we've found that punishment often loses its force entirely when the family environment is devoid of positive incentives for appropriate conduct. So in this program, before you learn to establish consequences for *negative* behavior, you're going to relearn how to establish incentives for *positive* behavior. You won't believe what a potent strategy this can be.

• *Practicing forgiveness.* We have a tendency to blame our teens for their defiant behavior or ourselves for our mistakes in parenting. But you now know that defiant behavior is the result of many factors and no one person is to blame. You can become demoralized and sink into learned helplessness or perpetual anger if you play the blame game. You need to forgive your teen for her defiant behaviors and forgive yourself for any errors you've made. Hold your teen accountable for her actions, but do forgive her in your own mind. Forgive yourself in advance for any errors you make using our program—things won't go perfectly. Forgiveness will help you stay on an even keel as you approach the task of helping your teen change defiant behavior.

Briefly, here's what you'll be doing in the behavior management segment of the program:

Step 1. Making Positive One-on-One Time a Habit

Before you can make any headway against defiance, you have to shift your attention away from the negative. Here you'll learn to catch your teen being good, offer praise when you do, and spend time together outside the usual conflict circumstances.

Step 2. A New Way to Manage Behavior

Here's the groundwork for establishing consequences effectively. You'll start learning to be more specific, consistent, balanced, and judicious in what you ask of your teen and to make requests and commands effectively.

Step 3. Contracts and Point Systems: How Teens Can Earn Privileges

Now you can give consequences some teeth, using either a behavioral contract or a point system to reward your teen for complying with requests and incentives for positive (instead of negative) behavior.

Step 4. Making the Punishment Really Fit the Crime

Only after you've made a habit of rewarding the positive should you start imposing fines or penalties for the negative. Here you'll also learn how to make grounding work.

Step 5. Tackling Additional Issues with Rewards and Penalties

Now that you know how it works, you can learn how to make contingency management work for you on those big issues that never seem to get resolved.

Step 6. Addressing Defiant Behavior in School and Conflicts over Homework

Whether or not you need to address behavior problems at school, almost all parents with defiant teens have problems making sure homework gets done. Here are ways to address these issues.

If you work your way successfully through the first six steps of the program, you'll regain some control or influence over your teen's behavior. If your teen was still a child, that might be all you'd need to avert defiance for the foreseeable future. But, as Chapter 3 pointed out, the need to become independent of parents is one of the primary tasks of adolescence. Your interactions with your teenager must not only allow that to happen but facilitate it. So the second half of the program teaches you and your teen to negotiate points of conflict through effective problem solving and communication.

If your teenager's defiance is very mild, the sources of conflict or tension between you are few, and your teen is average or higher in social maturity and intelligence, you may be able to go right to Step 7 and focus on communication and problem solving. But most of you were drawn to this book because your problems are more severe, and you'll need to proceed through the steps in order. Focusing on problem solving and communication training might put you in the awkward position of trying to negotiate over areas where you have no immediate control or authority. If you decide to work through this program with the help of a professional, the therapist will help you determine whether you should change the order of the steps. Otherwise, follow this rule: First reestablish control; only then can you negotiate. Your teen is not your equal in the home hierarchy, but you should be willing to negotiate once the balance of power is restored because teenagers don't become adults overnight. This is your chance to help your teen develop the skills needed for successful conflict resolution in adulthood, without sacrificing family harmony and tranquillity in the process. You'll do so in Steps 7–10 by keeping these caveats in mind:

• *Independence must be granted slowly and gradually.* If you look back at the nine principles in Chapter 6, you'll see that three of them (5, 6, and 7) urge you to help your teen become independent while maintaining adequate structure and supervision. The problem-solving skills taught in Chapter 14 can help you usher your teen toward independence without letting go of the reins too soon. The path of least resistance is forged by gradually granting your teen independence: You grant a little bit of independence from your restrictions, and when your teen handles it responsibly, you grant the teen a little more freedom. You need to be prepared to pull back when, as inevitably happens, the teen makes mistakes in handling newfound freedom, but never pull back to the "nothing" position, another trigger for certain defiance. Let's say your teenager wants to stay alone at home while you go away for the weekend. For this freedom, you expect the teen to lock up at night, clean up after himself, keep all the household possessions safe, take care of the yard or houseplants or pets, and refrain from having wild parties. Instead of throwing him into this situation all at once or denying him any stays alone at the house, you break up the goal into smaller steps. First he stays in the house alone for an evening, then for a whole night, then for two nights, and finally for the whole weekend. If, after any individual step, he shows he can't handle the responsibility, you go back to the previous step and try the next step again at another time.

- *The nonnegotiables must be absolutely clear.* The bottom-line issues that relate to basic rules for living in a civilized society (values, morality, and legality) usually include drugs, alcohol, aspects of sexuality, religion, respect, and violence. But they truly are unique to every family, and everyone in the family needs to know without a doubt which issues are not subject to negotiation. You can use communication skills to discuss the nonnegotiables, but essentially you list the basic house rules explicitly and make sure they are understood. The fact that they are inviolable will become crystal clear when you consistently use the behavior management techniques learned in Steps 1–6 to enforce them.

- *Teens are more likely to follow rules they helped create.* The goal regarding the negotiables is to compromise. It's not to get as much of what "your side" wants (at your teen's expense) as you possibly can. Therefore, the single most important principle of parenting an adolescent is to involve your teen in decision making about the negotiables. Don't expect a teen who has no say in them to cooperate with your rules, plans, or activities. You'll probably be pleasantly surprised by the novel solutions your teen will come up with.

Here's what you'll be doing in the problem-solving/communication training part of the program:

Step 7. Using Problem-Solving Skills

No matter how much you think you'd like to do so, you can't just dictate to your teenager about everything. But the non-deal-breaker issues don't have to be bones of contention; they can be negotiated using a proven set of steps for problem solving, which you'll learn in this step.

Step 8. Learning and Practicing Communication Skills

Everyone seems to forget how to listen actively and to speak respectfully and honestly when defiance rules the house. Here you'll relearn these basic skills of positive communication and begin to identify negative communication patterns that have only fed conflict.

Step 9. Dealing with Unreasonable Beliefs and Expectations

You've been hacking away at defiance brick by brick. Now we get to an important part of its foundation: negative beliefs and exaggerated expectations that tend to make defiance and conflict a self-fulfilling prophecy.

Step 10. Keeping It Together

It's not over till it's over, as Yogi Berra said. And it would be foolish to expect defiance to be "over" altogether. Even after you've reduced it considerably, a problem may arise post-training. Here are tips for examining where your skills and techniques lapsed so you can get back on track.

How Long Will It Take to Get Results?

If your problems with defiance are few and rather mild, you can work at the program once or twice a week in formal sit-down sessions. More severe problems often require more frequent practice of each step before its lessons and skills will be instilled and you can move on to the next one. Typically, we see families twice a month and give them 2 weeks for each step. This gives everyone time to learn the techniques, do some troubleshooting, and really make the methods a habit. You may be able to move faster, but it's wise to expect to spend 1–2 weeks per step.

What to Say—and Not Say—to Your Teenager about This Program

You can—and probably should—start this program on your own, without announcing your intentions to the teenager in question. Saying that you're about to use a step-by-step self-help program to reduce conflict (or, worse, to get your teenager back in line) only gives your teen another opportunity for resistance and oppositionality. You don't need that. Besides, much of this program is, as you now know, based on your making changes in the way you behave that are intended to elicit change in your teenager. You don't request or demand that your teen do something differently. If all goes well, the teen will eventually find him- or herself behaving differently, possibly without even noticing. You, of course, will notice.

Each step of the program tells you how to go about following the instructions and models how to inform your teenager of what you're doing. You won't need to ask permission. That does not mean, of course, that you won't encounter resistance. It's highly likely that your teenager will refuse to cooperate with behavior contracts when you first introduce them. We'll tell you how to stick to your conviction to use them, though. And before you get to that point, you're simply changing the way you pay attention to and talk to your teen, so there's no need to explain anything. Just follow the instructions.

Once you get to the problem-solving steps, your teen will start being more involved. But by then you should have eased conflict between you enough that your teen is more open to your suggestions. Besides, she will probably be fairly receptive to the idea of having a say in working out areas of disagreement between you, even if she balks at the idea of spending any of her time at a formal family meeting.

What If You Need a Therapist?

Deciding to work through this program with a therapist is a whole different story. Somehow you're going to have to get your teenager to go to the therapy sessions. And that's no mean feat considering that often it's the more severe cases of defiance that require professional help. This only means you're probably already dealing with a pretty high level of oppositionality.

Remember Mark, the 17-year-old you met in the Introduction? As we said in Chapter 4, Mark's defiance is severe enough that he almost meets the criteria for conduct disorder. His family will definitely need a therapist in conjunction with the program in this book. So how do they get a kid who treats their wishes like jokes to go to therapy appointments? In cases like this, where intervention was needed a long time ago and there's no time to waste, parents may have to pick a privilege that's very important to the teen and make the continued granting of it contingent on attending therapy. The choice of privilege has to be thought out carefully. It needs to be desirable enough to the teen to provide an incentive, and it needs to be something in the parents' control. In Mark's case, the choice was driving the family car. Mark's parents were not currently in control of whether he stayed at home or left the house, but the car keys were definitely in their possession, and they could keep it that way. They told Mark that he would be able to use the car if he attended therapy sessions with them for the next month. After that, they said, if he was cooperating with therapy, they would start to put a certain amount of money a week into a savings account to be used for the purchase of a used car for him.

Mark didn't take his parents seriously at first. He skipped the first two sessions after paying lip service to the idea that he'd attend. But after he saw that his parents were not going to relent and let him use the car anyway, he started to go to therapy sessions. Progress was slow in his case, but by the time he left for college his parents felt he was back on track and no longer in danger of thwarting his own future.

Gina's parents had a little more difficulty getting her to participate in the program. She had recently decided that she hated being on medication for ADHD and went through a period when she refused to take it. But eventually even she admitted that life was harder for her without her medication and she started taking it regularly again. Therapy, however, was another matter. She found it humiliating to imagine that one of her friends might see her going into the therapist's office and categorically refused to go. Gina and her mother set up an incentive system like Mark's family, but rather than taking away a privilege, Gina's mother rewarded Gina with computer time for going to therapy sessions; she received a little additional daily time after every session she attended. After a few sessions, Gina's therapist agreed that she didn't really need to come in twice a month and that the family could continue with the program in "guided self-help," whereby the therapist would be available for consultation when they got stuck.

What You'll Find in Each Step

Each step will begin with a brief list of goals to be reached during the 2 weeks spent on the step. You can refer to this list of goals as a reminder as needed. Then we'll provide explicit instructions for what to do, as numbered instructions within each goal. Interspersed throughout the instructions are illustrations of how various families have applied the directions. Because communication is so important, we sometimes model how you can put things to emphasize the positive and keep the potential for conflict low throughout the steps. We'll also offer troubleshooting ideas that will help you figure out why things aren't working as they should. Because younger teens (ages 12–15) are so different from older teens (ages 16–18), we'll offer a range of application ideas for these two different age groups where warranted.

What You Stand to Gain

Marla was sure she was losing her daughter, and Jenna was only 14. Not that her daughter necessarily was leaving home or running away, but that their relationship had become so bad that she feared it had been damaged forever. She had to do something. She chose to try the program in this book. (If you need a reminder of this family's circumstances, we introduced them in Chapter 2.)

Marla started by biting her tongue and ignoring Jenna's snappish responses to most of what Marla said. At first Jenna stood there waiting for her mother's retort. When she didn't get it, she often tossed out a sarcastic "Helllllooo. . . ." Marla either went about her business or smiled at her daughter and innocently said, "Yes?" Once Jenna got used to the fact that Marla really wasn't just giving her daughter the cold shoulder as another form of punishment, the disdainful responses began to wane a bit.

Meanwhile, Marla did her best to notice when Jenna did something she approved of, to comment on it briefly, and to otherwise demonstrate some respect and recognition for what her daughter had done. Instead of confronting her after school with "Jenna, most of your laundry is still all over your bed, and it's a total mess!" she said, "Hey, honey, you got a great start on your laundry—thanks for pitching in on the family work around here; it really helps out!" When her daughter had finished only one subject's homework by the time her mother was on her way to bed, Marla bit her tongue and, instead of saying "Oh, my God, Jenna, how are you going to get a good night's sleep if you haven't even started your English or history reading?" she would take a look at her daughter's math and say, "Wow, I wish I had had the same knack for numbers in high school that you have! Good luck with the rest of your homework! Good night, honey."

What Marla still wanted more than anything was to have the close relationship with her daughter that she'd always imagined, but she knew that Jenna had continually rebuffed her when she suggested lunch or a shopping trip. So she started watching for the moments when her daughter wasn't texting on the weekends and making a studiedly casual invitation like "Hey, I made some popcorn to go with this movie that just started. Want some?" Suspicious at first, Jenna gradually started taking her mother up on such offers. Once they even missed the whole second half of the movie because something on the TV screen reminded them of a favorite funny family incident, which led to a long storytelling session and lots of laughter.

A few days later Marla invited Jenna to do an activity of her choice with her. Jenna brushed her mother off. Marla simply said, "Maybe another time," instead of breaking into a negative stream of communication. By the third time she invited her daughter to do something together, Jenna accepted. Mother and daughter had a lot of fun making a scrapbook for Jenna's cousin's 16th birthday. They continued to do activities together several times a week and found they could indeed have fun together, despite their disagreements.

When Marla got to Step 3 in the program, she immediately felt like she and Jenna had taken a giant step backward for the few baby steps forward they'd managed. Jenna screamed at her mother that she knew Marla was up to something and just wanted to keep her under her thumb. "Why should I have to earn texting time at all? It's *my* cellphone. You *gave* it to me!" Marla held her ground and told Jenna that she wanted to help her control the way she spoke to people because she'd get along better with everyone—not just her mother—if she did and that every time she answered her mother civilly when she spoke to her, she'd earn 5 minutes of texting time for the day. By the end of the week, Jenna was texting as much as she always had and was generally answering her mother's call to her with "Yes, Mom?" instead of "*What?!*"

Over the next few weeks Marla picked other defiant behaviors that bothered her and added them to the behavior contract, eventually adding minor penalties for *not* behaving as expected. Jenna was never going to be a calm, happy-go-lucky teenager, her mother reasoned, and she was no neat freak, but the whole household, after about a month and a half of the "training," was a lot more tranquil than it used to be. Jenna's room now looked more like a tremor had hit it instead of a major earthquake, and her daughter seemed to be making regular efforts to think before she blurted out whatever she instinctively thought when interrupted by a parental request.

After successfully starting a behavior contract, Marla made a list of her nonnegotiable issues: (1) no alcohol or drugs, (2) no friends over without a parent present, (3) talk to people with respect (and especially no cursing), (4) follow curfew, and (5) contribute to the family by doing chores. Jenna objected vehemently, insisting she wanted a say in her curfew and chores. Prepared for these objections, Marla seized the moment to highlight how nonnegotiable and negotiable issues come in pairs. That Jenna would have a curfew was nonnegotiable, but the time of the curfew and the conditions for possible exceptions were negotiable. That Jenna would contribute to the family by having chores was nonnegotiable, but the exact chores, when to do them, and the consequences for completing them were negotiable. Marla then introduced Step 7, problem solving, to negotiate the details of the curfew and chores problems. To her great surprise, Jenna got into the problem solving because she wanted to have input into things impacting her life. Mother and daughter were able to reach agreements surrounding chores and curfew.

Problem solving was not always so easy for Marla and Jenna, though. Later, Marla and Greg tried to involve the entire family in a problem-solving discussion. Marla and Greg included the little kids because they decided to tackle Jenna's lack of consideration for other family members when she wanted to play Wii in the family room. The little kids felt she bullied them so she could take over the TV. Marla and Greg just couldn't stand the volume and were tired of having to trudge downstairs to yell at her to turn it down since she couldn't hear them from the living room or kitchen. Sometimes by the time they got to the point of going down there, they were so angry that they reverted to their old ways of threatening all kinds of dire punishment. One of those times Jenna responded by turning the sound up so she didn't have to hear them. Greg turned the Wii off so forcefully he broke the power button. When Marla tried to start a problem-solving session with the whole family, everyone started expressing their complaints at once—and loudly. Jenna said they were all ganging up on her and ran out, locking herself in her bedroom.

Problem-solving sessions can be a family affair in many cases, but when the focus is a defiant teenager, it's best to limit the participants to the teen and the parents. Younger kids may not be old enough to contribute, and parents don't need to add any sparks to a potentially volatile interaction. The parents can represent the interests of the younger children in such conversations. Once this family had shifted gears, they came up with a solution that ended up suiting everyone's needs—the younger kids were consulted about whether the solutions were acceptable to them, but outside the meetings themselves. The family set up a schedule that gave each member a time of day to use the Wii or Xbox, and Jenna was allowed to use the TV at any other time, but she had to keep the volume below a certain maximum level unless she was the only one home. It had to be even lower after 9:00 P.M.

Meanwhile, Marla and Greg started observing how the whole family communicated with each other, and everyone started making an effort to speak with respect and to listen—really listen. When Jenna tried to talk to her mother, Marla either gave her a sign that she'd be with her in a minute, or she stopped what she was doing, looked up at her daughter, and then made sure she'd understood what Jenna had said by repeating it back to her and asking if that's what she meant. In Marla's opinion, this form of attention alone headed off numerous skirmishes. Jenna still couldn't seem to control the impulse to utter the occasional profanity in front of the younger kids, which her parents had labeled a nonnegotiable rule. So they added it to the behavior contracts and kept working at it.

One day when the program was winding down, Marla suddenly realized she was right where she had wanted to be for so long: sitting in a restaurant booth, laughing with the daughter who was sitting across from her, with plans to do a little shopping right after lunch. "This is great, honey," she said a little shyly. Her daughter smiled back at her. Then Marla took the opportunity to explain a lot of what she had learned in recent weeks about what she had expected from Jenna and why it had all gone so wrong—from expecting 8-year-old Jenna to understand that she was too busy chasing 2-year-old twins to play Monopoly, to failing to tell her what a huge help she'd been with the little kids back then, to simply forgetting to tell her how smart she thought her daughter was and what a great future she had ahead of her. Jenna admitted she had thought her mother was "just horrible" a few months ago and that she should stay out of her life. Neither one had to say it, but they were both glad she hadn't.

Taking Action

Tackling defiance in a teenager is a worthy but sizable task. It's important not to set your sights too high or to make your goals too large, diffuse, or ambiguous. You don't really need to have specific goals other than to reduce conflict and improve your relationship with your teen, but if it will make the magnitude of your task seem more manageable, you might determine broadly what your goals are and keep your eye trained on those as you work through the program. Here are some of the overall goals that families we have treated have set—and met—using this program. Take a glance through them and circle one to three that you would like to achieve—or write your own on the blanks that follow.

"Improve communication between my teen and me."

"Resolve negotiable issues without an argument."

"Establish consequences for specific defiant behaviors and stick to them."

"Figure out how much freedom my teenager needs and deserves."

"Make sure my spouse and I are on the same page with rewards and punishments."

"Write up a complete list of nonnegotiable house rules."

"Do something to reduce personal stress from _____ [marital conflict, illness or injury, financial issues, emotional distress, etc.].

"Start scheduling time with my teen that's just for fun." "Help my teen develop his/her artistic talents."

"Praise my teen at least once per hour."

"Develop reasonable expectations for homework."

"Stop family members from taking sides against each other."

Make a list of your goals:

_____

_____

_____

_____

_____

Step 1. Making Positive One-on-One Time a Habit

Take a minute to think about what your teen has been up to over the last few days. How would you put it? "Making himself scarce—at least when there's a job to be done"? "Arguing over every little thing"? "Having nothing good to say about anything or anyone"? As we explained in Part I, a history of conflict can leave everyone focusing solely on the negative. When you feel like you've been getting "the worst" from your teen, that's what you start to expect—and we often see what we expect to see. So you're not alone if reviewing your teen's actions over the last day or two produces a list of transgressions, from talking back to blowing off all his or her obligations to whining and complaining.

It's not a pretty picture. Because we know that looking at your teen through a negative lens only feeds conflict, it's time to start making a new photo album. The first thing you need to do to reverse defiant behavior in a teen is to start to recognize the positive and act like you expect it.

GOALS FOR STEP 1

Here are the goals for this very important first step:

- Start replacing negative with positive attention to change the tone of interactions.
- Break the seemingly endless cycle of negativity between you and your teenager by spending quality one-on-one time together.
- Translate your positive attitude into effective praise to give your teen an incentive to comply.

Replacing Negative with Positive Attention to Your Teenager

When your main goal is to get control over a defiant teen's behavior, learning to pay attention, spending some positive time together, ignoring minor misbehavior, and offering praise may seem to be digressions at best. It may also be difficult because of the resentments and hostility that have built up in your relationship lately. After all, nearly every interaction with your teen may be fraught with negativity. But this is an absolutely essential step. Praise and quality one-on-one time are critical to breaking the logjam of negativity between you and your teen. So don't skip over or minimize this step, however difficult or trivial it may seem to you. Extensive research and clinical practice have shown that parents who carry out this step effectively have more success using the remainder of this program than parents who minimize or skip it.

Remember what we said in Chapter 7 about being proactive? You don't have to be a sitting duck, waiting for your teenager to attack and then scrambling around to avoid the gunfire. You can start to take specific, very simple, small measures to shift the tone of the interactions between you. The place to start is with learning to pay positive attention some of the time, instead of paying negative attention all the time. Your teenager still does some things that are positive, yet he may feel you're taking him for granted, like nobody at home appreciates the good things he does to contribute to family life or his unique qualities as a person. If you look closely, you'll see what these are.

In this chapter you'll learn to remind your teen that you don't think she's "all bad" by spending some short periods of time together without criticizing or even questioning her. You'll also learn to ignore minor misbehavior rather than coming down hard on it. Once you've established the idea that every moment with your teen doesn't have to be spent in conflict, you'll learn to start expressing your positive attention directly and aloud through praise. With a couple of weeks of practice in these deceptively simple techniques, you'll be prepared for the goal of Step 2: to make your commands and requests more effective so that they are more likely to be obeyed.

If you're tempted to skip Step 1, thinking you don't need this, read on.

1. *Review your "management" style: Are you a good supervisor?* Your teen wants recognition for her good qualities and achievements in the same way you want to be recognized for the skills you bring to your job, your volunteer work, or your friendships. The boss we willingly work for over the weekend isn't the one who constantly threatens us with loss of employment or complains that our productivity isn't up to par. It's the one who makes a point of acknowledging our positive achievements, even if it's just to say "I know I really loaded you down, and I appreciate your trying to get the report done"—even if you didn't quite finish it on time. The one who picks out the parts of the report that you thought were particularly well done and congratulates you on them is the one who's likely to find the next report on her desk a day ahead of the deadline. You've been there. Why should your teenager be any different?

The simple fact is that we all respond with more enthusiasm, goodwill, and cooperation to positive attention than to negative attention. The trainer we want to work with is the one who says "You can do it!" and then cheers us when we do. The grandmother we want to visit is the one who thinks we're the "cat's meow," not the one who always has "a little advice" on how to do everything we do better than we're doing it now. The power of positive attention is virtually limitless. So why is it so easy to forget to wield it?

We Get So Busy . . .

Sometimes it's just a matter of efficiency. Most parents of teens have an awful lot of obligations. You may have younger kids to chauffeur around, aging parents who need extra help and attention, a career that's at its demanding peak, finances and a household to be managed, and maybe even health issues you didn't have when you were younger. Sometimes it can seem like your life is one long to-do list. So you're to be excused for focusing on all the items delegated to your teen that haven't gotten done. But imagine what it feels like to your teenager to be greeted the minute he gets home by a long list of what he's done wrong, what he's forgotten to do, and what he has to get done in the immediate future. One 17-year-old we know once said in this situation, "Wow, Mom, why are you so mad at me all the time?" When her mother looked at her in bewilderment, she explained, "Sometimes it seems like all you ever talk to me about are all the things you're mad at me for." This mother hadn't thought of herself as being critical and didn't actually feel angry; all she had intended was to mention these things before they slipped her mind and therefore remained undone. Sometimes because we don't mean to be negative, we forget to make an effort to be positive.

Yet how much more likely would any teen be to cooperate if Mom or Dad greeted him with something positive: "Hey, honey, your room is really beginning to look good; thanks for starting to get it in shape before the party on Saturday. You're saving me a lot of time." Or what if Mom or Dad just didn't bring up the chores first at all?

We Haven't Been *Trained*

Another reason we may not exploit the power of positive attention is we've simply never learned how. It's not that we're bad supervisors; we just haven't *been* supervisors. Supervisors—at least the good ones—in the workplace have been taught specific ways to motivate their employees. For instance, among the best-selling business management books of all time was a thin book titled *The One Minute Manager*, the sole purpose of which was how to motivate employees by spending more time circulating among them, giving positive feedback and praise, and spending less time shuffling papers in an office. If you've never been in this position, you may never have had a chance to develop these skills and may never have realized that they are just as important within a family as they are at work. This step in the program will show you how.

2. *Take a sabbatical from teaching . . . and judging.* Where teenagers are concerned, being positive means a lot more than acknowledging the positives we observe and laying off the criticism. Whether it's showing them how to tie their shoes or how to drive a car, we've been teaching our kids since birth, so this is a hard habit to break. But by adolescence helping and teaching can seem just as negative as direct criticism. Teens are getting too old to want our help all the time, and "help" in a context of mostly negative interactions is always going to be viewed as another negative ("You're not doing it right!"). Even asking questions, no matter how benign, can be taken as a challenge or "the third degree." Your questions can put a teen on the defensive even when you meant no offense. If your teen has been ignoring your requests, neglecting chores, blowing off homework, or otherwise failing to meet your expectations, you've probably been asking a lot of questions to get the teen to do what he should be doing. *So start avoiding directions, instructions, and questions.*

Scheduling Quality One-on-One Time

1. *For the next week, spend at least 15 minutes, three or four times, doing something one on one with your teen.* During this brief period of one-on-one time, *ask no questions, give no directions, make no corrections, and give no instructions.* One of the main goals is to allow the teenager to direct the interaction—and questions from

WARNING: *Don't use one-on-one time as a reward or a punishment.* The whole point of this exercise is that it's positive time given freely by you that you allow your teen to direct. If you use it as a consequence, even a positive one, it becomes associated with judgment.

you shift that directing role to you. If you make no corrections or judgments and give no directions, you will have a brief period of nonjudgmental observations, which can facilitate a subtle shift in the tone of interactions between you.

There are two main ways to arrange one-on-one time:

- *Let your teen choose something enjoyable (within reason).* Maybe your daughter would like to take a drive to the mall, shoot some hoops, or play a video game for a little while. Just say you have a little free time and would like to spend it with your teen—what would she like to do? Younger teens, in particular, may surprise you with their enthusiasm. Let your teen choose any activity as long as it isn't illegal, destructive, or overly expensive. Let your teen direct the activity. If your teen chooses a game and cheats or violates the rules of the game, go along with the "new rules" during one-on-one time. If your teen picks a video game, ask your teen to teach you how to play the game. Be completely accepting of your teen and try to recapture the fun you used to have playing with your teen when your child was young.
- *Or make a point of noticing when the teen is doing something he enjoys—watching a show, working on a hobby, or pursuing some artistic talent—approach him, and make some positive, nonjudgmental, and brief comment* such as "I see you're using the new pastels we bought the other day" or "That movie looks like it's really funny." Then just stick around and find positive things to say for a few minutes—for example, comment about how well the project is going or how nice it is to hear him laugh or just how fortunate you feel to have her in your life. If you must ask questions, make sure they

are completely benign and couldn't possibly imply criticism: "Isn't this a neat movie?" instead of "Did you finish your homework before starting the movie?" Gina's mother chose a moment when her daughter was sketching her cat to approach her and compliment her on the drawing. Because her daughter's ADHD pulled her away from tasks like homework so readily, she had to try hard to avoid telling her to get back to her homework instead of spending the 15 minutes observing and commenting on the drawing.

The key to approaching your teen is to be relaxed and casual. This alternative may be a better choice for older teens, who have not failed to notice that suggesting spending time together doing whatever they want is a change and may react with suspicion, or for teens who usually leave no doubt that they are not interested in spending time with their parents.

2. *For the second week of this step, see if you can increase the number of one-on-one times you schedule with your teen.* Dr. Kenneth Kaufman, a psychologist in New York who has specialized in parent training for over 30 years, has found that one-on-one time can be even more effective if it's done at the beginning of the longest time of the day that you and your teen are together. So when you're looking for additional opportunities, keep this in mind. Often teens remain in a positive mood for several hours after an enjoyable one-on-one experience with a parent. Homework, chores, and other responsibilities may then go more smoothly than at other times. Although we don't yet have research to support Dr. Kaufman's findings, our personal experience with helping families confirms them.

3. *Ignore minor misbehavior.* Start using this tactic during one-on-one time, then try extending it to other settings if you feel it's not causing an increase in defiance or disruptiveness. What you do is ignore something your teen does that's annoying or irritating but not disrespectful or a violation of a household

THINK AHEAD

Don't let lack of planning get in the way of making one-on-one time work.

- Before you start this exercise, think about how you'll manage to be alone with your teen. Can you schedule this time when your other kids are out of the house or occupied with some predictable activity like homework or their favorite TV show?

- If you're so busy you feel like you don't have a free 15 minutes—ever—how will you fit this time into your schedule? Can you delegate a chore or errand to your teen's other parent to free up the time? Tack the time on to the end of an errand if your teen is likely to want to drive somewhere? Schedule the times mainly on the weekends and only once during your busy weekdays?

- What do you think your teen will likely choose as an activity? Will it be what you consider reasonable? If you know he'll suggest certain activities that you won't consider "within reason," can you anticipate alternatives to offer? For example, Kevin wanted to go to the game store 20 miles away because that's where they have the best selection. His mother offered to play any game that Kevin already had at home or to do any other activity around the house. The parameters are up to you to set, but one way to keep things reasonable is to exclude activities that involve driving or spending money.

- Remember that the goal is to catch your teen when her guard is down and spontaneously spend time together then, but that doesn't mean you can't think ahead about when these times usually occur. When is your teen usually involved in something she likes doing? At what times of day is there usually no work to be done? Knowing when you're likely to catch your teen relaxed and absorbed by something fun allows you to plan to approach her casually at times when one-on-one time is most likely to be positive.

WARNING: *If you're using this technique outside of one-on-one time, be careful of trying to ignore minor misbehavior in interactions involving hot-button issues.* You can quickly make them into something larger than they are. So if you know that conversations over the use of the car are always fraught with conflict between you and your teen, can you shift the responsibility for having these discussions to your child's other parent for a while? This way if your son starts to increase the volume in making his case to have the use of the car, you won't get roped into turning this minor misbehavior into a major infraction. Your husband (or wife), for whom this topic isn't a hot button, won't be as likely to overreact to the loud voice and can just ignore the volume and turn away until his (or her) son tones it down.

rule. Kevin's parents would just clam up and turn away when he started to interrupt in the middle of a conversation, as he was so prone to do. Lauren's parents decided to stop telling her to stop texting just because they didn't like how much time she was spending on it (instead telling her to do so only when she really had to be doing something else that was necessary right then, like come to the dinner table). Mark's parents ignored his refrigerator raids (but not his drinking beer). Gina's parents closed the door to avoid seeing her messy room and then invariably complaining about it. The key is to review your list of nonnegotiables to remind yourself where the line is between something minor and something that needs to be corrected.

When something you know is a minor irritant occurs, briefly turn away, stop talking until the behavior stops, even for a split second, and then make a positive comment. If the behavior escalates into a more serious problem, stop the one-on-one time and correct the behavior.

Q. *My 16-year-old just sneers at me when I suggest spending time together, and when I try to walk up to him when he's doing something by himself, he just gets up and leaves. How can we possibly spend positive one-on-one time together?*

A. When you get this kind of resistance, sometimes you have to grab whatever time you have together and turn it into positive one-on-one time. If you have a 15-minute drive to school or home from sports practice, you can practice the same principles described. Many parents find that being in a car together is their best chance to talk nonjudgmentally—especially since you're not looking at the teen while you drive. Don't worry about it even being for 15 minutes; start with making just 1–2 minutes of positive commentary. But by all means start doing it, because the relationship isn't going to move to being more positive if you yourself don't become more positive.

Q. *I can't seem to come up with the right way to talk to my daughter during one-on-one time. I get totally tongue-tied trying to speak in such a different way. What should I do?*

A. Some parents just think of themselves as sports commentators and narrate what their teen is doing. Others act as "reflective listeners," meaning they repeat back whatever the teen has said and ask if that's what the teen meant just to get the teen to elaborate and direct the interaction. You don't have to say too much, and it will get easier with practice. Hang in there; it's worth the effort, and any awkwardness will pass. You might also ask your spouse to role-play talking to your teen in a totally accepting way with you. Your spouse plays your teen and gives you feedback about your comments; this will help you catch and correct your negative statements in advance of actually talking with your teen. And sometimes words aren't even necessary. Try just going up to your daughter, putting your hand on her shoulder or arm, affectionately squeezing it briefly, and nonverbally conveying how much you care for your child. Touch implies intimacy and often speaks for itself.

Using Praise to Give Your Teen an Incentive to Comply

You need to be able to see the positive in your teen, but don't stop there. When was the last time you took the trouble to praise your teen for something good you caught him or her doing? Or for just being grateful that you even have a son or daughter to care for in your life? We often lose sight of how much we appreciate having children in our lives because of the onslaught of day-to-day activities and details, but how would you feel if your teen were suddenly gone? Use that feeling of being fortunate to have your teen to care for to overcome your resentments and hostility and generate positive comments about how much you really do value having the teen in your family.

If defiance has been entrenched, it might have been quite a while, yet I bet you can remember how your kid's face lit up when you praised him in his younger years. You need to learn to praise your son or daughter again when it's warranted. Only once you've learned the methods for paying and expressing positive attention should you try to learn to change the way you ask your teenager to do what you want him or her to do.

1. *Catch the teen being good.* During the next 2 weeks, try to catch your teen being good every day. Not being extra good, just being acceptable. Look for these three types of opportunities:

- When you're busy and your teen isn't interrupting you with a demand or some other disruption, stop what you're doing for a minute and thank him for not disturbing you. This could be as simple as mouthing your thanks while you're on an important phone call.
- *Anytime* your teen volunteers to do something helpful, be sure to thank her for it, no matter how small it seems, even if it is just wiping up soda spilled on the counter while pouring it into a glass. She might not seem to care at first, but your attention will have a cumulative effect and she'll start working to earn your thanks.
- If your teen starts to do what you ask, *immediately* praise him for complying.

2. *Set up opportunities to praise your teen by making offers he or she can't refuse.* If it sometimes seems that your teen is *never* good, then you'll have to use the content of your commands to set your teenager up to be good.

THINK AHEAD

Does your child have a strength that you identified at the end of Chapter 4 that you can tap in coming up with easy-to-obey commands? This can be as simple as asking your son to get something that's out of your reach because he's taller than you to something like telling your daughter to show her younger brother the map she made for her geography class because she draws so well and he needs a good example for his own homework. Or it could be telling the overactive, fidgety teen—as many defiant teens are—to get a Ping-Pong or volleyball tournament started at a family party. You're killing not two but three birds with one stone here: seeing the positive in your teen, playing to his strengths, and reinforcing the benefits of compliance. As you'll see too, by getting him to do something positive, you're making it hard for him to do something negative. No one can do both at the same time.

Not all commands, after all, are created equal. If you say to your teen "Turn that computer off, go upstairs, and finish your homework," you probably expect resistance, and you probably get it. But if you say, "Go get yourself a piece of that cake I just baked," what kind of response would you expect?

The goal here is to contrive some commands over the next couple of weeks to elicit compliance *and then go out of your way to praise your teen for complying.* When you say "Watch out for that puddle," you're using *content* to set the teenager up to start adhering to the *process* of acceding to your request. What's so great about this practice is that there is a whole world of commands in between "Do your chores!" and "Take a twenty-dollar bill out of my wallet and go spend it on whatever you like." So get creative. Check the list in the box on page 140 and then add some of your own ideas. Even the simplest of commands, if it doesn't seem onerous to the teen, is still a command. When she obeys it, you praise her, and before very long the connection between complying and receiving praise gets internalized and becomes more automatic.

Commands That Teens Are Likely to Obey

"Turn on the football game; it's about to start." [for teens who are fans]

"Go get yourself a soda."

"Take a break from your homework and relax for 10 minutes."

"Try on my new earrings; they'll probably look good with that top."

"Please pass me the salt." [at the dinner table]

"See if there are any good movies coming out this weekend."

"Take the front seat so you can choose the radio station."

"Hold the door for a minute."

"Check your e-mail."

"Text five friends."

"Go talk to your friends on Facebook."

"Take the last piece of chicken."

"Sleep late tomorrow; it's Saturday."

"Stay up another 15 minutes; this show is almost over."

"Tell Dad that hilarious story you told me today."

"Play us a song from that new CD."

"Take a long, hot shower tonight; it'll relax that muscle you pulled in the game."

"Hand me a tissue, please."

"Tell me if my glasses are on straight."

Your ideas:

_____

_____

_____

_____

_____

Whatever content you choose, make it attractive or easy to obey and then scrupulously praise compliance.

3. *Praise your teen for not being "bad."* What do you usually do when your teenager interrupts your conversations, talks with his mouth full, leaves a trail of dirt that he's brought inside the house, or breaks other household rules? Chances are you yell at him to stop or redirect him to something less disruptive. How has that response worked? If you have a defiant teenager, it probably hasn't been that effective. Now think about what you do when your teen is *not* breaking these rules. If you're like most parents, your answer is probably "Nothing." Why should you? The teen isn't defying you, so you don't need to take any action to correct his behavior.

And nothing changes.

So why not try the opposite? Pick some common misbehavior that you'd put in the category of defiance, and when your teen does *not* do it, praise her for it. Think of this strategy as the opposite of "Let sleeping dogs lie." Your teenager isn't a mad dog that will bite if you disturb her when she's not biting. She's an intelligent human being who will learn that if she gets credit for not biting, not biting is what she'll want to do.

To pick a common misbehavior, go back to the list of symptom behaviors in Chapter 1. Do the behaviors you identified in your teen mainly fall into one or two of the four categories? If so, that's probably where you should target this practice because that's where you would normally expect your teen to cause trouble frequently. With 17-year-old Mark, there were so many problems that his parents had a hard time figuring out what to praise him for. Their therapist helped them start small, suggesting they praise him just for respecting everyone's property and not "borrowing" his brother's clothes or iPod or ransacking the

WARNING: *Watch out for the temptation to be sarcastic.* Saying "Thanks so much for not beating Tina to a pulp" when your son isn't bugging his little sister with little slaps and nudges as he often does is not what we have in mind. While such irony may be the coin of the realm these days in comedy news programs and young people's social interactions, sarcasm is not what you need right now to help your relationship with your teen.

refrigerator after school. Lauren's problems were mainly verbal. When she wasn't withdrawing from her parents entirely, she was whining, complaining, and arguing. Her parents had also realized that she had always had a problem with adapting to new situations or unexpected change, so they started by praising her for not complaining when they had to spring an unforeseen obligation on her, like having to go help Grandma move some furniture, instead of taking Lauren to the mall. Gina's mother praised her for not starting to watch a show in the middle of her homework. Kevin's parents praised him for letting his little sister talk about her day at school during dinner without interrupting with sarcastic jokes and mockery.

Q. *Every time I say "Thanks," Lisa gives me a sarcastic "Oh, you're so welcome" or just sneers "Yeah, sure." Am I doing something wrong?*

A. No. Many teens are suspicious of a sudden shift in your behavior from previously being critical to now using praise or appreciation from a parent who hasn't offered it in a while. They naturally assume you want something from them or have some other ulterior motive. Just keep it up, and eventually your daughter will realize your motives are pure.

Q. *I caught Jose being good every chance I got for 2 solid weeks, but he still acts suspicious and hasn't really gotten more cooperative at all. What should I do differently?*

A. Has Jose had the same amount of conflict with his father as with you? If so, you may have to make sure that Dad catches him being good too. Otherwise Jose may feel like he's still not going to get credit for being good at home *because it's not offered consistently by the two of you.*

Q. *When I tried praising Tia for just doing the little things I asked, she'd make some nasty remark, and she's still doing it, so the praise doesn't seem to be making her more cooperative. Why not?*

A. How do you respond when she says something sarcastic or obnoxious? If you tend to snap at her and tell her to watch her mouth, or something similar, you're playing her game and shifting the emphasis away from the process you're trying to reinforce. Try using the technique you learned earlier in this step and just ignore these remarks—turn away briefly, and when the nasty remarks stop, thank her again for doing what you asked.

Understand that this can be the most important step in this program because it hinges on developing a newfound respect, appreciation, and approval of your teen that may have been lacking or downplayed in your previous relationship. As Stephen Covey says in his book *The 7 Habits of Highly Effective People*, every positive comment you make is a deposit into your emotional bank account with your teen, whether the teen formally acknowledges it or not. Be patient, stay with the positive commentary, and things will slowly improve. But know that in some families negativity between parents and teenagers is so deeply entrenched that you may not see results on your own from following this step. If you follow our advice in this step for several weeks and get no results, that is a strong indication that you are going to need the help of a mental health professional to carry out the remainder of this program.

No longer completely at the mercy of your teenager's defiance, you have now started to craft the context of your interactions so that your teen will naturally be inclined to comply. This will not happen overnight, but after 2 weeks you should begin to see some positive progress. At the very least, you've flooded your household with positive feedback, which is certainly all good. Now that you've shifted the balance back toward the positive, we can address how to start dealing with the negative. In the next chapter you'll learn the principles of behavior management and how to apply them to making your commands more effective.

Step 2. A New Way to Manage Behavior

After making efforts to shift the tone of the home environment toward the positive, many parents report that their teenager already seems more cooperative. Some teens need only concerted reminders of their parents' goodwill to start doing as they ask more often. Sometimes an infusion of benevolence and compassion simply eases tensions enough that family members are no longer so tightly coiled and ready to strike. You might find that your teen doesn't balk at every request, that you no longer comment on every little annoyance, and that in turn your teen doesn't seem to grab every opportunity to be snide or sarcastic. It's a not-so-vicious circle of interaction that can only expand with time and positive perseverance.

For most parents, however, eliminating defiance by creating a balance between positive and negative interactions with a teen requires more than increasing the positive. You probably also need to learn ways to directly reduce the negative. That starts with increasing compliance by giving more effective commands. Notice that we're not talking about getting your teenager to cooperate by imposing a deterrent for disobedience. We're not even going to talk about punishment until you learn everything you can to reduce the frequency of misbehavior, and thus the need to be punitive in the first place. This approach is based on two major principles that you've already met and that you're going to run into throughout this program:

- The positive will always come before the negative.
- Parenting style = power. Changing what *you* do to elicit change in your teen is being a proactive, effective parent rather than a reactive, frustrated parent.

Never confuse a willingness to change with weakness or giving up your authority. Living with a defiant teenager has a way of making parents feel incompetent and ineffectual. It's only natural for parents frustrated by feelings of helplessness to try to assert their dominance by forcing their teenager to change. The problem with that tactic is that it doesn't work. Remember what we said about the difference between *authoritative* parents and *authoritarian* parents? The former set fair, reasonable, but firm rules, expect them to be met, yet are open to negotiation around many of those rules. The latter rule by tyranny and usually incur revolt. You're showing your strength and your parental authority when *you* make changes that elicit your teenager's cooperation, not when you try to coerce your teen to change through threats, punishment, and verbal attacks.

Taking this message to heart is critical. Unless you subscribe to it, you won't be able to commit to making the kinds of tried-and-true changes that you'll start to make during this step. It would be like having a state-of-the-art computer at your disposal but trying to rely on an abacus to calculate the amount of principal and interest you'll pay on your mortgage over the next 30 years.

GOALS FOR STEP 2

- Start to apply the principles of behavior management to your daily interactions with your teen.
- Learn to give effective commands.

If you looked closely at the ways you've been trying to get your teenager to do what you want and show you the respect you deserve, you'd see how entangled you've become in the coercive behavior pattern introduced in Chapter 2. Like a puppet on your teenager's strings, you've given in when you didn't want to; been drawn into diversionary blowups that get the teen out of whatever you asked her to do; and punished the same infraction lightly sometimes, severely at other times, and not at all at still other times. The only thing that either of you could predict about most interactions is that they'd involve an argument. It's time to change that pattern of interaction through a proven approach known in the field of psychology as *behavior management* or *behavior modification*.

You'll be learning behavior management techniques throughout much of this program. At this step we offer some suggestions for applying the principles of behavior management in a preliminary fashion to the way you deal with your teenager. The main idea at this point is simply to engrave these principles on your brain so that you start to think in those terms. You'll be using them in a much more systematic fashion in coming weeks. At the same time, you'll adopt six important guidelines for giving effective commands. Remember to keep up the positive attention that you put into place in Step 1 throughout this step too.

Starting to Change Your Teen's Behavior by Altering Your Own

If your teenager has ADHD, you may already be familiar with the techniques and principles of behavior modification. The star charts, point systems, and time-outs that you may have found very effective in keeping your attention-challenged child on task when younger are all based on the same principles we want you to start adopting over the next 2 weeks. Even if your teen does not have ADHD and you've never used these tools, behavior modification is mostly simple common sense. It says that you can change someone's behavior through the use of rewards and punishments— what are collectively referred to as *consequences*.

You've seen this concept in action plenty of times. You just haven't seen it work for you all the time because you probably haven't been using it consistently. *Consistency*, in fact, is the byword of effective behavior management. But we're getting ahead of ourselves. Before you start to try to put behavior management to work, make sure you engrave the concept in your mind. It's as simple as the ABCs:

Anticipate → Behavior ← Consequences

As you can see from the directions of the arrows, there are two ways to influence or change behavior (B). You can either anticipate behavior or figure out what the antecedent (A) that often prompts it is, or you can establish a consequence (C) for either performing or not performing the behavior.

You used this ABC model throughout your teen's childhood. When your child was really young, because there were so many ways that he could put himself in harm's way, you often took great pains to anticipate what he might do and prevent him from doing it. You used the *A* part of the model to influence the child's behavior. A typical example is the use of plastic caps to protect a toddler from putting a curious finger into a live electric outlet. In cases where safety is the goal, you certainly wouldn't choose the other option, imposing consequences (C) for the child touching the outlet. But use of anticipation doesn't have to be limited to safety issues. Teachers use it all the time, such as when they seat a child on the opposite side of the room from his talkative best friend because neither of them gets anything done when they're side by side. By arranging the room so that both kids can concentrate, the teacher has effectively modified their behavior.

We usually tell parents that being able to think ahead and review previous experience to predict the future is like having money in the bank. These are "coins" you can use to modify your teen's behavior. Naturally, however, not all behavior is predictable, and that's where you also have to turn to consequences to modify your teen's behavior.

You undoubtedly won't be surprised to learn that positive consequences make it more likely that a behavior will happen again and negative consequences make it less likely that a behavior will happen again. Say "Good girl!" when your child reaches for the outlet, and she'll likely do it again; yell "No!!!" and she may think twice about it next time the urge comes upon her. Where things get tricky is that we often inadvertently reward a negative behavior, making it more likely to happen again, or punish a positive behavior, making it less likely to happen again. Since, as you reminded yourself during Step 1, positive attention is a positive consequence, catching your teen being good (or just acceptable) encourages a repetition of that behavior. Ignoring good behavior discourages the teen from bothering to try to be good (or acceptable). Coercive actions like loud arguing by your teen are negative behavior. If the teen gets out of what you wanted her to do because you finally give in just to stop the conflict, you have rewarded her negative behavior with a positive consequence. It will be used again—you can count on it.

Over time this coercive behavior pattern actually blurs the connection between behaviors and consequences for teens. They stop recognizing that there are positive consequences for positive behaviors and negative consequences for negative behaviors. That's why any attempts you may have made in the past to use rewards and punishments may have failed. The first goal to tackle during this step, therefore, is to ingrain three concepts that will keep the connection between behaviors and consequences crystal clear to your teen:

- Commands and consequences will be specific.
- Consequences will be immediate.
- Consequences will be consistent.

All we want you to do to begin this step is to start reminding yourself to be specific, to react immediately, and to be consistent. These are not easy changes to make, and they won't occur all at once. But if you start thinking of your interactions with your teenager in this way, you'll (1) notice where you haven't been following these principles and (2) make some preliminary changes in the way you deal with your son or daughter.

1. *Be specific.* For one chore or other task that has become a bone of contention between you and your teenager, think of a way to make your typical command more specific and use only that way of phrasing it over the next 2 weeks. Boy, do teenagers love loopholes. Tell your teen to do the dishes, and he may fill the dishwasher but not run it or not wash the pots and pans. Remind your teen to take out the garbage, and when you ask an hour later why it's still sitting in the kitchen, she'll turn an innocent face to you and say without guile, "Oh, I didn't know you wanted it done now." Ask him whether he's doing his homework, and he'll probably answer "Yes"—without mentioning that he's also talking to 10 friends on Facebook and downloading music at the same time as he's trying to write a term paper.

If you want your teen to do as you expect, you have to make it quite clear what that is. Say "Fill and run the dishwasher, wash and dry all the pots and pans, and scour the sink before you leave the kitchen." Say "Take a break from what you're doing and take the garbage out right now." After your son says he's doing his homework, say "Do *just* your homework—turn off Facebook, turn off your cellphone, and don't download any music. You'll get your homework done faster and *then* you can have those electronic privileges."

Make consequences clear too—not "You'll be in big trouble if you don't make your bed" but "If you make your bed, you can use your cellphone; if you don't make your bed by 9:00 this morning, you won't be able to use your cellphone for the rest of the day." Your teen has probably heard threats of getting into "big trouble" and the like often enough to know that they usually amount to nothing, so they'll have little force.

2. *React immediately.* Over the next 2 weeks, make a point of praising your teen for one positive (or neutral) thing he does routinely that you take for granted the minute he does it. Each minute that passes between a behavior and a consequence weakens the connection in your teenager's mind between the behavior and the consequence and dilutes the power the consequence should have. This is true not just for negative consequences for negative behavior but also for positive consequences for positive behavior. You probably noticed during Step 1 that not much changed in your teen's attitude or behavior if your praise was always delivered long afterward. Saying "Thanks for taking out the garbage" in the evening, when your daughter took out the garbage in the morning, won't strengthen the behavior–consequence connection the way thanking her right after your daughter came back into the house would.

As to negative consequences, let's say your teenager breaks your nonnegotiable prohibition of using profanity in the house. You let it go because you have company and don't want to create a scene. Hours later you tell your teen that he can't use the computer that evening. I'm sure you can imagine the argument that might ensue: the teen complains that you're being unfair; that you didn't say you were angry at the time; that now he *has* to use the computer because he has a group project that he has to work on with some other students, and if he doesn't get online with them, they won't get it done on time and they'll all fail. Your teen knew that the consequence for profanity was no use of the computer for the day, but because you didn't impose the consequence when he expected it, he assumed he was getting a reprieve. There are a million variations on this theme. The point is that, although a delayed consequence is better than none at all, if your goal is to cement that connection between behavior and consequences, an immediate response is your best bet. This means it's particularly important to make consequences immediate over the next 2 weeks while you're reestablishing the connection in your teen's mind. What do we mean by "immediate"? Within 10 seconds is an ideal goal to strive for, but certainly announcing consequences within a few minutes after the misbehavior (or bestowing rewards for good behavior) has occurred should work well for most teens.

Note too that immediacy is paramount if your son or daughter has ADHD. You probably already know that the world these kids live in is *now*. The nature of their disability is that they can't think ahead or reflect on the past without assistance. Help them by imposing swift consequences.

WARNING: *Act, don't yak.* Many parents repeat themselves incessantly when their adolescent fails to comply with their commands. Adolescents quickly learn that Mom or Dad is all talk, no action. As Sam Goldstein, PhD, has been advising for a number of years, after you've decided on the consequence and issued a command, it's time to act, not yak. Do not repeat your commands or restate the consequences over and over again, making hollow threats or bantering. Go directly to implementing them.

If you happen to be in a public place (e.g., a restaurant or store) when your teenager breaks a nonnegotiable rule, it may be difficult to carry out an immediate negative consequence. State the negative consequence and when it will be implemented, give your teen a "ticket" by writing it out on a piece of paper just as the police do when you are caught speeding, and implement the consequence upon returning home.

3. *Be consistent.* Pick one minor household rule—something that you want followed but that isn't a huge hot button—and make a commitment to enforcing it without fail for the next 2 weeks. Talk about loopholes! Parental inconsistency is one huge gaping window for defiant teenagers to slip through. Are your rules enforced consistently, or do they bend with every whiff of the wind? Do you insist they be followed for days at a time but then let them go for the next few days? Is it a rule for Dad but not necessarily for Mom? Is it a rule only when Mom or Dad is in a bad mood? Is it a rule only when Mom is there but Dad is not or when Dad is there but Mom is not? Do you cut some of your kids some slack on some rules but enforce them religiously for others (without those differences being clearly stated parts of the rules themselves)? Is it a rule in some situations or surroundings, a guideline in others, a mere suggestion in still others, and not even an issue in the rest?

No one can be expected to be consistent 100% of the time. And many teens can figure out that Mom's rules differ from Dad's rules, that in some situations the rules are relaxed, and that there are predictable cases that call for strict adherence to the letter of the law. But for kids who are already defiant, it's all up for grabs.

How far the rules can be bent, how Mom or Dad is likely to react to violations, and what's really a rule at this moment is the subject of one big lab experiment. So to reinstill the idea that household rules are consistent and that violations of them will be followed with consistent consequences, you're going to have to be much more diligent than most parents in sticking to the drill.

4. *Over the next 2 weeks, take a good hard look at the consequences you tend to impose: Are they meaningful, frequent, and well balanced—or impotent?* To forge a strong behavior–consequences link, you need to give consequences for good or bad behavior that have real power. Your teenager is not currently motivated to work for you—that is, to cooperate. She also may be immature or ill equipped to defer gratification for other reasons, such as having ADHD or an impatient, emotional temperament. You can't expect a teen who habitually resists to suddenly start following requests and rules out of simple pride in accomplishment, a sense of responsibility, or respect for authority (yours). You have to make the consequences meaningful to your teen. This means that you must give tangible, exciting, fun, stimulating rewards for the behavior you want to see again and again. *This is not a form of bribery.* Bribery involves taking a large amount of money for something illegal and is a term that should not be connected to the practice of rewarding your teen for positive behavior. Nor does it mean you've given in, given up, and let your teen call the shots. It's a reflection of your understanding that positive behavior is reinforced by positive consequences and your way of conveying that understanding to your teenager.

Your teenager will need lots of reminders of this positive behavior–positive consequence connection, which means consequences need to be imposed a lot more frequently than you may be used to. We're not talking about your "going broke" shelling out tangible gifts and rewards. Remember that a positive consequence can—and should—often be a few words of praise, a smile, a thumbs-up, or a hug. For now that's all you really need to do, keeping in mind the possibility of offering a more tangible reward for a significant achievement of your teen. You'll learn to use a more systematic schedule of rewards starting in Step 3. This week and next, call into play all of the ways you expressed positive attention to your teen during Step 1 and keep the positive patter going. Having a running "tape" of positive reinforcement in the background will help your teen stay on track with positive behavior throughout the day. Think of yourself as your teen's personal trainer, the executive who's helping him learn a new job (managing his behavior), or the driving instructor who's prepared to use an extra set of controls until your teen can handle driving solo. You'll be able to back off from the constant coaching and cheerleading once your teen's behavior improves—but then again, you probably won't want to. Praise and other positive consequences will become so much a part of your way of interacting that it will just seem like the way to be with each other.

Substituting for Your Teenager's Internal Executive

Some teens become defiant strictly through an unfortunate pattern of interactions with their parents. But as you learned in Part I, many defiant teens were vulnerable to these behavior problems because they have trouble with things like impulse control, concentration, deferring gratification, patience, and planning. These are some of the abilities that fall into what scientists have started to view as a person's executive functions or skills: the mental abilities to control our reactions to the world around us and regulate our behavior and emotions. It's as if we all possess a manager in the mind who tells us what to do and not do, say and not say. Kids with ADHD can be viewed as having problems with executive functions, and so can many other teens prone to defiant behavior and attitudes— sometimes their executive functions work properly, other times they don't. When you use the behavior management techniques in this program, you are in a sense filling in temporarily for your teen's absent executive. You are your teen's "surrogate executive functions." Working your way through this program teaches defiant teens some of the skills that have not come so naturally to them. The ultimate goal is to turn over the reins to them and let them be their own executive as much as may be reasonably possible.

One last way to make consequences powerful is to make them well balanced. We've been talking about positive consequences, but of course you'll have to impose negative ones as well. The trick you started to learn in Step 1 was to reestablish a balance between the negative and the positive by concentrating on positive attention and downplaying negative attention for a couple of weeks. Teenagers quickly become demoralized and lose their motivation to cooperate if negative consequences are imposed much more frequently than positive ones. This is why you need to learn to issue effective commands, the second goal for this step. You'll be applying all the preceding principles.

5. *Based on the principles of behavior management and your observations of your interactions with your teen over the last 2 weeks, review your most recent list of nonnegotiable issues.* It's hard to be specific, consistent, and immediate and to impose consequences with teeth if even *you* don't have the conviction to back up the rules. Now that you've looked closely at whether you act according to the principles of behavior management, and where you've had trouble doing so, ask yourself whether each rule is one you really want obeyed all the time. If not, delete it. Now ask yourself if there are others you've omitted that you want followed all the time. If so, add them. Also consider whether you can really follow up on enforcing these rules. What do your observations over the last 2 weeks tell you? Will you really mean it when you tell your teen to follow the rule? Do you have negative and positive consequences planned? If the answer to either question is "No" for any of your rules, delete it for now. Working toward the next goal will help you begin to know how to follow through on the rules you really do want to uphold.

Giving More Effective Commands

Over the next 2 weeks, follow these six guidelines whenever you need to issue a command to your teenager:

1. *Make sure you mean it!* It's amazingly easy to toss out an order to a teenager and a lot harder to follow through. So, before you tell your teen to do *anything* over the next couple of weeks, stop and ask yourself whether you mean it seriously. Do you have the time and energy to follow through and make sure the command is followed? Do you have a consequence planned for non-compliance? Are you prepared to give sincere positive feedback if your teen complies? Is it really important enough to make an issue of, or should you just ignore it? If you answer any of these questions with a *no,* bite your tongue. Unless all of your answers are *yes,* the command will be weak and ineffectual and will just keep the cycle of defiance going.

2. *Present the command simply, directly, and in a businesslike tone of voice rather than as a question or a request for a favor.* You can give choices, but draw the line between legitimate choices and illegitimate ones. It's legitimate to ask "Do you want to do your homework now or after dinner?" but not to ask "Do you want to do your homework?" when what you really mean is "Do your homework."

3. *Give one command at a time.* Teenagers tune out adults after the 10th word. You want to reinforce the connection between behavior and consequence. If you issue a string of commands, it will be harder to follow up with immediate consequences to each, and it will be hard for that strict B–C connection to sink into your teen's brain. If your teen has ADHD or other problems concentrating, this guideline is critical. If you need to give a complex or large command, break it down into individual smaller commands.

4. *Tell the teen what to do rather than what not to do.* Telling an oppositional teen what not to do is inviting her to jump over your line in the sand and disobey you just to prove she can. Remember how important pride is to your maturing teen. Saying "Put your shoes in the closet" tells her exactly what she should do, whereas

"Don't leave your shoes in the middle of the living room" doesn't signal what her next move should be and leaves her vulnerable to failure. Your goal is to make it *easy* for her to succeed.

5. *Make sure you have your teen's full attention when you give a command.* Avoid giving commands when there is a competing distraction going on. Distractions like the TV or iPod will just make it harder for some teens to pay attention to what you're saying and set them up for failure. Avoid giving commands from another room; face your teenager when you give him or her a command.

6. *Be cautious about commands that involve time limits.* Look back to your checklist from Chapter 1 of this book. If most of your teen's defiance falls into the "passive noncompliance" category, you're probably already experiencing lots of problems with unfinished tasks. If, in Chapter 4, you identified characteristics in your teenager that indicate difficulty concentrating, persevering, planning, or thinking ahead, telling the teen to put away all the clothes strewn on his bedroom floor in the next 15 minutes

THINK AHEAD

Know how to make sure your teen hears you. You may already know that a certain glazed look means that no matter what your teen says, she hasn't actually heard you. But we parents can't always tell where their minds are. Remember that teenagers tend to be preoccupied by all kinds of events and issues in their lives, and the fact that the TV is off, your teen isn't in the middle of a conversation, she's not using her Xbox, texting on her smartphone, and her iPod isn't plugged into her ear doesn't mean she isn't distracted. Try prefacing your commands with something like "I need to talk to you" and then wait until your teen is looking at you and at least seems to see you. To make sure she did hear your command, ask her to repeat back to you what you just said.

or be ready to go to an appointment at 1:00 P.M. will not make it easy for him to comply. Give this type of teen an aid such as a digital clock or timer or simply put as many commands as possible in the context of "now."

Q. *We gave our son a clear, direct command to do his homework and set the consequence that he'd have to study for an extra 5 minutes if he didn't complete all of his algebra homework by the time we came home from work. However, things got worse instead of better. Why isn't this working for us?*

A. First of all, although your command was clear, you violated the first principle of using consequences: incentives before punishments. Simply loading on more punishments usually won't work unless you already have a strong reward system for completing homework. Second, parents must monitor defiant teenagers during the homework completion process; you set yourselves and your son up for failure by requiring him to get the homework done before you came home from work. In addition to a positive incentive and being around during homework completion, you might try breaking up the homework into smaller segments and praising your son for completing them. This may keep him on track. You'll learn more about tackling specific problem situations with behavior management in the next two chapters.

Q. *Our 15-year-old son, Hiroshi, has ADHD. He is a consummate wise guy. He's often very funny, so we have a hard time keeping his banter, which regularly crosses the line from witty to mean, under control. To keep him from dominating the dinner conversation, which often leads him to cross that line, we made a strict rule that he has to let everyone finish speaking before he starts talking. The consequence for any interruptions is that he has to be totally silent for the next 5 minutes, even if no one is speaking. This has not worked. Hiroshi either explodes into some verbal tirade or starts making wild gesticulations as if choking himself to avoid talking, thus dominating the conversation anyway. What should we do?*

A. You have to respect biology when establishing consequences for problem behavior. It's very difficult for teens with ADHD to refrain from talking for 5 minutes; this is an example of an executive function deficit that follows from the neurobiology of ADHD. Your consequence is unrealistic. A better solution here is to rely on "antecedent control"—anticipating behavior and analyzing antecedents, as we discussed earlier in the chapter, instead of focusing on consequences. Establish a concrete antecedent for each person in the family to "have the floor" during dinnertime. Select an object such as a gavel, which a speaker must be holding to have the floor. Pass the gavel from person to person as each person has a turn to speak. Make a rule that each person has 2 minutes and then the gavel is passed on. This way the same rule applies to everyone and Hiroshi won't feel like you're all ganging up on him. Build in a positive incentive for Hiroshi to cooperate with this system; perhaps he can earn a privilege such as iPod, smartphone, iPad, or computer time or a small amount of money for each dinnertime during which he adheres to the rule about the gavel.

Q. *Our daughter's room always looks like a bomb hit it. She comes up with a million excuses for avoiding even something as simple as making her bed—"I put my clean laundry on it"; "I'll make my bed after I put my clothes away after school"; "I'm going to wash my sheets later, so there's no point in making the bed now"; and so on—so we decided to break the order "Clean your room" into several steps. But it still doesn't get done. We come into her room and find each individual task half done and Raven absorbed in a magazine that was under her bed or some note she found that a boy had sent her at school 2 months ago. What else can we do to get her to do this job?*

A. Try writing the list of steps down and posting it on the back of her door where she can refer to it. Some kids get distracted so easily that they can't stick to even a single, uncomplicated task without some kind of reinforcer. Another way to reinforce the individual commands is to attach positive consequences to each, which you also write down after each task. Positives could all be of the same kind, such as 10 extra minutes of screen time for completion of each task, adding up to a maximum for cleaning the whole room that includes a bonus, such as picking a new movie to download or just an extra 15 minutes of screen time for the evening.

We'll get into this system of rewards more fully in Step 3, but it may be worth trying out here, especially if you have an attention-challenged teen. Completing homework was a perennial issue for Gina, so her mother had to get very creative with rewards. One system she came up with was to hold on to Gina's iPod and let her earn 5 iPod minutes for each pair of math problems she completed. After doing all the problems and sitting quietly with her mother while Mom checked over the homework, she would get her smartphone or iPod for the number of minutes she earned.

Q. *I'm being very specific and firm and making sure I don't phrase my commands to Jared as questions, since I can now see that giving him choices like that just gave him enough rope to hang himself as far as defiance is concerned. So I say "Please take out the garbage" or "I would appreciate it if you would put all the dishes in the dishwasher now." Jared still doesn't do what I ask. Why not?*

A. You answered the question yourself: because, in a sense, you are still asking, not telling. It can be hard to be businesslike and no-nonsense in issuing commands when we've spent years trying to model how to speak courteously and respectfully to others. And many of us also took to heart parenting advice to show respect and empathy for our kids and their right as human beings to be self-determining. But now is not the time for niceties. Just gird yourself to be brief and to the point and say "Jared, take out the garbage" and "Jared, it's time to put all the dishes in the dishwasher." You'll probably be able to return to saying "please" and couching your instructions in other polite phrases at a later time. But for now the goal is to reestablish your authority, which means leaving no room for choice about whether to comply. You don't have to—in fact shouldn't—sound threatening, mean, or bullying. Just be straightforward. If you find yourself blurting out "please" or sounding unsure of yourself (ask your teen's other parent if you have any doubts about whether you sound authoritative), practice typical commands you'll need to issue over the next couple of weeks in the mirror—without "please."

Likewise, watch out for using "Thank you" in place of praise at this step. In Step 1 we encouraged you to say "Thank you" for the innocuous little positives and nonnegatives in your teen's behavior as a way of showing that you do pay attention to the positive things he or she does. But when you are directing your teen to do something you really want done, saying something like "Thanks for doing your homework" may create the false impression that your teen has done you a personal favor and that complying is optional rather than that the teen is expected to do as told.

As you can see from the preceding examples, behavior management is simple in theory, a little more difficult in practice. You should be starting to get an idea of how you can put to work what you learned in Part I about the personalities, habits, and automatic behavior and communication styles that factor into conflicts between you and your teen. The next couple of chapters will help you continue to use that information as you learn more about behavior management.

10

Step 3.
Contracts and Point Systems
How Teens Can Earn Privileges

Before you start on Step 3, stop for a moment and think about what has changed around your house. It's been about a month since you started this program. You might think of that time as a training period. You've been building up emotional capital with your teen, training him or her to expect more approval, praise, and respect from you. You're becoming a better supervisor and regaining confidence in your parenting. So even if you can't say your teen has made any radical behavior changes, you should be feeling a little better about yourself.

You undoubtedly feel relieved that the level of conflict at home has dropped, even if just a little, and you may also feel a bit less stressed, and possibly more energized. Giving effective commands takes a lot less energy and is a lot less frustrating than the scattershot approach of the past. It's tremendously liberating to know in your own mind that you've decided what you're asking is important enough to make an issue of it, that you've been specific enough that your teen has the information needed to get the job done, and that you have the authority to expect compliance and don't need to rely on emotional blackmail and other forms of coercion. Your teenager still may defy you, but you know that what you've asked and how you've asked it are above reproach.

You don't have to ruminate about how the encounter escalated into a fight or what you could have done differently or why you can't seem to get control of this kid. Change in your teenager's response will come in time.

Let's keep working on that: Your goal in this step is still to improve your relationship with your teen by reinforcing your teenager's positive behavior, but now you're going to make the consequences a little more concrete than a word of praise, a smile, or an affectionate gesture. To keep strengthening your teen's mental connection between behavior and consequences, you're going to take advantage of what your teen views as the positives in his or her life.

GOALS FOR STEP 3

- Learn the rationale for and principles of contingency management so they become second nature.
- Set up a formal system—a behavior contract or a point system—that makes privileges contingent on your teen's compliance.

You've already started demonstrating to your teen that there are positive consequences for positive behavior. But many defiant teens just don't believe it's possible to get a positive reaction no matter how good they are. They need evidence beyond your positive attention and praise. If your teenager is like most defiant kids, she believes that privileges and other rewards are doled out (or withheld) indiscriminately. She thinks you become magnanimous unpredictably because you're in a good mood or something has happened that has nothing to do with her. She believes you deny privileges just as capriciously because you're in a bad mood or mad at someone else—or to punish her for something you just remembered she did last week or because her transgressions have "added up" and you think it's about time to take drastic measures. The message your defiant teen needs to start hearing right now is that not only does good behavior have its rewards *but they are predictable.*

Even the youngest kids understand the concept of contingencies: I start to get ready for bed when Mom says to without arguing, and I get a bedtime story; I argue and stall for time and end up going to bed without one. Somewhere along the way, your teenager has lost touch with that concept. Now is the time to instill it again. The idea is called *contingency management*. You probably need to relearn the concept yourself. You've stopped requiring your teen to do what you want to get what *he* wants; you've let him believe he's in charge where he shouldn't be. Privileges have lost their potency. You're about to change that.

This is a step that you may find requires only a week, but don't give it less than a week, and don't yield to the temptation to extend the system to apply it all over the place. Follow the directions and take it slow. Make sure you're being consistent before moving on to Step 4. Two weeks is about right for most families to get the system set up and working routinely, so consider the first week more like a "shakedown" cruise of a new ship—a tune-up time for getting the program right.

Understanding How Contingency Management Can Reduce Defiance

Why do you need to bother with the formality of this step? There are three obvious reasons, plus a fourth that is more subtle but just as important:

- Defiant teens are motivationally challenged. Clearly your teenager hasn't been willing to do what you want in the past, so you need to supply the motivation externally. This is what contingency management does. It is a sort of motivational priming or nudging. By connecting behavior to immediate and desirable consequences, it results in the teen's being more likely to do what was requested. Over time, if all goes well, the idea of having to earn privileges through cooperation will become ingrained and internalized and become part of your teenager's modus operandi.

- Agreements between you and your teen need to be very explicit so that each of you knows what is expected of the other—what needs to be done and what is promised for doing it. This eliminates the ambiguity that can cause so much conflict.

• Contingency management is the way the adult work world operates. We get paid for doing our job. If we don't do our job, the paychecks stop. Creating contracts for work at home and in school helps prepare teens for this aspect of adult life. This type of motivational priming just makes the relationship between work and rewards explicit but by doing so makes it more likely teens will cooperate. Just as one does not do something for nothing, one does not get something for nothing. Point systems make it very clear that while there is no free lunch, there are lots of desirable items on the menu available for behaving well. It also makes a powerful ethical statement: No one owes you anything because you exist. What you seek to get you must earn.

• Your teen needs to know that his time and effort are valued. Our children are not slaves. Like anyone else, they deserve to be compensated for the work they do for others, including their parents. We'd never consciously think of our teens as our slaves, but sometimes we imply it when we act as if being part of our family means our kids owe us some debt. All of us have a limited lifetime. Since our time is limited, it is inherently valuable to us. If we are to spend it doing something for someone, generally we expect to get something of value to us in return. Point systems make this connection very clear. We'd expect to pay someone to cut the lawn, to clean the house, or to wash our windows, so why should our children simply be expected to do these things when told to do so? You may feel this is a fair trade since you feed, clothe, house, protect, educate, and otherwise support your kids. *But that's your job*—what you implicitly agreed to do when you decided to have children. Your children, on the other hand, had no say in that matter and therefore have no debt to repay. Treating them as if they do is neither fair nor right and can often lead to conflict within the family. Contingency management provides a structure through which you treat your teen as you would anyone else who's doing something for you, not only showing more respect for the teen and his time and labor but also satisfying his innate sense of self-worth, fairness, and justice. The product of that shift? You'll get more respect from your teen too.

1. *Consider why your teen is no longer motivated to cooperate.* With the preceding rationale in mind, why do you think your teen doesn't cooperate with you? As explained in Chapters 5 and 6, your teenager has been in charge of too many things too much of the time. Maybe your teen has been in control of what she does and when with little parental input. Or your teen has had so many unearned special privileges and possessions that she's taken them for granted and is now actually in control of rewarding herself. Many teens, in fact, think of these privileges as rights or entitlements. Or you've been expecting slave labor from your teen in return for providing the basic essential support that any parent should supply. Without a lot of thought, which of these strikes you as likely to be instrumental in your teen's case?

Before we go any further, understand that setting up a system whereby your teen starts to earn privileges is not meant to be a diatribe against the one-sided selfish materialism of the 21st century or to divert attention to a discussion of whether kids are "spoiled" today. The point is not how much your kids have in the way of toys or trips or how much money any of it costs; it's whether you control these things so that your teenager understands that they are privileges rather than rights or entitlements. Our goal is not to impose our own definition of modesty, our own version of Calvinism (reward denial), or our own personal values on your family. It's to help you instill in your teen a renewed understanding of principles crucial to successful adult life: that there is a consequence for every behavior and that the way to get what you want is to meet the expectations of those in control of what you aspire to obtain.

2. *Know the difference between rights, gifts, and earnings/privileges.* As far as we're concerned, your teen may be entitled to the basic essentials of human life—food, clothing, shelter, protection, medical care, and education—and so these things are "off the table" as consequences to be used to manage your teen's behavior. They are entitlements, not privileges or consequences to be given or withdrawn contingent on teen behavior.

What about gifts? Anything you've given your teen as a birthday present, Christmas or Hanukkah gift, or the like is also off the table. That's what gifts are: noncontingent offerings to others. You wouldn't expect someone outside your family to do something for you because you happen to give him a birthday gift. But if you've found yourself getting angry at your teen for defiant behavior via the reasoning that the teen owes you respect or cooperation since you just bestowed a lavish gift on him, consider the possibility that expecting this kind of reciprocity could well be the source of some of the tension in your relationship. Remember, gifts aren't supposed to come with strings.

This means if you've given your teen a computer, cellphone, iPad, video games, fashionable clothing, or anything else on a special occasion as a gift, you should not be threatening to take it back when your teen does not do some work for you or behave as you've demanded. Doing so will instantly trigger your teen's sense of injustice and unfairness. So think carefully from now on when you give a large gift, especially a smartphone involving a monthly data plan. Do you expect to be able to use it as a consequence later? If so, you have to state how, explicitly, up front. For instance, you could give your daughter a smartphone for her birthday with the explicit qualification that the extra monthly payments on your phone bill beyond that first month are *not* part of the gift. That means that each month's *use* of the phone is a privilege to be earned. The same applies to computers like iPads—maybe your teen owns the computer given as a gift, but monthly Internet access charges are a privilege to be earned. We cannot emphasize this enough: you *must* make the distinction between owning something as a gift and monthly usage bills as a behavioral privilege to be earned very clear at the start. If you didn't, then don't expect your teen to do so naturally either. Your son probably thought the whole package of product and monthly usage was the gift. This gets trickier around gifts that have no monthly usage bills, like an MP3 music player or an iPod. Once you give it, you cannot take it back as a consequence. If you do, you can likely expect an argument with your teen, and rightly so. What you *can* use as a consequence is the ability to earn extra music downloads from websites to add to the teen's music collection on the player. Your son could earn gift cards, certificates, or other credits through cooperative behavior and work done for you. That's fair—those are things to be earned.

That leads us to earnings. These are the privileges, goods, products, or other services you can offer your teen as part of a contract you will be making with the teen concerning the teen's behavior and the work he or she does for you. They are earnings because they are contingent on the teen's conduct or efforts. Such things as allowances, time out of the house with friends, use of the family car and its fuel, special clothing articles, monthly usage fees for electronics, dining out with friends, and use of the family TV, family computer, and the like can be used as sources of potential earnings for your teen. Here again, understand that once a teen has earned these things, you cannot unilaterally take back what you gave because of some future infraction. That would be like your employer taking back one of your previous paychecks because you did something wrong at work later. You, like your employer, can withhold *future* consequences ("paychecks") for what your teen does as part of your contracts, but it's not fair for you to take back what the teen has already earned. Making these distinctions clear with your teen will bolster his or her respect for you and your sense of fairness, and it will also cut down on a lot of the arguments that arise because of ambiguity about what is a right, a gift, or an earning.

Ambiguity may, in fact, be the greatest nemesis of parents with a defiant teen. In families where defiance rules, parents have often taken away privileges to little effect because the teenager knows that the privileges are doled out indiscriminately and often ambiguously, which means there's probably always another one around the corner—to say nothing of the ones the kid already has stockpiled. (A kid who's not allowed to go hang out with her friends, for example, still may have an iPod, cellphone, and computer to entertain her and, in fact, to keep her in touch with her friends, even if in a more virtual way than an actual way.) Trying to reward a defiant teen for good behavior probably hasn't worked either. If the kid knows he doesn't need another toy or another privilege, he's hardly likely to be motivated by the promise of a reward. Rewards just don't mean enough to him when he's gotten so much else, even if that is mainly freedom and independence that he actually hasn't earned and isn't mature enough to handle. If you've been inconsistent and indiscriminate in monitoring your teen and enforcing rules, and ambiguous in distinguishing what are rights, gifts, and earnings, the teen *is* in charge—and she knows it. You don't have to have actively bestowed those privileges for your teen to know she already has them. Never forget what valuable commodities freedom and independence are to teens. If your teen has them, plus a lot of toys, what more does she need from you?

The only thing you can do in this case is level the playing field, taking back control of the many privileges you do in fact have control over and issuing them only contingent on your teen's good behavior. Rewards will never have the power to encourage good behavior, and removal of privileges will never have the power to discourage bad behavior, if you're not in control of these privileges to begin with. That's why it's so critical to make it crystal clear to both yourself and your teen what are rights, what are gifts, and what are the things that can be earned. Remember that electronic items that are given as gifts have to remain that way, but you always have the option of making usage fees or add-ons a privilege—*as long as you say they will be in advance.*

Also know that the nonnegotiable rules you've established will always "trump" gifts and privileges. That you shouldn't take away gifts as punishment does not give your teen permission to violate those rules. Imagine that a midnight curfew on Friday and Saturday is a nonnegotiable rule for your teen, but you gave him a car as a birthday gift. Your teen might try to argue that he can drive around with his friends past midnight because the car was a gift that should not be "taken back." Be prepared for this kind of limit testing when you define gifts, rights, and privileges and have to integrate them with your inviolable rules. In this case the midnight curfew trumps the gift, and your teen needs to get home with the car by midnight or face consequences. To preserve the integrity of the gift, however, you'd be wise to establish consequences other than taking away the car. (By the way, the periodic insurance payments are also privileges to be earned and not entitlements to be expected.) That's what you'll learn to do in this chapter and the next two. But always remember that the bottom line shouldn't budge: If the consequences you set prove ineffective and the only way to prevent your teen from coming home past curfew is to take away the car keys on Friday and Saturday, you should take away the car keys. While the teen may "own" the car, you own and control the insurance on that car and hence the use of it. The loss of the car for one or two weekends will be a sufficient consequence for most teens.

3. *Identify your teen's rights, gifts, and privileges.* You've got the theory under your belt; now you need to figure out which things are which in *your* family. The biggest problem most parents have with grasping the idea of contingencies is that they really don't understand the definition of privileges and really don't get that making desirable things and activities available to their teen is in fact largely in their control. Here's a revealing conversation between the parents of 17-year-old Mark.

> *Mom:* There's nothing Mark will work for; he has it all now and thinks of it as his right. He has a 21-inch flat-screen TV, a Blu-Ray player, and an iPad that connects to our wi-fi in his room. We gave him a smartphone for Christmas. We gave him keys to our cars so he could drive when he needed to and we weren't home. So he drives anywhere he likes, without our permission. His grandparents gave him a PlayStation for Christmas.

> *Dad:* Yeah, he acts like his electronics are his birthright, and he does have a lot of creature comforts. But what does he really have a *right* to, beyond a place to live, food, clothing, school, and medical care?

Mom: Well, nothing, I guess, but try to tell Mark that. Are you ready for World War III?

Dad: We already have World War III. Except he has us on the defensive with no ammunition and no weapons. We'll tell him what we're planning to do together.

Mom: I'd like to take away the car, the wi-fi access, cellphone, and iPad when he comes home past curfew or cuts out the back door of school after first period.

Dad: I'd like that too, but unfortunately we gave him that stuff as gifts and did not attach any strings at the time. So if we start taking them away now, World War III will go nuclear and we won't accomplish anything. They have to go in the gift column.

Mom: That's a really hard pill to swallow. Why shouldn't parents be able take away anything they want anytime they want? Who's in charge anyway?

Dad: I hear you, but we're stuck in a bad situation with a really defiant teen. You know from our past experience that arbitrarily taking away stuff just got Mark so pissed off that he started destroying things around the house— it just didn't pay off for us. The real question is how we can do things differently to spur Mark to clean up his act, as difficult as this may be for us.

Mom: I guess you're right. But we need to be be clear that while these devices were gifts, the monthly data plans are privileges to be earned, as is the periodic insurance premium on the car. We also need to be very careful about future gifts. We did give him a car, but we never promised him gas or insurance money; we gave him the cellphone and wi-fi modem but didn't promise to pay the monthly charges indefinitely. Couldn't we put these in the privileges column?

Dad: Yes, we have to. We don't have much else. He drives 300 miles a week and will have to earn his gas money, cellphone fees, and cable access fees even though he thinks these are his rights.

Mom: Let's make him earn electricity for the TV and DVD player.

Dad: I'd like to do that, but it's not practical to control access to the TV and DVD player when we're not home, and he doesn't care that much about them. Let's let that one go.

Mom: OK, but take clothing. Who ever said that Mark has a right to Marc Jacobs shirts and jeans? What about lattes at Starbucks and eating out with his friends at California Pizza Kitchen three times a week? He gets clothing and food, but these expensive and fancy things are not rights.

Dad: Dining out and special foods go in the privilege column. Basic food at home is his right.

Dad: OK, so let's see . . . Mark's rights are to basic household food, reasonable clothing, a room, school, and medical care. The physical gifts he has now—TV, DVD player, iPad, computer, cable modem, cellphone—we won't take away. But the monthly usage fees and the gas and insurance premiums he uses driving our cars are privileges, along with fancy foods and expensive clothing.

Mom: I agree.

You can see how Mark's parents struggled with the idea of not taking away gifts and defining true rights and privileges, but they were able to develop viable distinctions. Now try the little exercise on page 172 before you get started on creating your own contingency management system: Fill in the columns in the Rights, Gifts, and Privileges form that follows based on how you think your teen would view these things. (Feel free to make copies or to download the form from *www.guilford.com/barkley16-forms* if you need more space or want to use the form again later.)

Rights, Gifts, and Privileges

What are your teen's rights?	What were given as gifts?	What are your teen's privileges (things to be earned)?

From *Your Defiant Teen* (2nd ed.). Copyright 2014 by The Guilford Press.

If you're like most parents, you might end up with a form filled in on the left and middle columns but almost blank on the right. It's very easy to see why your teen may not be willing to work very hard for you. There is probably great confusion between the columns, especially the second and third ones. Your teen has been thinking of things like having the latest electronic equipment and using it monthly with its associated usage fees; being able to make decisions about where she goes, whom she sees, and what she does; using the car; having pocket money; and choosing her own curfew or bedtime as her rights or noncontingent gifts. You've probably already begun to see that certain items your teen controls could and should actually be in your domain. But don't forget about time away from home and other forms of independence from parental supervision. These are never rights or gifts; they're consequences to be earned. Your teen should earn independence by (1) behaving appropriately and (2) demonstrating the ability to handle the newly granted independence responsibly until your teen reaches the age of majority and has the legal right to be autonomous.

Meanwhile, your teen does have certain state-mandated entitlements, but they are limited to things like food, clothing, shelter, protection, health care, education, and general safety. You might also decide that your teen has the right to access to a bike he bought with his own money, for example. By contrast, a privilege is something earned, and by definition that means it's under your control.

Now go back and fill in the columns of the form a second time, using the new form on page 174; but this time do it from your new perspective and what you would like it to look like going forward. Differentiating won't always be straightforward, but you'll get the hang of it—if only by listening to your *own* sense of fairness. You might, for example, decide that you should be able to say when your 13-year-old takes off for a ride on his bike. But what if he bought the bike with his own money? What probably belongs in the rights column is your son's access to the bike; it's his and his alone. What belongs in the privileges column, however, is the freedom to leave home in the first place, by *any* form of transportation.

What did you put under the rights column that you would now move to the privileges column? Maybe you think your daughter has the right to wear whatever she wants of the latest fashions beyond the basics—they are, after all, her clothes. But did you pay for them? Do you do the laundry or pay for the dry cleaning?

Maybe it seems absurd to tell a teen who flips on the TV whenever he wants that he now has to earn that privilege. But it's

Rights, Gifts, and Privileges

What are your teen's rights?	What were given as gifts?	What are your teen's privileges (things to be earned)?

not ridiculous at all if you paid for the TV and also pay the bill for the electricity that keeps it running. Same for the family land line. The cellphone may belong to your daughter in the sense that she has her own phone number and this particular phone unit was given as a gift for her personal use only. But if you pay the monthly bill, you have control over the phone's use each month.

If you start to think of privileges as anything that you are providing beyond the basic rights and therefore have control over, you'll see that a lot more of your teen's life is made up of potential privileges than rights. You'll find it helpful in the beginning to sit down with your teen and share the information in the table with her so that both of you are clear about what's what: rights, gifts, and earnings (privileges).

Setting Up Behavior Contracts and Point Systems

Now you're going to start putting a contingency management system into place. You'll choose one chore or other request where you really want your teen to comply and make a privilege that's pretty important to your teen on a daily basis contingent on his compliance.

There are two options for this step: establishing a point system or creating a behavior contract. You can use whichever system seems most likely to work in your family, but generally we recommend the point system for teens between ages 12 and 14 and behavior contracts for those 14 and up. Both are effective, but the point system may seem childish to older teens because it's more like a game: the teen earns points for meeting certain expectations during the day and then can "cash in" those points for certain privileges. However, if you have a very immature teen older than 14, you can still consider adopting the point system, which we have used for teens as old as 18 years. Because the behavior contract makes a specific privilege contingent on complying with a specific request, it's more straightforward and may speak more effectively to the teen's pride in his growing maturity (kids play games and rack up points; adults make contractual agreements).

1. *Start by compiling a list of the requests or chores you want your teenager to comply with that she often doesn't.* These should be routine requests (things you ask your teenager to do generally every day) that are fairly specific and that must be done right after being asked so that you can respond immediately: start doing your homework, make your bed, put your dishes in the dishwasher after eating breakfast, and so on. They should all be things you want your teen to do. Don't list any behaviors you want your teen *not* to do: Don't swear, don't hit your sister, don't slam the door on your way out. Take those things and instead rephrase them as their positive opposites, the behavior you want the teen to show (speak nicely, solve conflicts with your sibling constructively and without violence, close the door quietly, etc.). Use the form below or create your own. You can copy or download the form from *www.guilford.com/barkley16-forms* if you need more space or want to use it again later. *As always, it's important to start by reinforcing the positive, and you cannot do that if you don't specify what behavior is positive.*

Routine Requests

Just "free associate" and list everything you can think of on the following lines. Some parents find it easiest to compile this list if they mentally run through their day from getting up in the morning to going to bed at night.

_____

_____

_____

_____

_____

_____

_____

_____

_____

_____

Here are some typical requests, running through the day from the time your teen gets up to the time he goes to bed:

Get up. [if you're in the habit of waking your teen rather than having him use an alarm clock]

Take a shower.

Hang your wet towels up when you're finished using them.

Brush your teeth.

Get dressed.

Make your bed.

Come to the kitchen and eat your breakfast.

Make your lunch. [assuming your teen takes lunch to school]

Clean up your breakfast dishes.

Check and make sure you have all your books and homework.

Get in the car so we can get going. [assuming you drive your teen to school]

Call me at work when you get home from school.

Stay home and watch your little sister until I get home.

Make the salad for dinner and have it in the fridge by the time I get home.

Have your gym bag ready with everything you need for soccer practice so it's ready to go when I get home.

Have your math homework done by the time I get home.

Finish your homework before dinner.

Set the table for dinner.

Clear the table and put the dishes in the dishwasher.

Take the garbage out.

Read a story to your brother before he goes to bed.

Study for the history test for half an hour.

Decide what to wear tomorrow and put your clothes on the chair before going to bed.

Put your dirty clothes from the day in the hamper.

Fold your clean laundry and put it in your drawers and closet.

Turn your light out; it's time to go to sleep.

These are pretty basic ideas. Some may be too childish for your son or daughter. Some may be things you don't expect or want your teen to do. Mentally run through your typical day and just list everything you can think of that you might ask your teen to do.

Now go back through the list and delete anything that isn't routine or that you can't respond to immediately. "Rake the leaves," for example, is a one-time chore. You may want it done today, but it's not something you'll be asking your teen to do every day or even every week. "Start your homework right after you get home from school" is something you can't respond to right away if you're at work when your teen gets home.

Is everything you've listed specific enough for your teen to follow? "Clean up after yourself" may be too vague a command after breakfast: Will your teen know that you expect him to put the orange juice back in the refrigerator, put his dishes in the dishwasher, and put the sandwich fixings that he used for his lunch away if you don't say so? If you find any requests on your list that are too vague, see if you can rewrite them to be specific; cut any that you can't make specific enough.

Now rank-order the requests in terms of difficulty, based on how much time and effort each will take and how likely the teen is to comply. Once you've numbered them in this order, rewrite the list in ascending order of difficulty.

2. *Now compile a list of privileges.* Remember the distinctions we made earlier in the chapter between basic rights, previous gifts, and privileges (earnings). What does your teen find highly desirable that she'll want, again mostly on a daily basis? You can start by jotting down general items, like screen time, but ultimately your goal is to write down a specific privilege, such as having 1 hour of screen time (maybe because less time doesn't seem valuable to your teen). Other possibilities may be things you think you "owe" your teenager, like rides to social events or use of a cellphone or even use of the family car if your teen is old enough to drive. If your teen has been taking these things for granted, they may not seem like privileges to you right away, so try to list anything your teen wants or wants *you* to do for *her*.

Don't list anything that your teen doesn't already get on a regular basis. This is not an opportunity to give him a chance to get that new video game or piece of clothing or trip to the huge amusement park. You already know that's not going to motivate him, as it's likely too far in the future for him even to be thinking about right now.

Also don't list anything you can't actually control. Returning to the bike example above, if your teen has bought her own mountain bike with money earned from being a lifeguard, you should not feel like this is a privilege you can control. But if she wants to ride it to the mall (leave your property or street and be independent of you), that aspect of using the bike is under your control and can be used as a privilege.

If you're having difficulty coming up with a list of privileges, consider the "Premark principle," named after the experimental psychologist David Premark: anything that a person does often will serve as an effective reward for anything the person does less often. Observe your teen and see what she does during her free time. If your teen sits in her room staring at the four walls or using social networking for hours but does homework for minutes, the opportunity to sit in her room or use social network devices is likely to serve as a reward for doing homework. If your teen likes to debate for hours but does chores for minutes, the opportunity to debate is likely to serve as an effective reward for doing chores; you simply have to be creative and playful about creating contingencies involving the opportunity to debate as a reward. One teen's reward is another teen's misery, so observe your teen and use your imagination in coming up with privileges. Use the Daily Privileges form on page 180 or create your own. Feel free to copy it or download it from *www.guilford.com/barkley16-forms* if you need more space or want to use the form again later.

Now rank-order the privileges in terms of their value to the teen. Don't think right now about their relative value to you; something your teen finds highly desirable may be very easy for

Daily Privileges

_____

_____

_____

_____

_____

_____

_____

_____

_____

you to dispense and therefore may not seem like a big deal to you, but that's irrelevant—what you should be concerned with is providing an incentive for the teen, not putting some objective price on the privilege. Relist the privileges in descending order of their value to your teen.

Keep both of these lists; you'll be using them for at least the next week, though after a week you might end up amending them.

3. *Introduce the contingency management system to your teen.* "*Why should I do what you want to get something I already have!*" Be prepared to answer that question when you tell your teenager that you're going to set up a system whereby she can earn privileges by complying with your requests. There isn't a defiant teen alive who will respond with "OK" and then immediately get with the program. You may have already addressed it when we recommended that you clarify with your teen what are rights, gifts, and privileges. But here are some other ideas for explaining why you're doing this in a way that may elicit at least tentative cooperation.

For starters, point out, directly and without invective, any evidence you can for the fact that conflict has lessened at home. Tell your teen how much it matters to you that the two of you get along better than you have in the past. But then also say that there are certain chores or other tasks that you need the teen to do and they're still not getting done. Say without emotional pressure that these things may seem minor to the teen but they are important to you—important enough that you're willing to reward your teen for complying. Tell her that you know she needs some incentive to do the things that need to get done every day and you're now willing to provide it. Mention that everyone is more motivated to do things that are hard or that they don't want to do by getting rewards for them.

When your teen says that it's not a reward if it's something she's already got, go back to distinguishing rights from gifts from privileges. Your teen may be right if what you're proposing as a reward is really a basic right or a prior gift. She may not be right if what you are proposing as a reward is some usage fee that you pay for electronics each month, her allowance, time away from home or with friends, or the use of your own property (your cellphone, TV, computer, etc.). Tell her that part of your reason for establishing a point system or behavior contract is to clarify just these kinds of distinctions for both of you and that it's also a way to keep you clear and honest—that you know you've confused your teen by being inconsistent in rewarding her for the good things she's done and that you're trying to change that. Say you hope this system will contribute to stopping all the fights over every little thing and keep things fair around the house. Emphasize the idea that what's fair is for your teen to know that if she does something good, there will be a predictable reward for it. Also let her know that her labor and efforts are valuable and that she deserves to be paid for them just like anyone else. (If she keeps listening to you without a lot of arguing and interrupting, by the way, call into play what you've already learned and issue some praise for hearing you out. Also smile and make it clear that while you're not budging on this, it's intended out of good-will, not as another sneaky way of punishing her.)

In the case of the behavioral contract, tell the teen he will get a specific privilege, chosen by you, for complying with a specific request, also chosen by you. If he doesn't comply, he won't get the privilege.

In the case of the point system, tell the teen that he'll get points for complying with requests and then be able to use those points to buy whatever privileges he wants from the list.

To head off continued resistance, also say that you will give out bonus points or a slightly enhanced privilege if the teen accedes to your request promptly and pleasantly. (You'll need to be judicious here, or these bonus privileges will dilute the force of the consequence altogether and just become another indis-criminate response from you.)

Q. *We followed your instructions to the letter and explained the concept of the behavior contract and told our son in no uncertain terms that this is what we were going to do. He told us that was idiotic and there was no way he was going along with it, and refused to sign the contract we came up with. What do we do now?*

A. Your most potent tool is the consequence. Even if your son doesn't sign the contract, you can enforce it as if he had. If you've chosen correctly, the privilege that you can now withhold is truly in your control, and you can just unplug the TV, disconnect any computer your son has access to, or whatever will amount to with-holding the privilege you've picked. Your son may very well come around once he has spent the week without a privilege he has come to expect. Be patient.

This point in the program can be a real turning point for some teens. It's one thing to smile and issue praise when your teen isn't misbehaving, but it's another to confront him with the loss of something he feels entitled to have. If you do unplug the TV or computer and he just keeps plugging it back in and using it in defiance of the contract, you and your teen are going to need professional help. Don't try to push a confrontation like this, which could end up getting physical. Call a therapist and proceed with this system only with his or her guidance.

Mark's parents encountered a similar response when they introduced behavior contracts to Mark. He cursed them out, refused to talk to them, stormed out of the house, and stayed out all night without permission. They realized that they needed a therapist and called Dr. Sanders, who interviewed them at the first session and Mark at the second session. Dr. Sanders called Mark on his cellphone and personally invited him to come to an individual session to talk about his gripes about his parents—this ploy was used to get Mark to attend a therapy session since he would otherwise refuse to cooperate. Mark met with Dr. Sanders and gave him a long list of gripes about his parents. Dr. Sanders listened empathetically and asked Mark which gripe he wanted to work on first. Mark indicated that he wanted his parents to stop nagging him about homework; he would be more likely to do his homework if his parents did not nag him about it. The therapist said that he would instruct Mark's parents to refrain from nagging Mark about homework for 1 week if Mark would show the therapist the completed homework at the next session. Mark reluctantly agreed. Mark's parents were very reluctant to give up the nagging because they feared Mark would not do any homework; Dr. Sanders pointed out that they had nothing to lose since he wasn't doing any homework now. They agreed. At the next individual session Mark showed the therapist half-completed homework, and the therapist asked permission to share this with Mark's parents. Mark agreed, and his parents were surprised that he had done any homework at all. The agreement was extended for another few weeks.

In this case the therapist served as the intermediary negotiating a contract between the parents and the adolescent, seeing them individually to prevent negative outbursts. Because the therapist was a neutral third party, Mark and his parents were able to compromise, something they couldn't do in a direct confrontation. The real challenge for the therapist is to address the negative parent–teen relationship, which will come later in the therapy. Note that the therapist never used the word *contract* but did actually work out a contract between Mark and his parents.

4. *Set up a point system (especially for teens ages 12–14).* Point systems work best for younger teens and for teens who may be older in years but lack maturity or have personality traits or psychiatric disorders that make it hard for them to stay motivated because they can't concentrate or pay attention or they are impulsive or disorganized. Using points may also work better for a kid who loves thinking in terms of scores or money. A point system is also more flexible and gives kids more choices of which privileges they earn for good behavior, so it may be more suitable for teens whose pride is tied up in being self-determining.

If your teen was defiant as a child or has ADHD, you may already have used a point system. If so, you'll be familiar with the instructions. The only real difference between the system you've used in the past and this one may be the sophistication of the privileges the teen can "buy" with points earned now that the teen is older and may have access to additional privileges as a result.

Working with your request and privilege lists, assign each request points in multiples of 25. We usually award 25 points for every 15 minutes of effort required of the teen. You can also award more points for additional difficulty, with "difficulty" meaning not how difficult you think it should be but how difficult it *is*, depending on your teen's relative abilities and temperament.

Now assign points to the privileges on the same scale (25 points for every 15 minutes of the privilege). But first add some privileges to your list that will be doled out only weekly, not daily.

Make sure your teen can earn all the daily privileges by complying with one-half to two-thirds of the requests (by point value). The other half or third times 5 should equal all the weekly privileges. This means your teen has a chance to earn the weekly privileges by acceding to your daily requests.

Here's a partial example (your lists may be longer):

Requests

Get up on time: 25

Check and make sure you have all your books and homework: 25

Shower and then hang your towels back up when you're finished using them: 25

Brush your teeth: 25

Call me at work when you get home from school: 50 [for a teen who has a lot of trouble remembering to do things on time]

Make the salad for dinner and have it in the fridge by the time I get home: 75

Have your math homework done by the time I get home: 75

Take the garbage out after supper: 25

Study for a test for an hour: 100

Put your dirty clothes from the day in the hamper: 50 [for a teen who is typically sloppy and disorganized]

Turn your light out; it's time to go to sleep: 100 [for a teen who has a lot of trouble unwinding and getting to bed at a reasonable hour]

Total that can be earned: 575 points

Privileges

Using the computer for 15 minutes after school: 25

Using the computer for 30 minutes in the evening: 50

One hour of TV time: 100

Using the wide-screen TV at a time when other family members want to use it for another purpose: 50

Having Mom or Dad iron favorite outfit for school tomorrow: 50

Getting a ride to best friend's house after school: 50

Picking what will be served for dessert after dinner: 25

Getting a ride to the mall (weekly): 100

Choosing a video to rent (weekly): 100

Going out to dinner with the family (weekly): 200

Going to the health club with a friend: 100

Note that this teen could earn all the daily privileges listed here by earning about two-thirds of the points awarded for the requests listed. We encourage you not to get too technical about this, however, especially regarding the weekly privileges. Set a price knowing that your teen is saving about a third of her daily income for these things.

Now set up a journal or an old blank checkbook register to use with the point system, or create your own sheets, one for each day, listing date, item, deposit, withdrawal, and running balance. Every time your teen complies with a request *the first time you ask*, tell her what she's earned, then enter the number of points for that request in the deposits column. Award no points if you have to ask more than once. Also remember to *occasionally* give bonus points for particularly prompt and pleasant compliance, but think of this as being like tipping and give a bonus of no more than 20% of what you would otherwise pay for the job.

Only you are allowed to make entries in the checkbook, though you should allow your teen to look at the book whenever

THINK AHEAD

Are you sure you know which privileges your teen values? When you've been indiscriminate in allowing your teen the use of things you've paid for or otherwise provided for the family, it may be hard to get a handle on what your teen really values since everything seems like a right to him. Before compiling your list of privileges, ask yourself whether your teen would really care if he didn't have it. Maybe you value weekly family dinners in a restaurant because everyone talks more openly when not distracted by the trappings of the home, but does your teen really care if he gets to come along? Worse, would he welcome the chance to be in the house by himself? Give careful thought to what is truly desirable to your teen. If you don't know, put off starting this system and observe your teen closely for a couple of days to get a better idea of what is truly valuable to him.

she wants. In fact, it's a good idea to encourage her to keep checking. If she knows she wants a certain privilege—say, her friends are going to be chatting on the computer tonight but she hasn't earned any points yet—she'll be motivated to start doing what you've asked before the day is up.

If your teen seems inclined to want to spend all his points earned every day, as many are, remind him that there are weekly privileges on the list too and that he won't have any points left for those privileges if he doesn't save some of his points.

Q. *We started the point system with our daughter, and it went fine for a few days, but then she got angry when she had a day when she didn't have enough points to get online with her friends, and refused to cooperate. She started sneaking around and trying to get her privileges without our knowing and stopped obeying any of the requests on the list. We got so discouraged that we just gave up. What should we do now that we know the point system doesn't work for us?*

A. But it *was* working. What your teen is doing is testing your resolve to see it through on a longer-term basis. Talking to her friends online is clearly a powerful reward if she would sneak around to obtain it. You don't really know the point system *can't* keep working for you unless you show some resolve. Understand that it is very normal for teens to periodically test limits you have set, but it's also just as natural for you to show that you mean to enforce the limit or rule you've set. There will be ups and downs. When things don't go in your teen's favor, it's hardly surprising that she'll try to go back to the way things were before, when she got a lot of what she wanted without doing anything to earn it. The most important thing to do in this program is to *follow through*. You have to show your teen you have credibility. If you're not ready to stick with the consequences you established, don't start the system until you think you can do so. If you don't have any idea of how to get to that point, talk to a therapist.

But you might try starting over and explaining very matter-of-factly to your daughter that the way things worked before wasn't working and give examples of how it really wasn't working

WARNING: *Beware of the credit card mentality.* What will you do if your teen hasn't earned enough points for a weekly privilege that she desperately wants now that the moment is upon her? Lauren had made a new group of friends in school, and she was supposed to meet all of them at the mall on Saturday afternoon. She knew she'd lose ground with this clique if she didn't show up and was afraid they'd all take the opportunity of her absence to gossip about her. She was distraught when she tried to explain to her mother that she just had to get a ride to the mall even though she didn't have enough points to get this privilege. Her mother couldn't help feeling deep empathy for her daughter. She knew Lauren didn't make—or keep—friends easily because she was so emotional all the time and she hated the idea of her daughter being lonely. So she caved in and gave Lauren a ride to the mall, calling out to her daughter as she quickly disappeared into the crowd, "You'll have to make up those points next week, you know!"

Do we have to tell you that her daughter didn't bother to respond? And what do you think happened next week, when Lauren's mom realized that if she made her daughter pay back the points she'd used on the ride to the mall, she wouldn't be able to get any of her daily privileges for a couple of days and would be "impossible to live with"? Yes, she "forgave the debt," and the whole system disintegrated. Remember, the goal of this system is to build your child's motivation to behave the way you want her to. If you don't stick to the program, the incentive won't be established.

Never let your teen use points that haven't been earned. No borrowing! Under this kind of circumstance, Lauren's mom could have explained to Lauren how badly she would like her to go to the mall with her new friends but that she had yet to earn enough points. However, if she would do X, Y, or Z in the next 30 minutes, it would get her the needed points and she could go. You can do the same: Use an unanticipated event to create a chore your teen can get done easily before it's time to go out. Just make sure the chore can be done easily in that time frame. There is no reason you can't negotiate contracts on the spot for such unexpected events. Just don't give your teen a privilege for doing nothing because you feel bad for him or her.

for her any more than it was working for you. Say that you're still committed to finding another way, and you're going to try this again, but this time you plan to stick to it. Then do so.

5. *Set up a behavior contract (especially for teens ages 14 and up).* Choose a request of relatively low difficulty from your list and a privilege of moderate value. For the teen whose requests and privileges are listed above for the point system, the request might be hanging his towels back up after taking a shower in the morning, and the privilege might be 15 minutes of computer time when he gets home from school. Tell the teen that he won't get the privilege unless he complies with that request.

Your contract might be a simple statement written up like one of the following:

- *I, Dan Jensen, agree that I will hang my towels up in the bathroom before I leave the bathroom after showering or otherwise using the bathroom every day. If my towels are hung up, I can text for 15 minutes sometime between 3:00 and 5:00 P.M. after school. If my towels aren't hung up, I can't text after school.*
- *I, Amanda Navarro, agree to set the table, clear the table, rinse the dishes, put them in the dishwasher, run the dishwasher, and put away the dry dishes by 8:00 P.M. Mondays, Wednesdays, Fridays, and Sundays. In return, my mother agrees to drive me to a friend's house after school on Tuesdays, Thursdays, and Saturdays at 4 P.M. and take me to the mall every other Sunday at noon.*

Or you can copy the form on page 191 and fill it in with the terms of your agreement. You may want to copy the blank contract or download it from *www.guilford.com/barkley16-forms* so you can use it more than once.

For a week, use just one contract. Don't be tempted to add other contracts just because this one seems to be working. In Step 4 you'll start writing contracts that penalize your teenager for doing something you *don't* want him to do, but not until the

WARNING: *Make sure you truly have control over a privilege you want to use in a contract.* Kevin's parents were sick of hearing his younger sister complain about how he harassed her unmercifully when the two were home alone together after school. So they set up a contract that made Kevin's use of the computer contingent on his being nice to his sister after school.

Kevin's parents not only don't have control over the privilege in this case—they're both at work and can't be there to ensure that Kevin doesn't use the computer if he hasn't been nice to his sister—but they don't have any way of determining whether he has earned the privilege in the first place. The request isn't specific—What does "nice" mean?—and cannot be monitored as no parent is there to observe the brother–sister interactions. No one is on hand to respond immediately to either compliance or noncompliance with the request. Under such circumstances, a babysitter or someone else really needs to be present to supervise the situation and ensure the safety of unruly children or teens. If qualified, the babysitter could be trained to monitor and enforce the contract. This has worked well with au pairs who are hired by a family on an exchange program from Europe to help care for their children for one or more years and who live in the home. In fact, a qualified au pair might be given this book to read.

idea that positive behavior has positive consequences is firmly ingrained. Then, in Step 5, you'll put it all together and write contracts for all the sticky situations from which you want to eliminate defiance. For now, just use one behavior contract and let the connection between behavior and consequence in this single case solidify for your teen.

Q. *We thought the behavior contract was going to work well. Our 15-year-old son has ADHD and has a hard time deferring gratification or thinking about the future consequences of present actions. Tying a behavior and a reward so closely together seemed like the ideal technique for him, but he still kept forgetting to do what we asked. What else can we do?*

A. Forgetting is a big problem for teens with ADHD. To deal with it, we recommend putting some kind of physical cue, sign, card, or other reminder at the point where the work is to be done to help them remember to do it. If your teen already has a

Contract

This contract between _____ (teenager) and
_____ (parents) is hereby entered
into this, the _____ day of _____, _____.

With regard to

_____ ,

_____ , (teenager) agrees to:

_____

_____

_____

_____

In return, _____ (parents) agree to:

_____

_____

_____

If _____ (teenager) does not honor the
agreement, the following consequence is agreed upon by both
parties: _____

_____

_____

All parties have read and discussed this agreement. Any exceptions
must be mutually agreed upon by all parties. If disputes arise,
changes to the contract may be negotiated in the future.

_____   _____
        (teenager)   _____
                                          (parents)

_____   _____
                             (Date)

cellphone, it can be programmed to give audible reminders with a text message. Since teens love cellphones, they may be more likely to use them for reminders. For your son, even though he's 15, the point system might be a better choice than the behavior contract because the checkbook, and frequent reference to it, makes it easier to stay on track. Gina, who also has ADHD, found it really difficult to get her homework done in any kind of timely fashion. Her parents set up a point system that was almost entirely aimed at getting homework done, with points earned for various increments of work done (e.g., five math problems completed) or time spent (e.g., 15 minutes of uninterrupted studying for the daily biology quiz). Gina could earn points for *every* five math problems done, so that she earned 200 points for the first five, another 200 for the next five, and so forth. The list of privileges her parents wrote up was also broken down into small increments: 15 minutes of time on Facebook, 10 minutes texting, and so forth, so that the privileges kept coming at frequent intervals. This helped Gina stay on track.

Q. *We spent a lot of time setting up a point system for our 13-year-old, but it just ended up frustrating everyone because he never seemed to get enough points to get the privileges he wanted, and that only made him accuse us of setting things up to punish him. Where did we go wrong?*

A. There are several possibilities. Maybe you assigned privileges that mean a lot to your son but put a price tag of too many points on them for him to earn, and that *would* seem like a stacked deck. Or you gave the requests too few points to reasonably add up to that privilege. In other words, check the math here for fairness. Other possibilities are that you didn't include enough low-cost privileges that your son really wants. If you've included a number of items that he just doesn't care about, he's not going to be motivated to work to earn points for them.

If, after a week, you don't think the point system (or behavior contract, for that matter) is working as intended, review your lists of requests and privileges, adding or subtracting from either list as seems appropriate and changing point values or totals too if that seems like a good idea. Don't succumb to the temptation to make it too easy, though. Just be aware that sometimes getting the right balance of weighted requests and privileges is a matter of a trial and error. In that case, do take a second week at this step before moving on.

Stay with It and Stay Realistic

Behavior contracts and point systems are powerful tools, but only if you stick with them. As we said earlier, if you're not ready to hold your ground and withhold privileges for noncompliance with the designated request(s), you won't get anywhere. And this is an important building block. You must be able to reward positive behavior with positive consequences like privileges before you can start getting your teen to stop doing what you want to discourage and before you can apply this strategy to the really problematic bones of contention between you and your teen. So be patient, stick with the program, and don't expect too much change from your teen right away. Again, remember that the main goal here is to change your parenting style. If you get any behavior change from your teen, that's a bonus for the week, but it may not happen till much later.

11

Step 4.
Making the Punishment
Really Fit the Crime

Positives first. We really can't say it too often. At the beginning of Step 3, you may have wondered how behavior contracts or point systems could possibly succeed. After all, you had taken away your son's iPod or your daughter's cellphone before, and the defiance continued anyway.

You now know that this may have been a result of inconsistency or some other lack of follow-through or sense of proportion. But it's also because there's a subtle yet powerful difference between threatening to penalize or punish a teen for *non*compliance and promising to reward the teen for compliance. Relying heavily on punishment and other negatives only encourages teens to try to coerce you into doing what *they* want. You've certainly seen this principle in action.

Your teenager already knows that negative behavior has negative consequences; what he's forgotten is that there is an opposite alternative: that positive behavior leads to positive consequences—*every time.* So in Step 3 your goal was to remind him that positive behavior begets a positive response from you in the form of the privileges that have meaning for your teen.

How has that been going? If the behavior your contract required of your teen was relatively easy to perform, and the reward the teen got for it was meaningful to her, she might have already started to comply. Or she might not have. Consider why not:

- Many teens try to hold out and feign indifference to doing without the privilege at first. Contingency management plans represent a loss of their control over what they do and don't do, and they don't want to lose that. Who can blame them? So they will often fight the entire system at first. Hang in there.

- If your teen hasn't started to comply after a couple of weeks, it's possible that you gave the privilege promised in the contract more weight than your teen does. In fact, whether it's providing an incentive or not, you should periodically rotate new privileges into the point system to make sure your teen doesn't get bored with the program.

- Maybe you gave too few points for a task that seems like a no-brainer to you but that your daughter actually finds much more onerous. Try adjusting the contract or point system.

- Or the behavior you targeted was too difficult. Try refocusing on an easier behavior for which you might develop another contract and try it for 2 weeks.

- Finally, if your contract or point system doesn't seem to be having any effect at all, consider consulting a therapist, especially if your teen has completely ignored the contract over the last 2 weeks. Deciding to impose a penalty for failure to comply with the request, as you're going to do during this step, when you haven't yet laid the groundwork of seeing your teen at least start to earn a privilege through positive behavior is fraught with risk.

The Importance of Sticking to the Agreement

Kevin's parents had always taken a certain amount of pride in the way their 15-year-old could verbally back almost anyone into a corner with his incisive and impassioned arguments. Now they felt hypocritical telling Kevin there would be no discussion about the terms of the contract they wanted him to sign. If he e-mailed his mother the daily journal entry that was his English homework before she left the office every day, he could use his skateboard after school the next day. Kevin's parents had found it impossible not to laugh a little when he had lambasted the assignment as "stupid" and for the "artsy people in the class who think they're writers," but now he was getting a D in English due to his failure to turn in these assignments. Kevin pulled out all the stops in arguing against the injustice of the contract, his voice getting louder and more and more scornful as he heard and then watched self-doubt creep into his parents' voices and facial expressions. Before they knew what was happening, they were looking at each other sheepishly, saying, "Well, maybe we were a little harsh. I mean, sometimes he really needs the skateboard to unwind before he can concentrate on his homework anyway. . . ." Kevin's parents rewrote the contract, substituting an hour of TV time for the skateboard use. The problem here was that Kevin didn't really care about TV, and so he started finding ways around sending his mother his journal entries after school: he'd claim the Internet was down and he couldn't send any e-mails, or he had a stomachache and took a nap before starting his homework, or he'd just snap and shout "So I haven't done the stupid journal writing yet—so what? Go ahead and punish me!"

You should *not* revise the terms of the contract before you've even instituted it and demonstrated to your teen that you intend to enforce it. When your teenager tries to coerce you out of continuing with the program, by arguing, getting belligerent, or refusing to obey the rules of the contract, *you have to stand your ground*. Giving in will only reinforce this coercion. You'll not only stall in eliminating defiance but probably end up undoing all the good changes you've made in the first steps of the program as you get sucked into the coercive behavior patterns that brought you to this book in the first place.

You very well may be already seeing some positive changes in your teen as a result of Step 3. If so, we offer you our congratulations on a job well done. *Don't let down your guard.* Make a particularly firm resolution to keep it up as you launch into

WARNING: *At no time should you engage in any form of physical confrontation with your teen.* Defiant teens who have felt largely in control of their own lives—and of their parents—may see behavior contracts as a serious threat to their autonomy and may do almost anything to fight them. Seventeen-year-old Mark has been in charge for so long that he burst into derisive laughter when his parents announced that he could go out with his friends in the evening only if he came directly home from school and then asked his mother what chores needed to be done. When he realized that his parents were serious, he swore at them and declared that there was no way he was going along with that—and they couldn't stop him if he decided to go out. Mark's father, Doug, saw red—and felt like he was right back in the middle of every frustrating battle he'd had with his son in the past—and yelled back that Mark damn well was going to go along with this contract, and his father certainly could—and would—make him do so. In the span of a few seconds, Mark and his father were facing off against each other like a couple of snorting bulls and Mark's fist was raised behind his head as if he was ready to strike.

Sandy, Mark's mother, also felt like she'd been here before. "Doug!" she called out. "Let's take a break for a minute." Drawing her husband into the family room, she wisely interrupted what could have turned into a father–son fistfight. After taking a few deep breaths, Doug and Sandy realized how quickly the small gains they had made with their volatile son could disintegrate and old patterns of interaction take hold. Sandy called the family's therapist, who helped them recognize the limits of their personal control over their son. The therapist also advised them to start discussing how they could protect everyone's safety. What could they do to keep an encounter like this one from escalating into a physical confrontation? Sandy and Doug needed to come to an agreement on what point at which they would seek outside help from the police, juvenile court, or state department of social services. They decided that physical violence, destruction of property, and running away would necessitate calls to the police for assistance.

Meanwhile, they agreed that anytime they felt like they needed to take a time-out from an encounter with Mark to avoid dangerous escalation, they would put in a call to the therapist for a debriefing.

Step 4. Dropping your businesslike attitude and getting overly emotional, relaxing your commitment to enforcing the contract, or awarding your teenager too many bonus points can all thwart your efforts to keep a taut, short string between positive behavior and positive consequences in your teenager's mind and will make it really difficult to add penalties without falling back into old counterproductive ways of interacting with your teen.

GOALS FOR STEP 4

- Add fines or penalties for noncompliance and unacceptable social conduct.
- Learn effective use of grounding.

Even if your teen has started to comply and is earning the privileges connected with that behavior, this approach isn't going to reverse all the defiant behavior you want to eliminate.

WARNING: *Beware of emotional blackmail.* In the last chapter we talked about how to avoid being deterred from imposing penalties by the fear of harming your teenager's self-esteem. Even if you were able to gird yourself on that score, you might be tempted to cave in when hit with "I hate you," "You're ruining my life," "No one else's parents are as mean as you are," or even "I'm going to report you." And hit you will be—maybe with both barrels—if your teenager senses that you're vulnerable to emotional blackmail. Depending on how much confidence you've developed so far in this program and the dynamics between you and your teen (have you been prone to give him what he wants in the past because you're afraid of losing his love?), you may need a therapist's support to remain firm and consistent in the face of emotional blackmail.

But one thing you can try when your teen says she hates you for what you're doing to her is to act like you're in the United Nations General Assembly with translator headphones on, and you have to run your teen's words through that translator if you already know that the consequences you're imposing are fair and just (see the litmus test on page 208). Then you can respond with your "translation" in your best businesslike tone of voice: "I know you don't like what we're doing, but it is what we're going to do."

Undoubtedly there are things your teen does that you *don't* want her to do. Your teen will occasionally violate your nonnegotiable rules. And there will also be requests that you want obeyed that may be hard to motivate your teen to obey without connecting them with a reward for obedience *and* a penalty for disobedience beyond withholding the reward. As you'll see, the former lends itself more to behavior contracts in many cases, while the latter may be easier to implement using a point system.

Either way, the most important guideline to follow in adding penalties to rewards over the next 2 weeks is that *the penalty must fit the crime*:

- Use removal of privileges or points for noncompliance with day-to-day requests to complete chores or for nonsevere violations of household rules.
- Use work chores (assigned work around the house) for mild to moderate violations of rules, which we've found particularly effective for the youngest teens, ages 11–13.
- Use grounding for more serious problems, including violations of nonnegotiable rules. Keep in mind, however, that grounding is unlikely to work with kids of 16 and older who have a driver's license and car and can just leave or even for kids who own their own smartphone, iPod, or laptop that you can't block them from using because they're not in your control. (In these cases, stick to penalties.)

Logically, it may seem as if you should be able to teach your teenager to behave well with positive reinforcers alone. And that may be mostly true for some teens, especially those who've been denied positive feedback for positive behavior for a long time. Depressed parents, for example, may be somewhat withdrawn and may just not have the energy and focus to positively reinforce their kids' positive behavior. These kids may be acting out just because they're dying for some sign of their parents' approval. Or you may have a very sensitive teen who simply needs more of this kind of reinforcement than most. What did you learn about your teen and yourself in Part I of this book? One sign that you might not need a lot more than positive contingencies to reverse much of your teen's defiance would be that your teen's positive response to the praise and attention you started to offer in Steps 1 and 2 exceeded your expectations.

But even in these cases, you should learn how to use penalties wisely and judiciously. Use of penalties is planning ahead rather than being reactive, a major principle underlying this program. If you're prepared to impose very specific and consistent penalties for predictable infractions—"predictable" in the sense that you've gotten very explicit about your household rules, so you know what a violation comprises—you'll probably find yourself relieved and relaxed in a way you never anticipated. Namely, you won't have to yell so often. You can just impose the penalty that your teen knew was a consequence of that behavior.

So even if you don't think you need it, learn to use penalties in this step. You don't know when you might need them. Without them all you have at your disposal is the yelling or physical punishment you tried without success in the past. The techniques you're learning in this program are meant to substitute for those more primitive, less productive measures. *There is no place in this program for yelling or physical punishment.*

Adding Penalties to Rewards

1. *Identify something you* don't *want your teen to do and connect it with a specific penalty.* **If you and your teen used a behavior contract in Step 3**, attach a meaningful privilege to the "do not" behavior that you can and are willing to withhold if the need arises. For example:

> *I, Antonia Salazar, agree that I will not swear at my parents. I understand that if I do, I will not get a ride to school in the morning and will have to take the bus.*

Due to the nature of the behavior contract, you've essentially already been withholding the privilege tied to a task if your teen hasn't complied. If your first Step 3 contract stipulated that your son would get ice cream after dinner when he set the dinner table when asked, your first Step 4 contract shouldn't say that if he doesn't set the table, he doesn't get ice cream. That was already a natural consequence of violating the contract. If you're using behavior contracts instead of point systems, choose an undesirable behavior (like swearing) that you want to see eliminated from your teen's daily repertoire.

As with the contract that you wrote in Step 3, review this new contract with your teen to make sure she understands it. Then have everyone initial it. Also as in Step 3, even if your teen refuses to sign the contract, you can conduct yourself as if she had, enforcing it without her sanction.

If you and your teen set up a point system in Step 3, add penalties for failure to complete a task on the list. So far your teen has merely not earned points if the task wasn't completed. Now she not only won't earn those points but will lose additional points.

Tell your teen that from now on failure to do a chore on the list will lead to an immediate fine/deduction of points. The fine is the amount you would have entered as a deposit to the

THINK AHEAD

Make sure you explain penalties to your teen in a way that leaves no room for misinterpreting this move as a return of the old regime. Explain in a businesslike, matter-of-fact way that there's still room for improvement in your teen's behavior. Give specific examples of how your teen did not obey the contract or earn the points at every single opportunity (this will undoubtedly be the case for most families), but again, report this dispassionately, making it clear that you're on your teen's side and trying to help her learn to behave up to her potential. Positive rewards are intended always to be the primary incentive. Convey in no uncertain terms that penalties are not a punishment intended to force the teen to comply but are intended to remind the teen to comply better.

teen's checking account if she had done the job. Gina's mom has been giving her 100 points for half an hour of studying for a test. When she didn't study, she didn't get those points. If she studied for 15 minutes, her mother gave her 50 points. But now Gina not only doesn't gain 100 points when she doesn't study but loses 100 points.

By the way, you may notice that these totals are higher than the ones we showed in the sample list in Chapter 10. Even though we often award 25 points for every 15 minutes of effort that a task takes, we advised a different system for Gina, who finds sticking to studying really hard since she has ADHD. Her mother thought she needed extra incentive. We also usually assign a "price" of 25 points for every 15 minutes of privilege (such as TV time) so that the reward seems to fit the behavior that earned it—15 minutes of effort is rewarded by 15 minutes of fun. Gina's mother decided to keep the price for 15 minutes of privilege at 25 points to underscore the desirability of Gina's doing her studying.

Also create fines for violation of two of your household rules, as with behavior contracts. What would you like your teen to stop doing? Whining? Arguing? Swearing? Taking things without permission? Teasing a sibling? Interrupting? Eating between meals? Lying? Look back at the list of household rules you compiled in Chapter 3 (and may have since revised) and create a fine for some form of violation of two of them. Be sure to assign smaller fines for less severe misbehavior.

When incentives have been tried and have not been sufficient to eliminate a negative behavior, a penalty should be added to the contract to strengthen it. Twelve-year-old Billy, for example, used curse words around the house eight to 10 times a day in conversation with his parents. First his parents established a positive incentive system for using appropriate language. They divided the day into three periods: (1) morning, from awakening until leaving for school; (2) afternoon, from returning from school until dinner; and (3) evening, after dinner to bedtime. Billy earned $.50 for each interval during which he used appropriate language, with his parents paying up each evening at

THINK AHEAD

Expect the institution of penalties to have negative repercussions and plan to offset them with extra positives. Let's face it, most teens are going to view penalties as a negative no matter how strongly you define them as reminders to comply rather than punishments. Expect your teen to balk or to act angry or hurt, and resolve to do what you can to keep the negative repercussions from overshadowing the positive work you've done so far by going out of your way to catch your teen being good and reward him or her with praise, bonus points, or spontaneous small rewards. This is yet another way to keep the positive in the forefront of your interactions.

Remember that your primary goal is to change your act, not to get your teenager "in line." When you remember that you're creating contingency management systems largely to rewrite your own script, creating clarity, honesty, and accountability, you'll be less likely to descend into guilt over whether imposing penalties is likely to harm your teen's self-esteem. When you worry about whether you're being unfair to your teen, take a look at this diagram:

The emphasis in this program is on warm (positive, loving) and firm (specific, immediate, consistent behavior). When you're afraid of using penalties for fear of being cold, you end up being soft, which allows coercive behavior to develop further in your teen.

bedtime. Over the first 3 weeks of this system, Billy's cursing dropped from eight to 10 times a day to two or three times a day; however, his parents wanted Billy to curse even less. They added a $0.25 fine for each episode of cursing. Billy did not curse at all for 1 week, and over the next month he cursed about one or two times a week. His parents did not expect perfection and considered this a reasonably positive outcome. They kept the incentive and fine system in effect indefinitely. The addition of a penalty to an effective positive incentive system often is just what you'll need to further reduce a negative behavior.

Q. *We wrote a behavior contract that made our son's use of Facebook contingent on his no longer slamming doors, which drives us both crazy. Things were going along pretty well last week, but when we introduced this contract Seth threw a tantrum like we haven't seen since he was a little kid. We were totally caught off guard and just backed off. What happened here?*

A. The penalties are supposed to be *mildly* aversive to remind the teen that compliance is more reinforcing than noncompliance. This means not only that no penalty imposed this week should be particularly onerous but also that each penalty must be proportionate to the crime. Slamming the doors may drive you and your spouse crazy; some people have a low tolerance for noise. But even if your 13-year-old son knows that being quiet underlies a lot of the household rules, boys at this age aren't particularly self-aware, and your son may not be deliberately breaking the rules but simply being somewhat unconscious of his own physical movements. What's his personality like? Also remember that boys at this age are going through lots of developmental changes, some of which aren't particularly comfortable for them. Do your overall observations tell you this is throwing your son off-kilter?

Even if these factors aren't coming into play with Seth, do you know how valuable Facebook is to him? Maybe being on Facebook is an important social medium for your son, as it is for many kids at this age, when relationships with their peers, maybe especially those of the opposite sex, become important and yet their conversational acumen in person has a long way to go. And what are your rules for socializing on school days? If you feel Seth is too young to go over to a friend's house after dinner, yet many of his friends get together then, he may feel that Facebook is the only way he isn't "totally out of it" and can stay in touch with peers. In other words, the penalty might not fit the crime in this case. Only you can decide how important no door slamming is to you, but make sure you know how important the privilege you're willing to withhold is to your son.

Seth's tantrum throwing may, in and of itself, be unacceptable behavior to you. But to figure out whether his reaction is really a huge overreaction, compare the penalty-and-crime ratio in this contract with the task-and-reward ratio in the contract(s) you worked with during Step 3. If this one seems out of proportion in comparison to the earlier contract, Seth may feel like there's a bit of bait-and-switch going on and that fairness has no place in your dealings with each other.

2. *Consider designating the first week of this step for defining the behavior you want your teen to abstain from before you start imposing the penalty.* Lauren and her mother, Jan, were constantly embroiled in battles over Lauren's "smart mouth." Jan wanted desperately to get her daughter to speak respectfully to her and was all set to write up a contract that imposed a penalty for "talking back." But the pair had so many arguments about what the term meant, with Lauren accusing her mother of laughing at her daughter's comebacks sometimes and grounding her at other times, that Jan realized she had to make sure Lauren knew exactly what she was going to be penalized for before the contract was put into effect. So they added a 1-week training period to the beginning of this step. Jan spent this week pointing out (labeling) the behavior whenever she observed it and warning Lauren that when the week was over the behavior would be fined. "That's what I mean by talking back," she would say. "Starting next Monday you will lose 100 points if you talk back." You can take the same tack if you want to write a contract for a behavior whose definition has caused battles on its own.

3. *Resolve never to fine your teen more than twice in any interaction.* One of the biggest pitfalls for parents starting to reintroduce penalties is what we call the "punishment spiral," in which a fine elicits a negative response or coercion and then the parent fines that response, escalating the negative behavior, then the fines, and so forth ad infinitum. To avoid the punishment spiral, adopt the rule of fining no more than twice. After that, redirect your teen so he'll cool off away from the situation: "Go to your room," "Sit at the dining room table until you can calm down," and the like. If the teen won't remove himself, *you do it: remove yourself to terminate the interaction.*

4. *Use time-outs to defuse conflicts in danger of escalating.* For an emotionally volatile, "temperamental" teen, taking a time-out can be an important anger management strategy. By "time-out" we don't mean the punishment version of time-out used with younger kids, where you withhold reinforcement by having the child sit in a corner or some other isolated spot. Here "time-out" means telling your teen to leave the room or sit down and be quiet until he cools down. If the teen is highly volatile, you can always tell him that if he does not remove himself until he calms down, he'll face a penalty or grounding.

5. *Use work detail or work chores as a penalty for younger teens.* If your teen is 11–13 and moderately oppositional, assigning the teen work like dusting, vacuuming, cleaning the toilets, mopping, laundry, and so on can be an effective penalty. Work chores make sense to teens as natural punishments for failure to carry out their regular chores and responsibilities around the house—but will work only if the teen is in fact likely to accept the punishment. If you try this form of penalty and your teen balks, go back to other penalties. Older, severely oppositional teens can successfully thwart parents from carrying out work details, creating a secondary power struggle over compliance with the punishment, and the same may be true for some younger teens. You definitely do not want to set yourself up for more battles than you already have.

Pick a chore that is unpleasant but can be accomplished in a relatively short period of time—5–15 minutes is quite sufficient. Explain in advance the negative behavior that will result in having to do the work chore. Be brief, clear, and businesslike in your explanation. For example, "If you fail to take out the garbage by 7:00 P.M. Tuesdays, you will have to clean the toilet in the upstairs bathroom Tuesday night." "If you fail to make your bed before you go to school, you'll have to fold the laundry when you come home from school." Assign only those work chores that you can be around to supervise. Don't hover over your adolescent while she's completing the chore, but do check up to make sure it's done properly. If your teen fails to comply with the work chore, impose a fine or penalty as a backup punishment; don't add more work chores since this is unlikely to be effective.

Q. *My daughter has developed a bad habit of lying to get what she wants or to evade the consequences of her behavior. But sometimes she makes me feel so guilty about not trusting her, insisting that she is telling the truth, so I give in, feeling I should treat her like she's innocent until proven guilty. So if lying is the behavior I want to eliminate, how do I do it?*

A. Lots of parents have brought up this problem. They want to establish fines for lying but say it's unfair because they can't be really sure of what happened. Here's a case where it's important to be an *authoritative* parent. You're in charge. Believe it or not, you can be both judge and jury. You can and should weigh the evidence to the best of your ability as a mature adult and then pass judgment. It's better to make it clear that lying won't be tolerated and risk a mistake than to allow your teen to lie without consequences. You know your teen and are probably right when you suspect she's lying; if it turns out you were wrong, you can always apologize. If it turns out you're wrong frequently, then you know to trust your teen more than you have been doing. But be sure to tell your teen that it's her job to remain above suspicion. The onus is on her not to give you any cause to suspect she's lying. You should feel comfortable under the preceding conditions fining your daughter for creating the suspicion of a lie, for which no

The contract is probably fair and just if . . .

- The time your teen has to spend complying with a request is roughly equal to the time period for the privilege granted or penalty imposed (e.g., do a half-hour job, get half hour of screen time).
- The rule at issue is a true nonnegotiable. (You never consider swearing in the house acceptable, and the rule applies to all family members.)
- The task, the privilege, and the penalty would all get around the same number if you rated them from 1 to 10 in importance.
- Your teen is capable of fulfilling the task or obeying the rule. (Expecting a teen to do a "spring cleaning" of his room in one afternoon after school is unrealistic, even if a fond dream.)
- It gives her plenty of chances to be good. (You don't let your teen mouth off to you for an hour and then suddenly ground her; you remind her that there is a penalty for talking back in this way, and she has now incurred it, and that if she continues to violate the contract a certain number of times or after a certain amount of time, the penalty will increase to grounding.)

real evidence is needed. A key idea here is to act on the suspicion of a lie and not just wait for a lie to be proven beyond all doubt. If you wait for the latter, you'll be waiting a long time and throughout many lies without giving consequences for lying.

Understanding the Function of Grounding

Grounding is like a time-out for younger kids; it means time without reinforcement, during which you withhold all forms of positive activity as punishment for behavior more severe than that for which you usually impose penalties like fines. Grounding denies your teen not only privileges that he values like social media sites and his smartphone, but also the reinforcement of his friends as well as you.

A couple of caveats about this part of Step 4:

Grounding generally is effective only for younger teens. If your teen can drive and has access to a car, it may be difficult to prevent him from just leaving the house, meaning grounding is a penalty you can't practically impose. And as with removal of privileges, if your teen has bought his own iPod or pays for his own cellphone or the like, you may not be able to cut him off from using it while grounded, in which case this penalty won't have much force and you may have to stick to the other types of fines. But also, by the age of 17 or 18, many teens are developmentally too mature to respond constructively to this strategy. The physical size and cognitive independence of older teens make it easy for them to resist parental efforts to limit their activities. For these teens you'll instead want to establish a hierarchy of penalties so that you have appropriate penalties—ones you can realistically impose because you control them—to use should severe misbehavior crop up.

During this step, avoid actually grounding your teen. Remember, the goal is for you to relearn to use penalties effectively, and that means to make them mildly aversive. Trying grounding when you haven't had enough practice in more garden-variety penalties may catapult you right back into the negative, punishment-oriented reactions to your teen that contributed to defiance in the first place.

1. *During these 2 weeks, instead, observe your teen's misbehavior and try to get a handle on what you consider the most severe rule violations and other defiant behaviors.* We'll give you opportunities to decide to try grounding in Step 5. Also reflect on how you used grounding in the past and where it failed because you didn't follow these guidelines:

• *Grounding means having no access to anything you define as a privilege.* Many parents make the mistake of limiting grounding to "house arrest," but while confined to the house the teen is allowed to watch TV, use her smartphone and laptop, listen to music, and so forth. Sure, she's denied the physical company of friends, but there are so many other diversions that can ease the pain, and these days teens can text, talk on Facebook, and find other ways to stay in touch with friends when confined to their homes.

• *You have to be on hand to supervise and enforce the terms of the grounding.* Your authority will be undermined significantly if you ground your teen and then leave the premises—leaving the teen to her own devices, which will probably mean violating all the restrictions you've imposed.

• *Grounding should never last more than 2 days.* This may be the biggest mistake most parents make. How often have you said impulsively "You're grounded for a week!" (or a month or even longer)? Grounding can be as short as a couple of hours but should never be longer than 2 days, such as a weekend, for these reasons:

—There's bound to be some important event scheduled for your teen during a period of 7 days, and once you remember one, you're likely to let your teen off, which undermines your authority and robs this penalty of its teeth.

—Especially if your teen has ADHD or other problems with attention, after a couple of days he's likely to forget what he did to earn this penalty to begin with. All he'll get out of the grounding in that case is a lot of built-up resentment for you; the penalty won't provide motivation for avoiding the misbehavior in the future. Moreover, the length of the penalty itself after a few days can become yet another issue of contention between you and just one more reason to fight.

• *The teen must be made aware of what will be cause for grounding.* As with the other penalties, you need to tell the teen exactly what behavior will lead to grounding. If you're using grounding as a last resort when other penalties don't work, tell your teen that he'll be warned that he is about to be grounded (e.g., if the teen is throwing a tantrum, you could start by removing a privilege, then give one warning, then follow up with grounding if the tantrum continues).

• *Consider including some kind of work for your teen to do while grounded.* See the earlier discussion of work chores. This is up to you, but there's no reason you can't take advantage of your teen's "free time" while grounded to get her to do something constructive (without pay, of course). If you're going to do this, be sure the teen knows this is part of the deal ahead of time.

• *When the grounding is over, you can matter-of-factly remind your teen of what got him grounded, but don't harp on the incident.* Go about your business as you would ordinarily and show your teen that once he's paid for his crime, his "debt to society" is paid and you won't drag out the punishment by castigating him for the infraction over and over.

As with the other penalties, limiting grounding in these ways may be a relief. Instead of losing your temper and grounding your teen "for life," you can make grounding a sharply defined consequence that's to the point and doesn't leave you floundering for ways to get out of enforcing an impulsive and impractical sentence.

12

Step 5.
Tackling Additional Issues
with Rewards and Penalties

At this point in the program you've put a solid month into learning contingency management. You started by showing your teen that good behavior is rewarded. You then showed your teenager that "crime does not pay," but that the "payment" for violating nonnegotiable rules and defying your authority will now be fair, just, and proportionate to the "crime."

Dabbling may have left you champing at the bit to apply rewards and punishments to every bone of contention you have with your teenager, but we hope you've resisted any temptation to jump ahead. Awarding or withdrawing points or privileges for several issues before the concept has had a chance to sink in can send you right back where you started with your teen. The same way you need practice on the "bunny hill" before you can negotiate moguls with confidence when learning to ski, you need time to build confidence in your ability to manage your teen's behavior. Trying to control too much too soon will leave cracks in your confidence that invite inconsistency and wavering resolve to slip through. Overwhelming your teen with a barrage of behavior contracts all at once, or making daily life one long session of scorekeeping, will quickly cost you all the emotional capital you've built with your teen and make your efforts going forward even more difficult to sustain.

It's enough for the first few weeks to get used to the idea that you have the right to make a privilege like smartphone use contingent on your teen's making her bed in the morning. It may not sound like an ambitious goal, but even if your teen actually started making her bed pretty regularly as a result, you all need to make contingency management a comfortable habit before extending it to other chores and issues. Establishing this solid foundation is so important, in fact, that ensuring its integrity is the first goal of Step 5.

GOALS FOR STEP 5

- Resolve any problems you've had so far with contingency management.
- Start using contingency management systems for all behavior problems, especially those of greatest concern.

Resolving Any Problems You've Had with Contingency Management

Take a close look at how things went over the last month to see where you might be able to resolve any glitches that came up so they don't affect your success at this step.

1. *Learn to recognize and head off lapses in consistency.* Kathy and Jay set up a simple behavior contract requiring 14-year-old Andrew to set the table for dinner to earn a ride to and from the mall on Saturday. Andrew scored a perfect 100 for the whole week, so his mother drove him to the mall that Saturday. Andrew continued to do well the second week and was driven to the mall by his father. For the third week, his parents figured they had done their job and no longer had to reward their son for doing this chore. So, on Friday night, they informed Andrew that they were both busy and unavailable to drive him to the mall Saturday, and now that he had acquired the habit of setting the table, rewards were no longer necessary. Andrew had arranged to meet a girl he really liked at the mall and was very angry at his parents, accusing them of "cheating on the contract." He walked 3 miles to the mall in the rain. The next week, he refused to set the table. They were dumbfounded at their son's "overreaction" and the return of his defiance.

Kathy and Jay made a few mistakes here. Their first was assuming that a few weeks of reinforcement of Andrew's positive attitude were enough to make table setting a permanent behavior. Jay assumed that by this point his son had "gotten the idea" that it was his job to set the table and that he shouldn't need to be rewarded "forever" for doing "his part around the house." So he didn't think he owed his son a ride anymore just because Andrew had set the table every night that week. But parents who've been battling defiance almost certainly need to keep at it a lot longer if they want to see positive behavior last after removing the contingency. So long as the job is required of the teen and the family's life circumstances remain the same, the contract should stay in force. After all, would we keep working at our jobs if our paycheck were stopped after several weeks because we had learned how to do the job and no longer needed a paycheck as reinforcement?

Sometimes natural transitions such as a teen going away to college or a reallocation of household responsibilities will result in the cessation of behavioral contracts. Other times, as teens mature, they tell their parents that they no longer need a reward to accomplish a task. Many families convert formal contracts into informal understandings with praise or intermittent reinforcement instead of continuous reinforcement after each time the chore has been completed. In a minority of cases, when none of these events occur, parents need to continue certain contracts until the teen reaches adulthood.

Kathy and Jay should have kept this contract going, but it would have been a lot easier to do that if they had not made mistake number two: choosing a privilege they couldn't manage to deliver without fail. Jay was usually available to drive his son to the mall on Saturday, but not always, and he didn't always know too far ahead of time when something would interfere. Kathy had a part-time weekend job that kept her from being available to drive her son to the mall on about half of the Saturdays. So there were weekends when Kathy and Jay couldn't fulfill their part of the bargain when their son had already performed his part. Unless they had an alternate driver waiting in the wings, they shouldn't have chosen this privilege for the contract. Of course, we parents are only human and can't be expected to anticipate every possible twist and turn in life. This is where reviewing and revising contracts comes in—which we'll introduce later in this chapter. But this poor choice of a privilege might also have been avoided through problem solving, a time-honored process that you'll learn to do, *with* your teen, in Step 7.

Then there's mistake number three: not keeping the teen informed. Kathy and Jay should have told Andrew that the contract was no longer in force before he set the table for an entire week. The fact that they didn't is why their son called his father a cheat. Even if Jay didn't find out that he wouldn't be able to drive Andrew to the mall until it was too late for Andrew to choose whether to set the table, he could have averted a lot of damage by acknowledging that he was unable to fulfill his part of the bargain at the last minute and offering to compensate his son in some other way—or at least offering a sincere apology. But in the back of his mind, Jay knew that he'd blown it and his confidence in his own authority was shaken. He became defensively authoritarian instead of authoritative, convincing himself that he didn't need to "explain himself" to a "kid." Some parents let regaining a modicum of control over their defiant teen go to their head and believe they can just revert to the parent–little kid balance of power they used to find so comfortable. It rarely works.

2. *Make sure you can keep up a united front if your teen has another parent.* This can be even trickier, especially if the teen's other parent is an ex-spouse and there is animosity between you (see Chapter 5). Let's say Kathy and Jay had the same contract with Andrew, but it was understood that sometimes Jay would do the driving and other times Kathy would, depending on who was free. Several times during the last month Kathy had felt sorry for Andrew, who hadn't set the table because he was texting to arrange meeting up with the girl he was interested in, who apparently was "toying with her son's affections" (Kathy's words); she didn't want him to lose out on meeting this girl, so she drove him to the mall even though he had skipped 2 days of setting the table. Until the parents sat down and retraced everyone's actions to figure out why their son's table setting was still so spotty, they didn't realize that Andrew had gotten "free rides" to the mall because his mother did not want his social life to suffer. When Kathy and Jay made their own pact to hold the line on granting this privilege, Andrew began to set the table pretty consistently. The first time he did it with a smile instead of a grunt, his parents rented the latest sci-fi movie for him.

If you and your child's other parent (or another adult who is sharing the parenting responsibilities with you if there is one) are having a hard time staying on the same page with your contingency management plans, review where the problem lies:

• *Do your work schedules make it hard for both of you to enforce the contract equally?* Sam leaves for work at 5:00 A.M. and gets home at 4:00 P.M. His wife, Bonnie, works the 3:00-to-11:00 P.M. shift at the local hospital. Sam is the "enforcer" for the homework contract the family signed. Bonnie wakes up for just long enough to kiss high school freshman, Jordy, good-bye before school and ask him questions like "Did Dad ask you about your homework? Did he check it? Did he tell you to put it in your bag?" Jordy honestly answers "Yes" to all of these questions, which were, after all, about what his father had done, not what he had done. Bonnie sometimes found out later that a major battle had erupted between Sam and Jordy after school over homework and it had never gotten done. After a couple of weeks of this, the couple had to revise their approach: Sam would monitor Jordy while he did his homework after school, then Bonnie would take the time to check it the minute she got home from work and ask him to show her that it was all in his bag the next morning. This is also a situation where technology can help—Sam and Bonnie could leave each other voicemail, text, or e-mail messages about the status of Jordy's homework.

• *Are you in agreement on your philosophy about discipline?* Go back to Chapter 5 and see how you'd define yourself and your partner in terms of parenting styles. Are you in total agreement, diametrically opposed to one another, somewhere in between? Until you've got a lot of experience with contingency management, try to write contracts that don't tap into any differences in parenting philosophy. Disagreements can arise in areas you never expected. Maybe it made sense to stipulate that if your daughter stayed at her desk after school until she had done all of her homework, she could be on the computer between 7:30 and 9:00. Your spouse thinks this means she doesn't eat with the family if she's still working at dinnertime. You think there are more compelling reasons for her to participate in family meals and insist that she be allowed to break for dinner. There are now more fights between you and your spouse over whether your daughter should be allowed to come to the table than you used to have with her over the homework. Many problems like these can be solved by doing advance troubleshooting. When you and your spouse are discussing the terms of a contract you want to write with your teen, spin out the "what ifs" and see if the contingency makes sense given all kinds of circumstances. If not, amend it before writing the contract. Making sure your teen can't use the "divide and conquer" strategy against you will be very important before you try to extend the use of behavior contracts and point systems in this step.

• *Is one parent shouldering too much of the burden for managing and monitoring?* Who is managing the checkbook register or keeping track of the contracts? If one parent is responsible for too much, the system may very well fall apart. The overburdened parent will become resentful and weary and start to give in to the teen, or the teen will try to take advantage of the less invested parent. The resentful parent may become overly controlling to make up for the other parent's laxness. Or the less involved parent may sabotage the overburdened parent by precipitously making unreasonable requests of the teenager and putting responsibility for carrying out the discipline on the spouse. In all these situations marital trouble is brewing. Jordy took advantage of

Bonnie's sleepy state to get around performing his part of the contract. Sam resented having to be the "heavy" every afternoon and reverted to his authoritarian ways with his son, which only sparked conflict. When you're exploring the "what ifs" in advance of writing a contract, be sure to ask yourselves whether the balance of work between you is fair. Try to write contracts that will allow you to swap roles regularly so that neither of you has to do all of the record keeping or all of the monitoring and enforcing.

3. *Use anger management techniques to keep conflict from escalating around penalties.* No teen reacts to the reintroduction of penalties with joy and glee, so tempers are almost guaranteed to flare. What's important to monitor, though, is whether any anger on your teenager's part or yours was kept in check. If anger tended to escalate out of control when you fined the teen or took away privileges, you may need to devote extra effort to using anger control techniques:

• Leave the room. Remember what we said about the efficacy of teen–adult time-out in Chapter 11. If your teen follows you out of the room, go for a walk around the block.

• Be businesslike in discussing the contingency management plan with your teenager. This might be easier said than done, but you can get used to this with practice. If you have trouble speaking in a modulated, businesslike, matter-of-fact way that invites no rebellion, try practicing in front of the mirror or asking your spouse to listen to you practice and give you feedback about body language and tone of voice. Or . . .

• Let the other parent serve as moderator for your discussions with your teen. Use this tactic sparingly because using it too often can either overburden the moderator parent or give the teen the false impression that the other parent is more sympathetic and possibly more easily manipulated.

Be sure you feel comfortable using one or more of these techniques before launching into the work of this step.

4. *Address any problems you've had with the mechanics of keeping the checkbook register.* An advantage of the point system for those who are using it is that all the earnings and losses are right there in black and white for your teen to see, cutting down on opportunities to discuss whether a privilege has been earned. Unfortunately, having a physical record is also an irresistible temptation for some teens to tamper with the amounts. Get in the habit of memorizing the teen's balance each day so that you know when an unauthorized change has been made. You need to know that you can prevent this before extending the system to additional chores and rules. Consider using an unusual-colored pen for the entries and keeping the checkbook inaccessible to your teen so that you can easily spot any changes made by anyone but you. Back up the register electronically on your computer or iPad.

5. *Keep the privilege list fresh and interesting.* This may require a little creativity on your part. Be alert to any new interests of your teen's and to the latest trends, and tap both of these to come up with new privileges. Switch them around, putting movie rentals on the list one week and game rentals the next. It's important to keep your teen motivated to earn those points. Many of you using the point system instead of contracts will have teens who need the extra reinforcement of a list of privileges to choose from, so the effort will be worthwhile. When you start adding chores and other behaviors in this step, you'll need a good selection of privileges to inspire your teen to keep up the good work.

Extending Contingency Management to Other Behavior Problems

What you're going to do for the next 2 weeks is simply expand your use of contracts and point systems to apply it to other behaviors. You won't be doing anything brand-new, but the fact that this makes the step "simple" doesn't mean it will be easy. All the advance troubleshooting of the preceding goal is intended to help you avoid the many pitfalls that can occur with contingency management, but it's not going to be a smooth and easy path even with a lot of vigilance and diligence on your part. Think "trial and error" and cut yourselves some slack for not being perfectly successful at this right away. It takes time. And again, take it slow. When we say to tackle three or four new problems, we do mean three or four, not a dozen. And keep them as simple and straightforward as you can. As you'll see, contracts often need to be revised to address unforeseen circumstances. These revisions often end up making the contracts more detailed or more complicated by themselves.

If you find yourselves mired in problems you don't know how to solve, speak to a therapist. But also know that we're going to give you some powerful new tools and techniques to boost your effectiveness in the second half of this program.

1. *Go back to the list of chores and household rules you wrote in Step 3 and pick the three or four that you'd most like your teen to comply with.* Also look at the list of household rules that you compiled back in Chapter 3 and used in Step 4. If there's one you really want obeyed that hasn't been, check that off too.

If there's another parent or other supervising adult, make sure the two of you agree on your choices. If you can't decide—or the two of you can't agree—take a few days at the beginning of this step to observe your daily interactions with your teen and start "thinking contract": When things come up that cause a conflict, ask yourself whether a behavior contract would help here. If so, jot it down when you have a chance or record it in your smartphone.

Or maybe everything on your lists seems equally in need of action, so you're having a hard time prioritizing. In that case, try carrying around your list and putting a little checkmark next to each item whenever the fact that your teen doesn't comply with it or doesn't obey the rule crosses your mind.

After those few days have passed, get together with your spouse and review what you've observed. If there are new chores or new rules that you hadn't listed before but that are problematic, add them to your list and consider whether any of these are pressing enough to tackle during this step. If you've been checking off "hits" on your existing list, see which three or four have the highest number of checkmarks and whether you can agree to target these over the next 2 weeks.

2. *Now write out behavioral contracts for each chore or rule, choosing incentives and penalties that are both meaningful to the teen and of reasonable impact (the penalty must fit the crime), as you did in Steps 3 and 4.* If you're using the point system, just keep doing what you've been doing, but if you have now added new chores or rules to your list, assign them points that can be earned for compliance and points that will be deducted for noncompliance. Consult your teen regarding the choice of incentives—review the list of incentives you made in Chapter 10 with your teen and ask which incentive your teen prefers to earn. Honor that preference when it's reasonable.

In Chapter 10, Dan Jensen and his parents signed a contract that allowed him to use his smartphone for 15 minutes after school if he had hung his towels back up in the bathroom after using them earlier in the day. For the first week, he kept forgetting to hang up his towels, and he would become enraged when denied the privilege of using his smartphone. But his parents stuck to the deal, ignoring his brief tirades, which happened less frequently after a week. During the second week of Step 3, Dan started hanging his towels up—not every single day, but he was clearly trying to remember to do this small task.

During Step 4, his parents added a contract that penalized Dan for taking food out of the refrigerator without asking. It's not that they didn't want their growing son to, well, keep growing. It was just that he had a tendency to scarf down integral parts of the dinner planned for that evening; once he ate the subs that his mother had left as a snack for his sister and the friend who was coming over after school to study with her. This contract had proved more problematic because the penalty, loss of Internet use for a whole evening, had seemed to Dan to be way out of pro-portion to the "crime" of just eating something out of the family fridge when he came home from school "starving."

Dan's parents had wanted to make sure the penalty was a significant deterrent because having to come up with something different for dinner at the last minute was a major inconvenience for them, which they had told him repeatedly, and because they wanted to discourage Dan's disrespect for his younger sister. Dan was actually quite hurt by being banned from the refrigerator; it made him feel like he wasn't an equal member of the family, and he didn't understand why his mother didn't get how hungry he was after school. But the idea of expressing hurt feelings made him feel weak in a way that offended his adolescent pride, so instead he focused his ire on his sister, once going so far as actu-ally taking money from her wallet to go out and buy himself a fast-food snack to "pay her back for causing all this trouble over nothing." In addition, he stopped hanging his towels up in the bathroom after using them.

This example also illustrates two points about contracts: (1) adding a second, unsuccessful contract too soon after starting the first contract sometimes undermines the success of the first contract; and (2) contracts imposed on a teen are not the best way to handle problems that are partly a function of biological/developmental needs. Increased appetite is normal for growing adolescents, although Dan's approach to satisfying his increased appetite was inappropriate. Instead of imposing a contract with a penalty on Dan, his parents should have involved him in a mutual problem-solving process designed to reach a compromise solu-tion to this negotiable issue. In Step 7 you'll learn how to use problem-solving skills for such situations. Dan and his parents used problem solving to revise the contract to be more specific about what Dan could and could not eat without permission, making it much less likely that he'd incur the penalty, which they kept as it was because deterring disrespectful, inconsiderate behavior was so important to them. Dan also was required to pay back his sister her money, with some interest, as a consequence for his theft, which is not to be treated lightly.

Meanwhile, though, they chose the following other issues for new contracts:

I, Dan Jensen, agree that I will do my laundry on Saturday morning before lunchtime. If my laundry is washed, dried, and put away by noon, I can go to the gym for 2 hours in the afternoon with my friends. If not, I can't go to the gym that Saturday and have to stay home until my laundry is done.

I, Dan Jensen, agree not to swear in the house. For every time I do swear in the house, I will lose $1 of my allowance, which will be $5 a day. For every day I speak respectfully to others without profanity, I will get an extra $0.50 added to my allowance.

I, Dan Jensen, agree to put my breakfast dishes in the dishwasher and put away any food that I've used before leaving the kitchen. If I do clean up, I will earn 15 minutes of video gaming time for that evening. If I don't clean up, I will lose 15 minutes of time.

I, Dan Jensen, agree to take the garbage out when I get home from school. If I take the garbage out, I will earn 15 minutes of gaming time for that evening. If I don't clean up, I will lose 15 minutes of time.

I, Dan Jensen, agree to ask my mother if she needs any help with dinner when she gets home from work. If I ask her, I will earn 15 minutes of gaming time.

Dan's parents seemed to have struck a nice balance with these contracts. Dan's sloppiness was another major sign of disrespect for the rest of the family to them, so most of the contracts focused on his being neater and also helping out more around the house. They also were well aware that Dan enjoyed video gaming and that earning gaming time was paramount to him. So they gave him three opportunities to earn gaming time each day. Only two of them came with a built-in loss of gaming time if he didn't do the chore. They thought it was a stretch to get him to ask his mother if he could help in the kitchen, but they wanted to encourage this kind of thoughtfulness, so they made it a chance for Dan to earn extra gaming time without penalizing him for not doing this. This way, they were using contracts that, combined, had the flexibility of a point system, allowing Dan to gradually build his compliance and respect for his family while providing just enough incentive to earn his gaming time.

3. *Over the next 2 weeks, monitor your teenager's behavior stipulated in the contracts and scrupulously enforce them as you did during Steps 3 and 4.* If you find it helpful, jot down notes about how well the system is going so that you know where you've hit obstacles, why, and what seemed to work particularly well. You'll be applying that knowledge to revising these contracts as necessary and creating new ones in the future. Create a binder where you can keep all your contracts and any notes you decide to take. This repository will be especially useful if you are now, or end up, working with a therapist.

4. *Make sure to praise your teenager daily for compliance with all of the contracts!*

Q. *We wrote four more contracts and started to enforce them, but our son dug in his heels and started insisting, "Go ahead and take it away; I don't care!" This has gone on for a week. Maybe he really doesn't care, in which case he'll never do what we want. What should we do now?*

A. Our best answer is still "Hang in there." When a little kid insists he doesn't care about being denied something of value, you can usually tell pretty quickly that he does care because he can't hold out for very long. Teens are different. Their pride and, in some cases, their ability to defer gratification can make them pretty stubborn. It doesn't mean that they really don't care, and in time they'll realize you're not fooling around and they might as well do what you want if they ever want to see their iPod, smartphone, or favorite TV show again.

But be sure you're sure. That is, give it a little more thought and ask yourself whether your gut instinct tells you your teen really does care about this privilege or reward. Most parents know their kids pretty well. They know what's of value to them because they've been closely watching their interests develop over the years. They may also be able to read their kids' body language, facial expressions, and so forth. If everything you know about your teen says this privilege does matter to her, ignore the "I don't care" claims and just keep enforcing the contract. Also, make sure the bar for achieving the reward has not been set so high that you've forced your teen into quitting because success seems out of reach to her even if it does not to you. Starting with smaller work quotas or lower standards for doing the task you wanted done and then gradually raising the goal (as you increase the value of the reward) are ways around that sort of problem.

5. *Periodically, you and your teen's other parent, if there is one, should sit down and review how well things are going.* Are you feeling comfortable with enforcing the contracts? Is the responsibility for doing so being shared equitably? Would you say you're regaining confidence in your parental authority? Is your teenager beginning to be less defiant? These are pretty general measures you should look at first. If you decide to take time to review only once a week, any notes you've taken will make it easier to answer objectively. Otherwise you may base your assessment on the most recent encounter with your teen, which could mean putting too positive or too negative a spin on your progress.

These notes will also help you discover whether revisions of the contracts are called for, generally to respond to a few typical occurrences:

• **The contract didn't define the task well enough.** Dan Jensen started throwing out the garbage even if there was only one thing in the bag, which infuriated his mother, who felt he was wasting garbage bags. They rewrote the contract to specify that he should check the kitchen garbage, and if the bag was at least half full he was to empty it; otherwise he was to wait until the next day.

Samantha Rivera's parents spent a couple of weeks in aggravation over their daughter's half-completion of the task "clean up after dinner" until they finally rewrote the contract to be very specific: "I, Samantha Rivera, agree to clear the dishes from the table, rinse them off, put them in the dishwasher with soap, and turn the dishwasher on by 8:00 P.M. on Sundays through Fridays. . . ." The Kravitzes were just as frustrated with their son Neil's scattershot attempts to perform the "clean your room" part of his contract—until they listed out what they meant by the chore:

We consider the room to be clean if:

a. *The bed is made with four hospital corners.*
b. *The trash basket has been emptied.*
c. *All books, papers, sports equipment, and so on are off the floor and in a drawer, on a closet shelf, or neatly placed on a bookshelf.*
d. *The carpet has been vacuumed (i.e., we heard the vacuum cleaner running for at least 5 minutes and there is no visible dirt on the carpet).*
e. *All dirty dishes have been returned to the kitchen and put in the dishwasher, and all food wrappers and other trash have been placed in the trash basket.*
f. *All dirty clothes are in the appropriate clothes hamper and not on the bed or floor.*

• **Unanticipated problems with making the privilege available came up.** The Riveras had agreed that if their daughter cleaned up after dinner as stipulated in the contract, that they would drive her to and from a maximum of three school special events (not practices) or dances a week. But Samantha accused them of reneging when she sprung a need for transportation on them at the last minute and they were unable to drive her. So they added a condition to the contract: "Samantha has to give us 24 hours' notice when she wants to be driven to a game or dance."

• **The privileges needed to be more flexible.** The Jensens, for example, realized that their laundry contract wasn't working ideally. When Dan didn't do his laundry on Saturday morning, he spent Sunday through the next Friday begging his parents to let him go to the gym and sometimes threatening to just go without their permission. They also realized that their gaming privileges weren't working quite as planned. The only time Dan asked his mother if she wanted help in the kitchen was when he realized he had not cleaned up after breakfast or taken the garbage out that day and would therefore have earned no gaming time at all. They debated whether to attach a penalty to the contract requiring him to ask his mom if she needed help or to try something else. They decided after weighing the "what ifs" that the best move was to terminate that contract altogether.

But a better solution might have been to give Dan the option of earning gaming time or gym time from doing each of the chores they desperately wanted him to do and also for not swearing. That way Dan could decide to sacrifice his weekly gym time if he was really involved in a particular game that day, and this might have dissuaded him from then whining about the loss of gym time since the reward had been his to choose.

Neil Kravitz's parents were very specific about how they would assess whether his room was cleaned and what reward options he'd have if they decided he'd done his job:

> *Mrs. Celia Kravitz will inspect the room at noon on Saturday. If the room meets all the criteria in this agreement, Neil earns any one of the following privileges:*
>
> a. *Go to the movies with a friend that evening. Parents pay for his ticket.*
> b. *Rent two videos that evening.*
> c. *Five dollars' allowance.*

• **A plan for review and revision needed to be included in the contract.** For some families (perhaps especially where both parent and teen have ADHD or there are so many environmental stressors that follow-up is challenging), it makes sense to build in an agreement to review the contract at a specific time: "This contract will be in effect for 2 weeks from the date it is signed, and then it will be reviewed for modifications in a family meeting." This can be helpful also when the teen is highly resistant; knowing that the system will be reviewed may convince the teen that by then the whole system will have blown up, so maybe 2 weeks won't be so bad. Don't prove your teen right—stick to the contract, and he may just see that even when the system hasn't blown up, it isn't so horrible to live with.

• **Instead of resolving one behavior problem, the contract plants the seeds for another.** One day Dan Jensen was accused of not having done his duty when he insisted that it had been his sister who had taken the orange juice and English muffins out of the refrigerator. The Jensens realized they couldn't always be in the kitchen to see who was using what when, so they started to wonder whether this contract was just too difficult to monitor and enforce. Then they decided that, since Dan was older, it was perfectly OK to say that if he was the last one in the kitchen, he was to put all the food away—and that they would speak to his sister about putting away what she had used first, but that the buck would stop with Dan. Unfortunately, the Jensens had no idea what they had wrought; thus began the battle of the breakfast dishes, a problem that illustrates one way that you can use contracts creatively to tackle more complicated behavior problems, as described below.

6. *Revise your contracts to make them more specific or complex as needed.* Behavior contracts can be short or long, simple or complex. You can in fact, learn to draw them up to suit any behavior management need. But always start with the simple. You can (and should) then refine them (making them longer and more detailed) to respond to problems that come up. For Neil Kravitz, the original contract required him to clean his room on Saturday to earn the privilege of going to a movie on Saturday night. The detail above was added by his parents after they realized that they were constantly battling over what "clean your room" really meant. *When a contract causes a conflict instead of replacing one, it needs to be revised.*

Sometimes a contract causes a new conflict because no one lives in a vacuum. In the Jensen family, there was already a lot of tension between the siblings. The Jensens didn't realize they were going to feed that tension when they created a contract requiring their son to clean up after himself following breakfast or that their first contract revision would make things even worse. Considering the rivalry between the two teens, they probably shouldn't have made Dan responsible for cleaning up after his sister. But, on the other hand, the war that broke out over the breakfast cleanup revealed that, even though their daughter didn't have a particular problem they would define as defiance, her willingness to take responsibility for cleaning up after herself could use some work, as could her dedication to trying to get along better with her brother.

So first they rewrote the breakfast contract, making both kids responsible for cleaning up the kitchen when they were both eating breakfast, rewarding and penalizing them equally. This worked out so well that they decided to extend the idea into a more complex contract designed to foster peace in the family: they divided each day into three periods of time: before school, after school until dinner, and after dinner. For each interval that Dan and his sister treated each other respectfully (no teasing, hitting, stealing), they each earned 50 cents. So they could earn $1.50 per day, or $10.50 per week, for getting along. In the first week, Dan's sister earned $8.00 while Dan earned only $1.50. His parents then discovered that Dan's grandmother was slipping him $10 per week ("Because you're the oldest and I know you probably want to take all the pretty girls out"). When she agreed to make her money contingent upon Dan's decent treatment of his sister, she pushed him into deciding to go along with the contract. He earned $9.00 from his parents the second week. One weekend, the Jensens were astounded to overhear the two laughing as they competed to see who could get the dishes in the dishwasher faster after breakfast.

7. *Start "thinking contract" throughout the day.* You may already have some ideas of how you could use behavior contracts on the spot if you took notes about typical daily conflicts at the beginning of this step. Using contracts in this way is very valuable, but again, it requires caution and practice to use skillfully. There's a fine line between saying "If you refrain from bugging me to buy you things while we're shopping for Dad's birthday, you can get two new lip glosses on the way out of the store; otherwise you'll lose your allowance for this week" and saying "If you don't stop bugging me, you're going to be grounded for a week!" You already know everything that's wrong with the latter. The trick is getting to the point where you can come up with something like the former with little notice. One way to get used to that is to have some desirable but not-too-huge rewards in mind along with some not-too-harsh but meaningful penalties that you can call up. It also helps if you start pairing these in your mind with proportionate infractions typical of your teen. Make a list— at least mentally—of the types of spontaneous rule violations or other problems often perpetrated by your teen, then (again, even just in your mind) think about how long the problem usually goes on. If your teen is prone to sudden bursts of profanity that don't last, make the penalty small but meaningful too. If your teen has to resist the urge to beg for purchases for 4 hours while she helps you shop, then two lip glosses (instead of the more modest one) might be a fair reward.

This kind of spontaneity is something you probably shouldn't try to implement yet, but you can take incidents that would call for on-the-spot intervention back to the drawing board with you and use them to come up with contracts in the future. Meanwhile, situations will come up that require an immediate response that might be amenable to a contract, while allowing you enough time to do a little thinking. Bruce announced to his parents one Saturday at 7:00 that the girl he was "crazy about" had finally agreed to go out with him that very night, but that now they'd have to go to a late movie, which would mean he wouldn't be back by his usual 11:00 P.M. curfew. His father started to put his foot down and refused to budge on the curfew. His mother immediately went in the opposite direction and wanted to suspend the curfew for the night, considering how important the occasion was to Bruce. The two could have ended up embroiled in a conflict of their own but decided to step back and look at whether a behavior contract could help. This is what they came up with:

I, Bruce Noonan, agree to come home by midnight. If I am more than 5 minutes late, I understand that I will be grounded from electronic privileges from Sunday through Tuesday.

This contract proved so successful that Bruce's parents decided to make midnight their son's new Saturday curfew and keep this contract in place until they were sure that he would continue to handle this new independence responsibly. What we haven't shown here is the process by which the three family members arrived at this contract. It's called problem solving, and it's a technique by which you involve your teen in decision making once you have completed the first part of this program, which you are about to do. You'll learn about it in Step 7. First, though, because school-related issues are so problematic for many teens and parents, we'll wrap up the behavior management segment of the program with a focus strictly on school.

Step 6. Addressing Defiant Behavior in School and Conflicts over Homework

This is a good time to take a deep breath. Now that you've learned how to take back your authority as parents (the first part of this program), you can work on the second part: rebuilding your relationship on a new, adult-to-almost-adult basis. The remaining steps will help you keep defiance under control *without* tripping your teenager up on the inexorable and essential march toward independence. You're going to learn to use effective problem-solving and communication skills and to examine beliefs and expectations that tend to trap us all in false assumptions and harmful attitudes about one another.

These are ambitious, though worthy, goals. So this is a good time for a pause. For the next week or two, we're going to switch from a focus on home to a focus on school. Some defiant teens have problems only with their parents. If yours is one of these, you may not need this chapter at all and can skip to Step 7. But if your teenager's defiance affects his or her academic performance or classroom behavior, or a lot of battles erupt over homework and you haven't yet dealt with that issue via behavior management, you'll find help in this chapter.

Understand, though, that an individual teen may do poorly in school for a wide variety of reasons: failure to complete homework, failure to turn in completed homework, low test scores, poor study habits, spacing out or failing to pay attention in class, coming to class without the correct books or materials, poor understanding of the material, poor classroom participation, sloppy handwriting or inaccurate math computation, arguing with teachers, disrupting the class, getting into fights with peers, and truancy or skipping classes. Many of these concerns—poor understanding of the material and poor study skills, for example—need to be addressed with the teen's teachers and other school personnel. If your teen is experiencing such problems, the school may need to provide informal accommodations to help him or her succeed academically or conduct an evaluation for an individualized educational program (IEP) to provide special education services. A full discussion of these issues goes beyond the scope of this book's focus on defiant behavior in teens. The Resources at the back of this book will steer you to additional sources for help.

In this chapter we'll concentrate on defiant behavior in the classroom—arguing with teachers, disrupting the class, and the like—as well as conflicts over homework. The skills presented so far in this book (and in the following chapters as well) can help you with these aspects of school functioning.

GOALS FOR STEP 6

- Use a home–school report system to decrease defiant behavior in the classroom.
- Establish an effective homework contract.

If your teen doesn't have any school problems related to defiance, or you're already addressing them with positive attention, praise, and behavior management, you can skip this step or take another week or two to refine the work you began in Step 5—not a bad idea if you feel there are still significant kinks in your behavior management system. But even if you don't think you have any school-related difficulties, you might benefit from reviewing that arena of your teen's life.

Decreasing Defiant Behavior in the Classroom via Home–School Report Systems

The home–school report system is a proven effective tool you can use to monitor and modify defiant behavior or poor academic performance in the classroom even though you're not on the scene. At its simplest, this system involves three basic components: (1) a list of target behaviors monitored by your teen's teachers, (2) a method for the teachers to communicate the monitoring data to you on a regular basis, and (3) consequences administered at home based on the monitoring data provided by the teachers. Together with your teen's teachers, you select the list of target behaviors and determine the methods for monitoring and communication. Then you select the consequences to be administered at home, with some input from your teen regarding positive incentives.

1. *Select the target behaviors.* By phone or in a face-to-face meeting with your teen's teachers or guidance counselor, you should figure out together which behaviors to target for change. As you undoubtedly know if your teen's defiance extends to the school setting, teachers often volunteer information about negative behavior. You may already have been told that your teenager clowns around in class, talks out of turn, socializes when he should be working, uses disrespectful language, disrespects others' property, argues back, arrives late for class, or comes to class unprepared. Whatever seems defiant to the teachers can be targeted for change. But as with the behaviors you've been targeting at home, it's always better to state the target behaviors positively than negatively. You want to be able to tell your teen what she needs to do rather than what she needs to stop doing. For example:

> Follow posted classroom rules
> Talk when given permission

Stay on task during independent work time
Use respectful language
Express disagreements appropriately
Talk to peers courteously
Come to class on time
Bring books and planner to class daily

As you've done at home, it's also wise to start with just three to four target behaviors to make the system manageable. You and the teachers or guidance counselor can always target other behaviors after your teen has reached the initial goals.

2. *Agree on monitoring methods and frequency.* Your teen's teachers will likely be happy to hear that you're invested in helping resolve any behavior problems your teen is bringing into the classroom. But the easier you can make the home–school report system to adopt, the more likely it is that you'll get full and enthusiastic cooperation. The first thing you can do is supply a form for reporting the teachers' observations, but first ask if it's needed. If the school has its own form, the teachers will probably want to use the school form because they are accustomed to its format. If you're supplying the form, photocopy the one on page 236 (there are blanks for filling in subjects your teen has other than math or English) or provide it electronically (see below) if you and the teachers plan to communicate by e-mail; you can download it from *www.guilford.com/barkley16-forms.*

How frequently you should ask your teen's teachers to monitor the target behaviors depends on how serious and pervasive his or her school problems tend to be. Ideally, you might like to have daily feedback if your teen's problems occur every day and it's important to get some control over them quickly. If you start with daily report cards, once your teen can go for 2 straight weeks with two to four *Nos* (the equivalent of about one per class) on the form, you can drop back to either twice-weekly (such as doing evaluations on Wednesdays and Fridays) or once-weekly (on Fridays) evaluations.

Weekly Home–School Report

Name: _____   Date: _____

Math:		Yes	No	N.A.
	Followed posted rules	Yes	No	N.A.
	Talked respectfully to others	Yes	No	N.A.
	Paid attention during lectures	Yes	No	N.A.
	Came to class with book, planner	Yes	No	N.A.

Comments:

Teacher signature: _____

English:				
	Followed posted rules	Yes	No	N.A.
	Talked respectfully to others	Yes	No	N.A.
	Paid attention during lectures	Yes	No	N.A.
	Came to class with book, planner	Yes	No	N.A.

Comments:

Teacher signature: _____

_____				
(Subject)	Followed posted rules	Yes	No	N.A.
	Talked respectfully to others	Yes	No	N.A.
	Paid attention during lectures	Yes	No	N.A.
	Came to class with book, planner	Yes	No	N.A.

Comments:

Teacher signature: _____

_____				
(Subject)	Followed posted rules	Yes	No	N.A.
	Talked respectfully to others	Yes	No	N.A.
	Paid attention during lectures	Yes	No	N.A.
	Came to class with book, planner	Yes	No	N.A.

Comments:

Teacher signature: _____

_____				
(Subject)	Followed posted rules	Yes	No	N.A.
	Talked respectfully to others	Yes	No	N.A.
	Paid attention during lectures	Yes	No	N.A.
	Came to class with book, planner	Yes	No	N.A.

Comments:

Teacher signature: _____

But keep in mind that busy secondary education teachers may not always be able to provide you with daily feedback. You should request weekly feedback if your teen's problems at school occur just a few times a week and are less serious. After all, in most cases, the teachers see your teen for only one class period a day—less in the case of block schedules. Many target behaviors may not occur daily and take time to be monitored and time for a change to be noticed. A weekly evaluation therefore may work for many teens at the start. Again, let the frequency and seriousness of the teen's school behavior problems determine which schedule of feedback to choose at the start of this program.

3. *Develop an effective home–school communication system.* There are three different possibilities for getting the form completed and sent home weekly (listed here in descending order of our preference):

a. Ideally, since many teachers now have e-mail at their desks, every Thursday you e-mail a blank form to the teachers. On Friday, the teachers fill it out and e-mail it back to you. This is quick, avoids paper shuffling, and your e-mail serves as a reminder that it's time to evaluate again.

b. A counselor, teacher consultant, or social worker collects the forms from each teacher on Friday and faxes them to you, or you call the identified individual and get reports on your teen by phone. This requires a lot more coordination on everyone's part.

c. According to the old-fashioned approach, your teen picks up a blank form like the one above from the school office, carries it around to every class, asks each teacher to complete it at the end of class, and then brings it home. You give the office a supply of forms. If your teen has been defiant at school as well as at home—or especially if he's been *more* defiant at school than at home—for some time, he's clearly not going to like being monitored in this very specific way. Be prepared for a number of evasive tactics from the teen, from "forgetting" to pick up the forms to "editing" the ratings, perhaps claiming that certain teachers

didn't fill them in or vociferously protesting the teacher's libel-
ous or wildly unjust ratings. As with your behavior management
at home, you'll have to stand your ground: make it clear that you
have ways of checking with the school about whether your teen
showed up to collect the forms and checking with the teachers
about whether they filled them out (again, e-mail comes to the
fore). You can ask the teachers to keep copies of each form in
their own file so you can compare what you get back with the
unadulterated reports. For all of these reasons, we prefer direct
communication by e-mail, fax, or phone from the teachers to
you.

   4. *Develop effective consequences at home for the data reported
by the teachers.* What do you do with all this data when you get it
every day or once a week? You either tie it in with your current
rewards and punishments system or you develop a new contract
for school behavior. If you use our monitoring form, for example,
you can give points for the ratings on each form (say 25 points
for each Yes circled by each teacher). Then enter the total points
in your checkbook as for home behavior. Shayla and her parents
wrote the following contract:

> *I, Shayla Johnson, agree to pick up a blank home–school note
> form in my first-period math class every Thursday morning and
> to have each teacher fill it out and sign it by the end of school
> Friday. I agree to bring it home Friday and show it to my mother.
> If 80% of the behavior ratings are YES, my mother agrees to pay
> me $20.*

   If your teen refuses to cooperate with the system and you're
stuck with the old-fashioned approach (his participation isn't
necessary if you're using e-mail, fax, or phone), you could write a
behavioral contract whereby he agrees to bring home (and drop
off in the morning) the report forms every day and tying a significant privilege to his doing so (and a penalty to his not doing
so).

Q. *Ricky has a lot of trouble with deferred gratification, so waiting till the end of the week to see whether he's earned enough points for privileges here doesn't seem to be enough to keep him on track during the school day. What else can we and the teacher do?*

A. By the time kids are teenagers, the kinds of reinforcers that are typically used to motivate younger kids have been phased out. And setting up a system that gives rewards in the classroom is problematic if it's not something that can be applied to the whole class. If you need to be able to reward your son more often than weekly, you'll need more frequent evaluations on which to base the rewards. This is one situation in which daily or at least twice-weekly report forms may be advisable. But if the teachers can come up with a way to reward your son without causing dissension by appearing to favor your teen over others, these are some of the kinds of rewards students of age 12 and over might be given *in the classroom*:

- A scribbled note saying "Thanks for contributing to the discussion" or the like, dropped discreetly on the student's desk
- A smile or discreet thumbs-up
- Extra computer time
- Being excused from the class to deliver something to another room
- Access to special materials for a project
- Leading the class (or a group) in a discussion or exercise

Other rewards can be *handed to your teen during class but take effect outside*, allowing more discretion:

A positive phone call to the student at home
Elimination of one bad grade
Being excused from a quiz
A no-homework pass

A small gift card (such as for iTunes, fast food, or free popcorn at the movies)

A pass to go to the gym or other recreation area during a
study period

5. *Customize the system for your teen's specific school behavior
problems.* Remember 17-year-old Mark? In Chapter 10 we let you
hear his parents debate how they could possibly withhold privileges when it seemed that Mark already owned everything he'd
ever wanted and had free rein over his life. His mother said she'd
like to withhold all kinds of things that seemed like privileges
every time he sneaked out the back door of school after first
period. Mark's parents know he's bright, and they want him to be
able to go to college. But they're worried about the repercussions
of his truancy. He manages to keep a C or C– average in most
classes by attending class just often enough and doing just enough
homework and studying. But Sandy wants him to get his grade
point average (GPA) up before the end of junior year. So Sandy
and Doug decided to work with the teachers on an attendance
recording system that would give their son an incentive to stay
in school all day. They made up a variation on the home–school
report system that required each teacher to stamp the card to
show that Mark had shown up for his or her class that day. Mark's
parents supplied unique rubber stamps to each teacher so that
Mark couldn't fake their stamps. He got a dollar toward his dinners with friends at California Pizza Kitchen for every class he
attended during the week. If he cut any classes during a particular
day, he was grounded from the use of the car for the remainder of
the day. If he cut more than three classes during any week, he was
grounded for Friday and Saturday. If he attended all his classes
for 2 weeks in a row, his parents would pay for the gas he used for
that month. If not, he had to take it out of his own bank account.

At first the system seemed destined for total failure. Mark
simply refused to take the report forms to his teachers, but when
Sandy called them individually to find out whether their son had
been in class, she was often told that he had been. It didn't take

long for them to realize that their son was just too old to tolerate having to carry these forms around like a much younger kid. So they switched to e-mail—which, after all, couldn't be faked either since Sandy could instantly tell whether an attendance report had come from a teacher's legitimate e-mail address. Note that this is one case where it's reasonable to expect the teachers to provide daily feedback since 1 week is too long to wait to find out whether a teen has skipped classes. It doesn't hurt, though, to acknowledge the extra effort they're being asked to invest. Sandy surprised the teachers about once a week with bagels from the local deli. As for Mark, he acted tough and rolled with the punches of loss of spending money and use of the car, but when he found his bank account dwindling from gas purchases he started attending classes regularly.

Creating an Effective Homework Contract

There are all kinds of ways to tackle homework problems, but if these issues have proved resistant to your interventions in the past, you're going to have to get creative. First, try to figure out what the problem is:

- Does your teen claim she doesn't have any homework when it turns out later that she did?
- Does your teen "forget" to bring home assignments or the materials needed to do them?
- Does your teen consistently claim to have finished his homework—but parent–teacher conferences reveal otherwise?
- Does your teen say she'll do it "later," which always seems to be after you've gone to bed?
- Does your teen refuse to study for tests, saying he's done it at school, during study periods?

Let's look at these problems one at a time.

- *If your teen claims not to have homework, and you continually find out she did have homework but didn't do it,* enlist the teachers' help in informing you directly of the day's assignments—by e-mailing you or by filling out an assignment sheet with some stamp or other unique "signature" to let you know you're seeing it directly from the teacher. Ask your teen after school what homework she has. If her report matches what the teachers tell you, reward her (via points or a behavior contract).

- *If your teen "forgets" assignments or books,* make him responsible for tracking them down from a classmate or borrowing the books. Establish one level of reward for following up and a higher one for the times he doesn't "forget." Also, see about leaving a deposit with the school so that you can keep an extra set of the teen's textbooks at home.

- *If your teen claims to have finished his homework,* but you consistently discover he hasn't, create a behavior report form just to track this problem with the teacher and make the points awarded (or subtracted) fairly significant.

- *If your teen is always saying she'll do her homework "later" and you can't check that she has,* write a behavior contract whereby she agrees to do her homework within a certain time period when you can monitor the work.

- *If your teen refuses to study at home,* write a behavior contract or award points for studying. Monitor closely to be sure your teen is actually studying, and consider incorporating your quizzing him at the end of that period as an extra check and building in an extra reward for doing well on the quiz.

As you can see, there are two key ingredients to homework reinforcement: being there to monitor closely so you don't have to take your teen's word for it and using rewards to motivate him or her to do what he is so loath to do.

Following is a sample homework contract for one high school student:

▬▬▬ Homework Contract for Miguel Hernandez ▬▬▬

I, Miguel Hernandez, together with my parents, teachers, guidance counselor, and principal, agree to carry out to the best of our ability the following homework plan:

I. Keeping Track of Assignments

    A. My teachers will write the assignments on the board every day. They will also give a copy of all the assignments for the week to Mrs. Smith, my guidance counselor, each Monday. She will keep a copy and fax or e-mail a copy home to my parents.

    B. I will write down the assignment from the board every day before I leave each class. I will write it on the back of the section divider for the section of my looseleaf binder for each class. I will read over what I have written down to make sure I understand it. I will ask the teacher to explain any assignment I do not understand.

    C. During my last-period study hall, I will read over each assignment that I have written down and make sure I understand what I am being asked to do. I will make a list of all of the materials I need to bring home and gather them from my locker. My study hall teacher agrees to give me a hall pass during last period to go to my locker and find any materials I need.

II. Bringing Home Materials

    A. I will bring home all the materials I have gathered as well as the binder in which I have written my assignments down.

    B. My mother agrees to ask me nicely one time without nagging to see my list of assignments. I agree to show it to her without a big hassle or an attitude.

    C. As a backup in case I forget to write the assignment down, I will pick a study buddy in each of my classes, get that person's phone number, and post those phone numbers on the refrigerator door.

III. Schedule and Setting for Doing Homework

    A. From Sunday through Thursday, I agree to work on homework from 6:00 P.M. to 8:00 P.M. If I finish early, I will show my completed work to a parent, and if he/she agrees that it is completed, I can do whatever I want.

    B. I will do my homework at the big desk in the den. I can listen to soft music with headphones, but no loud rock. If I find myself getting distracted, I will take a short break, do something physical (not using my smartphone), and start working again.

    C. My mother will remind me once without nagging to start on my homework at 6:00 P.M. I will start without an attitude.

IV. Daily Plan for Organizing Homework Completion

    A. With help from my mother, I will make an organized plan for each night's homework. This plan will guide me in which subject I will do first, second, and so on. It will also divide up homework time between assignments due tomorrow and long-term assignments. My mother agrees to permit me to determine the order of doing homework.

    B. My plan will estimate the time needed to complete each assignment, as well as how I will check each assignment for accuracy, completeness, and legibility.

    C. The plan will specify how often I will take breaks during homework time, how long the breaks will be, and how large assignments will be divided into smaller units.

    D. The plan will specify where I will put the completed assignments and how I will make sure I turn the work in.

V. Turning in Assignments

    A. As I finish an assignment, I will put it in the section of my binder for that class.

    B. I will do my best to remember to hand in each assignment.

VI. Feedback

My teachers agree to tell me how I did within 2 days after I hand in an assignment. They also agree to send my parents feedback on how many of the last week's assignments were turned in on time when they send the next week's assignment list. The guidance counselor will collect these materials from the teachers and fax or e-mail them to my parents.

VII. Rewards

My parents agree to let me use my smartphone for 20 minutes each night that I do my homework. If I do my homework for 5 nights in a row, they agree to let me use my phone for 45 minutes on the weekend.

Signed,   *Miguel Hernandez*   *Roberto Hernandez*   *Sandra Hernandez*
    Bill Jones, Principal   *Brenda Smith, Guidance Counselor*
    Millie Broadbent, Algebra   *Harold Milton, English*
    Darla Breeze, French   *Alfred E. Newton, Chemistry*
    Harry Buff, Phys. Ed.   *Maria Machiavelli, History*

THINK AHEAD

Write a biography of your teen's school experience to pass on to next year's teachers. Whether your teenager has an IEP or a Section 504 plan in place or not, if he or she had problems with defiance in the classroom, you'll find it very helpful to start writing a biography of your teen's school life, adding a few paragraphs each year. We suggest you meet with your teen's teachers or guidance counselor about 3 weeks into the school year, hand each one a copy of the biography, then tell school personnel about your teen's strengths and weaknesses, how you intend to help with the weaknesses, and what you'd like the faculty/staff members to do. If you start your child's biography during middle school, you'll have compiled a wealth of valuable information for the teachers by the time your teen enters high school.

Q. *Poor Jack. Our behavior contracts and other work have really started to make a difference at home, but he just can't seem to change his image at school. I guess his teachers are so used to him being "bad" that they can't see the change in him, so they keep coming down hard on him, and as a result he reacts with more defiance in class. We think the teachers are making everything worse, but how can we tell them that?*

A. Your best chance is probably to frame this to the school as a "poor teacher–student match" of personalities to minimize blaming the teacher and putting the school on the defensive. First, ask for a change of teacher for that subject. If the school refuses, seriously consider having your teen drop the subject and take it in summer school with another teacher or take it the next year, even if it delays graduation. Why rush toward failure? If the school refuses this too, as very well might happen, it may be up to you—or you and a therapist—to help your teen "sweat it out." You can encourage your teen to practice anger management techniques to keep a low profile and reduce the risk of further inflaming the teacher. Offer lots of support at home and maybe engage a supportive after-school tutor. Give the teen significant rewards for not "losing it" in that teacher's classroom.

Step 7.
Using Problem-Solving Skills

All your life you've been solving problems. Problem solving is a technique you've used for damage control, planning, and just to keep the gears of daily functioning running smoothly. You've probably used it over and over at work and in civic and volunteer endeavors, with friends and relatives, maybe even with your partner in life. And it's a skill that will be the mainstay of your future relationship with your rapidly maturing teen.

So why would you need to learn these skills? And if they're so important, why haven't we gotten to them earlier?

You need to learn these skills as part of this program because the skills we use adroitly in one setting don't always translate to another. When you're trying to figure out how to boost stagnant productivity at the office, elicit cooperation among volunteers at the local food pantry, or hash out a household budget with a significant other, you get somewhere because everyone (ideally) is starting from the same perspective: mature, respectful, open to new ideas, willing to compromise, interested in reaching a mutually agreeable outcome. Doesn't sound much like the prevailing atmosphere at home before you started this program, does it?

That's why you need to learn this skill from scratch in the home setting. Formal (re)learning and practice will help you do with your teen what you already do well elsewhere—and might very well have done when your child was much younger and dissension wasn't a given. You've already reclaimed your behavior management skills this way; now you can do the same with problem solving.

Actually, the fact that you relearned behavior management as the first part of this program answers the second question. We've waited this long to tackle problem solving because it's impossible to negotiate—what problem solving is really all about—with a teen who won't even talk civilly to you and has no respect for your authority. We hope that the strides you've made in the last few months, even if modest, have shifted your relationship toward benevolence just enough to create a fruitful environment for this new collaborative rational endeavor.

Skeptical? Wondering if you and your teen are ready to negotiate—or if you even want to? Maybe you feel like you've just started to get things under control and are loath to relax the reins for fear of ending up back where you started. That's understandable. But remember, you *have* started to take back control; *you* have changed your act, and this is no longer your teenager's show. Your newfound (or regained) ability to give effective commands, provide powerful incentives, and reinforce the behavior you want to see can be called into play in this arena too. We have tested the exact sequence of steps in which you're working through this program and found that more families stick with our program if they learn behavior management skills first than if we introduce problem solving first. But if you find that your initial problem-solving sessions with your teen push old hot buttons and things spiral out of control, you can use the tools you've acquired to manage your teen's behavior, including calling a time-out where everyone retreats to his or her corner and then comes out *not* swinging.

The fact is, for some families, the transition to this part of the program is more of a leap than a glide. Some families find themselves falling into old patterns of coercion when they try to follow the problem-solving steps taught in this chapter. Negative patterns of communication may be so entrenched that when the teen is brought into the decision-making process, the whole family erupts into conflict as if they had never completed the first six steps of the program. Or very deeply held negative beliefs (discussed in Chapter 16) come rushing to the surface when the teen is invited to negotiate with the parents, as if the mere suggestion has tapped a well of resentments and derogatory preconceived notions about each other—on the part of both parents and teen.

We want you to give the problem-solving process a very concerted effort and not give up at the first sign of friction. But if you really find yourself at a standstill or in repeated blowups, you may have to do Step 8 or 9 first and then come back to this step. We'll help you spot the signs that this is necessary throughout the chapter. But there's also a chance that you could use a boost in the right direction from a therapist at this point. Having an impartial third party ease you into the negotiation process—like hiring a professional mediator—can help you cross the divide to the second part of this program more successfully.

The Point—and Principles— of Problem-Solving Communication Training

Why does this divide sometimes feel like a chasm? Because we're making a switch from parents controlling the program to parents involving teens. You still have control over the nonnegotiables— the household rules you consider inviolate—through behavioral contracts and the other means you learned earlier. But now you need to find a new way to resolve conflicts regarding the negotiables. As we hinted in Chapter 13, using problem solving (along with the communication skills so integral to the process that you'll learn in Step 8) to work collaboratively on resolving conflicts is a way of recognizing your son or daughter's natural developmental push toward independence and of teaching him or her responsible independence-related skills. Now that you've reestablished your parental authority, you're free to start involving your teenager in the decision making that affects his or her life. This is not just a privilege but a necessity; problem solving

---

The Principles of Problem-Solving Communication Training

- Gradually grant increasing independence.
- Distinguish negotiable from nonnegotiable issues.
- Involve adolescents in problem-solving negotiable issues.
- Maintain good communication.
- Develop reasonable expectations.

---

will be one route by which you can grant your teen the gradually mounting freedom that we started talking about in Chapter 3. By this path, your teen should arrive safely at the threshold of responsible adulthood.

Problem-solving communication training (PSCT) is based on the fact that parent–teen conflict is mainly *verbal* conflict over specific issues. That's why you and your teen need to learn a different way of talking to each other when in conflict—especially conflict that escalates in frequency and intensity. Think of PSCT as similar to going to acting school: first you will learn a script (the specific problem-solving steps that will be applied to every issue addressed here), then you will work on "delivery" (how family members communicate with each other, Step 8), and then "attitude"—the unrealistic beliefs and expectations that family members often have about one another and that fuel angry feelings (the target of Step 9).

GOALS FOR STEP 7

- Learn the problem-solving model and practice it by using a mock issue.
- Rank issues that cause conflict to establish a list of problems to solve.
- Pick one or two low-priority or low-intensity issues to work on with problem solving.

Learning the Problem-Solving Model and Practicing It

If learning problem solving in a very structured way seems stilted, remember that one of its purposes is the same one behind being businesslike when you give your teen commands. As you've seen, a dispassionate, direct, no-nonsense communication style tends to keep high emotion from flaring and thwarting your objectives. Besides, following a strict format during scheduled family meetings will not be the way you do problem solving forever. The ultimate goal is to be able to use the techniques in impromptu problem-solving sessions (when a problem suddenly presents itself and you want to solve it immediately rather than get embroiled in an argument or let conflict brew) and also completely informally—applying the components of problem solving in all kinds of natural settings in which you and your teen find yourselves.

Please understand that getting to that point will require a lot of practice. We can't possibly illustrate all the nuances or walk you through this process inch by inch (whole books have been written on problem solving; see the Resources for a couple of examples that may be useful). You'll have to discover for yourselves, through a certain amount of trial and error, exactly what works for the dynamics in your family. The only way to do that is through practice, so please do your homework at this step!

1. *Start by introducing the next phase of the program to your teenager.* Have a family meeting or sit down with your teenager in a slightly less formal setting if you think the prospect of a "meeting" will get his hackles up, but be sure that the teen understands that you need to talk about something important—and in his interest. Tell your teen you're going to start learning problem solving together. Explain that this is intended to recognize his growing maturity and to find a way for him to participate in decision making that affects him. Be sure to praise him for any strides he has made in earlier steps and express confidence in his

THINK AHEAD

Don't be surprised if your teen expresses skepticism when invited to participate in decision making about her. Don't be surprised, in fact, if she uses less-than-ideal verbal gambits to express this skepticism, such as sarcasm, sullen silence, or mockery. Empathetically tell your teen that you understand her feelings, but you really value her opinion, and you don't want to impose solutions to negotiable problems on her—you really want her to have a fair say in solving these problems. Would she try it out once and see if you stick to your word? Just remain businesslike, but be prepared to conduct your problem-solving sessions in a way that will reinforce your intention to collaborate, not dictate. Stress that this is not just another way to force the teen to do your bidding, as she may suspect. Be very clear in explaining that solutions agreed on through this process will include a role for everyone and consequences for compliance and noncompliance for everyone. Also tell your teen that she will take an active role in problem-solving sessions, such as being the first "recording secretary" when you start brainstorming solutions. Before you have this conversation with your teen, talk to the teen's other parent about any other ways you can immediately demonstrate that your teen will be treated like an equal member of the problem-solving team.

It's not that likely that your teen will flat-out refuse to participate if you come armed with a couple of examples of issues important to your teen and note that you think these can be worked out to everyone's satisfaction through problem solving. This could pique your teen's interest, especially if you have refused to discuss one of these matters to this point out of fear of being unable to draw a line between negotiable and nonnegotiable. But if, in fact, your teen does refuse, this is a good place to make a significant privilege contingent on your teen's cooperation. You might even write a behavioral contract to ensure your teen's participation.

ability to handle new responsibilities. Recap and remind the teen of everything great that has happened in the family so far. Say you want to take this further and not only find ways to resolve issues between you the way adults do but make it possible for the teen to negotiate for what he wants and to gain more and more independence. If you feel like it will clarify the goals, quickly run through the nonnegotiables to remind your teen that these rules are not subject to problem solving; they'll be handled as they have in the past. If, however, you've discovered that there are certain aspects of the nonnegotiables that are negotiable, point out that those matters *can* be resolved in problem solving (e.g., that your daughter will have an established curfew is not negotiable, but maybe when and by how much the curfew will be extended as time goes by is negotiable).

2. *Explain the problem-solving steps briefly.* You and your teen's other parent (if there is one) should review the steps and be sure you understand them before this meeting so that you can answer any questions (or objections) that your teen raises. Have copies of the Problem-Solving Worksheet on page 254 ready and hand one to your teen so he can refer to it along with you as you explain each step.

a. *Define the problem—then stick to it.* Explain that when people disagree on an issue, they're likely to define the problem in different ways. The only way to start solving the problem is to know exactly how each person looks at it. They are also likely to blame each other for the problem rather than defining it in a neutral way. So each parent and the teen first define the problem in their own words, in nonaccusatory language, using "I" instead of "you" to avoid using this step as a way to lay blame.

Now each of you restates what the other person has said to make sure you understand. You correct any misunderstandings and then record the resulting problem definition on the designated line on the worksheet. Point out how different your respective definitions of the problem can be, *but note that you don't have to persuade each other to accept your opinion to discuss the issue.*

Problem-Solving Worksheet

Date: _____

Problem: _____

	Evaluations		
Proposed solutions	Teen + −	Mother + −	Father + −
1. _____	_____	_____	_____
2. _____	_____	_____	_____
3. _____	_____	_____	_____
4. _____	_____	_____	_____
5. _____	_____	_____	_____
6. _____	_____	_____	_____
7. _____	_____	_____	_____
8. _____	_____	_____	_____
9. _____	_____	_____	_____
10. _____	_____	_____	_____

Agreement: _____

Implementation Plan

A. Teen will do: _____

_____

by the following time: _____

B. Mom will do: _____

_____

by the following time: _____

C. Dad will do: _____

_____

by the following time: _____

D. Plan for monitoring whether this happens: _____

_____

_____

E. Any reminders that will be given. By whom? When? _____

_____

F. Consequences for compliance and noncompliance: _____

_____

_____

Poor definition	Good definition
Issue: Teen makes too much noise	
Parent: "You make all the noise around here, blasting those ridiculous songs from your iPod." Parent is accusing.	*Parent:* "I get upset by how loudly you play your music and by the inappropriate songs you listen to." Parent starts with an "I," states what bothers him, and gets specific.
Issue: Teenager's dirty, messy room	
Parent: "Your room looks like a pigsty. If you keep it up, you won't ever amount to anything as an adult." Parent is blaming, vague, and adds ruinous thinking about the future, in the absence of any evidence for such a connection.	*Parent:* "I get upset by the clothes on the floor, the books and papers all over, and the empty food containers under your bed in your room." Parent starts with an "I" and then makes a specific, nonaccusatory statement of what bothers her.

b. *Brainstorm: Think of as many possible solutions as you can.* Now you brainstorm solutions, taking turns coming up with ideas for solving the problem, with one person recording them on a worksheet (start with the teen, as suggested earlier, but then rotate this job at later problem-solving sessions). See if you can come up with 12 possible solutions, but even six to eight is a good start. What's most important is that you follow these guidelines:

- Don't judge the ideas.
- Get crazy and creative; let your imagination run wild and don't reject anything you think of, no matter how silly.
- Try to go beyond your initial position, or you'll get nowhere.
- Keep the mood light. Humor helps decrease tensions and maintain involvement.

Poor definition	Good definition
Issue: Teenager's curfew	
Teen: "You're ruining my life by making me come home early." In an exaggerated fashion, the teen blames her parents. *Parent:* "You could end up pregnant, addicted to drugs, and totally ruined if you keep up irresponsibly disobeying our curfew." In a blaming way without any evidence, the parent comes up with an exaggerated account of terrible things that might happen if the teen stays out late.	*Teen:* "I feel stupid and treated like a little kid when I have to go home before my friends." The teen starts with an "I" and expresses her feelings in a nonaccusatory manner. *Parent:* "I'm concerned about older teens possibly convincing you to do things you're not ready to do if you stay out too late." Starting with an "I," the parent honestly expresses her concerns about what might happen if the teen stays out too late.
Issue: Homework	
Teen: "You bug me too much about my homework; I don't need your stupid reminders." Teen is accusing.	*Teen:* "I get angry when you ask me over and over again whether I did my homework." Teen starts with an "I" and makes a neutral statement expressing her feelings.

c. *Evaluate your options.* Copy the possible solutions onto each person's worksheet, and then each of you evaluate the solution by asking these questions about it:

- Will it solve the problem?
- Is it practical?
- Do you like it?

Based on your answers, rate each solution with a plus or minus. Transfer each person's ratings to your own form so you can compare.

d. *Select the option most agreeable to all.* Point out that the goal is to reach a decision that everyone can live with and *with which everyone will have to give up something to get something*; this is the essence of negotiation. Now the "secretary" (still the teen at first) reads out the solutions that everyone rated with a plus. If there is one or more of these, everyone should be congratulated: you've found your solution—or solutions, which you can then combine into one overall solution. All you have to do now is implement the plan. (And you might consider rewarding yourselves for a job well done. If it fits with the way you and the teen get along these days, take everyone out for ice cream or a movie; if time with parents won't feel like a reward to the teen, maybe give the teen money for a movie ticket for him and a friend while you and your spouse treat yourselves to a dinner out.)

Surprisingly, agreement on solutions is reached 80% of the time. But if no single solution got all pluses, identify the solution(s) that were closest (say, one parent and the teen gave it a plus). Figure out and state out loud the gap between the positions. Brainstorm solutions that fall between your various positions. Now try to reach a compromise using these. (You'll find examples of how this works later in the chapter.) If that still doesn't work, ask the disagreeing parent to give in for now and just try the new solution for 1 week—after all, it's not a permanent solution; just a week-long experiment. The family can revisit the contract next week and change it if it is not working.

e. *Implement the plan.* Explain that to put the agreed-on plan into effect, you have to think ahead about all the details to ensure its success:

- Who will do what, when, and where?
- Who will monitor compliance with the agreement and how will monitoring be carried out (e.g., with graphs or charts or verbally)?

- What will be the consequences for compliance or noncompliance with the agreement? The teen should start out suggesting incentives and the parents punishments.
- What, if any, performance reminders will be given if these aren't already built into the solution?
- Exactly what constitutes compliance (e.g., how clean must a room be)?
- What difficulties are anticipated in carrying out the agreement?

Explain that it's really important that each family member have a role in implementing the solution, even if it's more verbal than active (e.g., Mom being responsible for reminding the teen to do what he or she has agreed to do; the teen and Dad thanking Mom for helping the teen and Dad get along). And it's just as important that there be consequences for the parents for compliance and noncompliance too, not just the teen. All this information should be added to the worksheet. Then the agreement should be put into effect.

f. *Evaluate the implementation of the plan.* After enough time has passed to implement the plan, review how it went. If everything went smoothly, great; you'll be able to integrate what you learned from this experience into future problem solving. But what if the plan didn't work at all or worked only partially? Then you all ask yourselves these questions:

- Did you try to implement the solution? If yes, where did it break down? If you didn't try, why not?
- Did one or more of you resist? If so, who and how?
- Did negative communication sidetrack you?
- Was there general mistrust and hostility?
- Did you "forget" to implement the solution?
- Did a new crisis with the teen (a run-in with the law, a failing report card, drugs or alcohol, etc.) arise and eclipse the solution implementation?

- Did real-life circumstances (business trips, busy teen sports schedule, visits from relatives, holidays, etc.) interfere?
- Did ADHD in either parent cause problems? (Did you get overwhelmed and distracted, go off task, or give up on the plan too soon, or is your family suffering from ongoing chaos that interfered?)

Depending on the answers to these questions, you have a few different options. But before you consider them, be sure everyone understands that this "failure" is a result not of malicious intent or sabotage but simply of insufficient problem solving. Taking this as another opportunity to point the finger of blame will only make things worse. Instead, try cycling through the steps of problem solving again, figuring out where you went wrong and renegotiating a more viable solution.

Now, does everyone understand the problem-solving steps? If not, review and discuss them again. If you feel any of you still need a better understanding, consider consulting a therapist.

3. *Practice the problem-solving steps using one of the three scenarios below as a mock issue.* You can try this practice at the same family meeting if things are going well and you sense that no one is running out of steam; running through a mock problem-solving session now may cement the steps and principles more firmly than waiting until another time. But if your teen is getting restless, you spot the signs that tempers are starting to flare, or you get any other indication that continuing will be unproductive, try picking up where you left off either later that day or on another day, preferably the next day.

If none of these scenarios appeals to you and your teen, make up your own, but be careful not to choose one too close to a real issue between you. We strongly recommend starting your own problem solving with an issue of low to moderate intensity—and it's not till the next part of this step that you'll determine which these are. So inadvertently substituting a real issue for a mock one at this point could abort the entire practice.

- **Scenario A:** Tony is about to turn 16. He wants to have a birthday party for 100 of his "closest friends," and he wants his parents to go somewhere else during the party. His parents aren't too happy about the idea; Tony says they will "ruin his life" if they don't let him have a "decent party like all his friends."

- **Scenario B:** Fourteen-year-old Aaron and his father are constantly at odds over Aaron's chores. Dad says Aaron is totally unreliable, either not mowing the lawn and taking the garbage pails out to the curb at all or not doing it on time. Aaron says that his father is completely unreasonable about the timing and that the chores "aren't that important anyway." Aaron's mother feels torn between the two and spends a lot of her time playing referee; she just wants to find a way for the chores to get done without starting World War III.

- **Scenario C:** Fifteen-year-old Bettina wants a later curfew because most of her friends are 16 or 17 and are allowed to stay out later than she is. Her parents don't like the idea because they're not comfortable with her spending so much time mostly with older friends, and they also think that Bettina is too immature to be given this extra freedom. She violates the curfew she has on a regular basis, despite the negative consequences they've imposed, and they're afraid that she'll do the same with a later curfew, meaning she'll be out even later.

Once you've picked a scenario, work through the problem-solving steps, filling out the worksheets as if this were your own issue. Keep this light and fun, treating it as a role-playing game. In fact, don't hesitate to let a parent play Tony, Aaron, or Bettina. This would give you an opportunity to demonstrate how creative and outrageous some of the brainstormed solutions can be without objections raised—and also shows your readiness to put yourself in the teen's shoes.

Compare your results with the filled-out worksheet for Scenario B, which follows, and the ones for Scenarios A and C in Appendix A. You may have come up with completely different agreements, but we hope you tried to make this as realistic as possible. Spin out the scenario you chose. Do you think the plan could be implemented effectively? Why or why not? Did your solution, or the plan based on it, lack anything that is evident in the plans shown on the worksheets produced with the help of a therapist? If so, how would you do things differently?

You're about to get a chance to find out by doing your own problem solving. But first you need to identify the ongoing conflicted issues between you and your teenager.

As you can see, the compromise the Bronsteins worked out ensured that the chores got done—without relieving Aaron of the entire responsibility, while permitting him some leeway in deciding when over the weekend he would do the work. This is a straightforward example of enforcing nonnegotiables and negotiating the rest in a way that grants the teen some self-determination.

As with the Bronsteins, the Santos couldn't find a single solution to Tony's party proposal that appealed to all of them, so they too had to find a middle ground. Not surprisingly (and as you can see from their brainstorming list in Appendix A), the gaps in agreement were in how many guests Tony could have and how adult supervision could be ensured without embarrassing Tony. The family brainstormed some compromise positions, talking over what number of guests (from their own experience and from knowing how many guests friends' teenagers had had at parties and how that number had worked out), and arrived at 40 guests as a total that would be manageable yet make Tony feel like it was a "real party." Tony's uncle, who was 25 (and thus likely to be viewed as cool by Tony's friends), would chaperone, enforcing the same rules that Tony's parents would have enforced (which

Problem-Solving Worksheet for Aaron Bronstein and Parents (Scenario B)

Date: 9/19/13

Problem: _Chores problem, e.g., Dad says Aaron does not mow the lawn or take out the garbage reliably and on time. Mom agrees. Aaron says his parents ask him to do the chores during his favorite TV shows or at other inconvenient times._

		Evaluations		
		Teen	Mother	Father
	Proposed solutions	+ −	+ −	+ −
1.	_No television until the lawn is done_	−	+	+
2.	_Aaron does the lawn and garbage any time he wants_	+	−	−
3.	_Aaron does the lawn right after school on Friday_	−	−	+
4.	_Mom takes out trash; Dad does the lawn_	+	−	−
5.	_Hire a lawn service_	+	+	−
6.	_Pay Aaron $30 for doing lawn and trash_	+	−	−
7.	_Replace lawn with rocks_	−	−	−

Agreement: _Aaron does the lawn by 10:00 a.m. Sunday and takes the trash to the curb by dinnertime Sunday._

Implementation Plan

A. Teen will do: _Cut the grass, bag the cuttings, clean & return mower to garage by 10:00 a.m. Sunday from May to November. Take the big trash pails from garage to curb_
   by the following time: _dinnertime or 7:00 p.m. Sunday, whichever comes first_

B. Mom will do: _Remind Dad not to lecture Aaron about chores and to give Aaron only one reminder as planned below_
   by the following time: _Friday and Saturday evenings_

C. Dad will do: _Remind Aaron one time Sunday morning of need to do the lawn and one time Sunday afternoon of need to take out garbage. Dad will not lecture on these topics._
   by the following time: _9:00 a.m. and 4:00 p.m._

D. Plan for monitoring whether this happens: _Dad will check on Sunday morning for the lawn. Mom will check on Sunday evening for the garbage. Will write on calendar on refrigerator whether Aaron did each of these chores._

E. Any reminders that will be given. By whom? When? _See above._

F. Consequences for compliance and noncompliance: _Aaron will earn $10 per week of his $20 allowance for doing the lawn. Praise is the positive consequence for doing the garbage. Aaron will lose all television privileges on Sunday night if he fails to do either chore on time, and will still have to do the chores. Dad and Aaron will both thank Mom for doing her part and helping them deal well with each other. Mom will do something nice for Dad if he keeps from lecturing Aaron about these chores. Aaron will say something nice to his dad for not lecturing._

made his parents feel comfortable that they were represented, the guests would be safe, and the house would remain intact). They also agreed that if Tony or his guests gave the uncle any trouble or brought alcohol, the uncle would immediately call the parents' smartphone and, if necessary, contact the police, especially if uninvited guests began to arrive, having heard there was a "party at Tony's place!"

For the James family, compromise wasn't really necessary; they found solutions to which they all gave a "plus." The only thing they had to deal with was that there were three of them. After discussing which made the most sense, they quickly concluded that everyone would be most likely to stick with the agreement if they combined the three solutions into an aggregate contract.

Ranking Issues That Cause Conflict to Establish a List of Problems to Solve

Now that you've had a chance to try problem solving in other people's shoes, let's get back to you and your teen and the issues that are causing conflagrations between you.

1. *Complete the Issues Checklist for Parents and Teens.* Fill out the form on pages 264–265 to record what you and your teenager have talked about *at all* over the last 2 weeks. If there is more than one parent or other adult who serves as an authority figure in your home, each of you, as well as the teen, should fill out the form. (You can make copies before you start.)

Circle Yes or No to indicate whether or not you and your teen have talked about each of the topics on the left. Be sure to do this for all 44 items.

Now look at all the topics for which you circled Yes and answer this question: How hot are the discussions? (Circle the number under the word that represents how hot the discussions were on the average.)

Issues Checklist for Parents and Teens

Go down this column for all pages first.			Then go down these columns for all pages.				
			How hot are the discussions?				
Topic			Calm	A little angry			Angry
1. Cellphone, texting	Yes	No	1	2	3	4	5
2. Time for going to bed	Yes	No	1	2	3	4	5
3. Cleaning up bedroom	Yes	No	1	2	3	4	5
4. Doing homework	Yes	No	1	2	3	4	5
5. Putting away clothes	Yes	No	1	2	3	4	5
6. Using the TV, computer; choice of shows to watch	Yes	No	1	2	3	4	5
7. Cleanliness (washing, showers, brushing teeth)	Yes	No	1	2	3	4	5
8. Which clothes to wear	Yes	No	1	2	3	4	5
9. How neat clothing looks	Yes	No	1	2	3	4	5
10. Making too much noise at home	Yes	No	1	2	3	4	5
11. Table manners	Yes	No	1	2	3	4	5
12. Fighting with brothers or sisters	Yes	No	1	2	3	4	5
13. Cursing	Yes	No	1	2	3	4	5
14. How money is spent	Yes	No	1	2	3	4	5
15. Picking books, downloading iPod songs, choosing video games	Yes	No	1	2	3	4	5
16. Allowance	Yes	No	1	2	3	4	5
17. Going places without parents (shopping, movies, etc.)	Yes	No	1	2	3	4	5
18. Playing music too loudly	Yes	No	1	2	3	4	5
19. Turning off lights in house	Yes	No	1	2	3	4	5

(cont.)

20.	Using drugs	Yes	No	1	2	3	4	5
21.	Taking care of clothes, videos, iPod, computer, and other personal things	Yes	No	1	2	3	4	5
22.	Drinking beer or other liquor	Yes	No	1	2	3	4	5
23.	Buying cellphones, games	Yes	No	1	2	3	4	5
24.	Going on dates	Yes	No	1	2	3	4	5
25.	Who should be friends	Yes	No	1	2	3	4	5
26.	Selecting new clothing	Yes	No	1	2	3	4	5
27.	Being sexually active	Yes	No	1	2	3	4	5
28.	Coming home on time	Yes	No	1	2	3	4	5
29.	Getting to school on time	Yes	No	1	2	3	4	5
30.	Getting low grades in school	Yes	No	1	2	3	4	5
31.	Getting in trouble in school	Yes	No	1	2	3	4	5
32.	Lying	Yes	No	1	2	3	4	5
33.	Helping out around the house	Yes	No	1	2	3	4	5
34.	Talking back to parents	Yes	No	1	2	3	4	5
35.	Getting up in the morning	Yes	No	1	2	3	4	5
36.	Bothering parents when they want to be left alone	Yes	No	1	2	3	4	5
37.	Bothering teenager when he/she wants to be left alone	Yes	No	1	2	3	4	5
38.	Putting feet on furniture	Yes	No	1	2	3	4	5
39.	Messing up the house	Yes	No	1	2	3	4	5
40.	What time to have meals	Yes	No	1	2	3	4	5
41.	How to spend free time	Yes	No	1	2	3	4	5
42.	Smoking	Yes	No	1	2	3	4	5
43.	Earning money away from house	Yes	No	1	2	3	4	5
44.	What teenager eats	Yes	No	1	2	3	4	5

2. *Create a list of issues by how hot the discussions have been.* Once you've done so, create a list that groups the issues by intensity level, from 5 (most angry) to 1 (mild). Obviously you won't all agree on how hot the discussions over each issue are, so note in parentheses following each item which of you (you can put parents together collectively) gave the issue this ranking. Here's a partial example:

> Intensity 5: Most angry
> Fighting with brothers and sisters (parent)
> Talking back to parents (parent)
> Who should be friends (teen)
> Coming home on time (parent)
> Getting to school on time (parent)
> . . .
> Intensity 3: A little angry
> Cursing (teen, parent)
> Helping out around the house (parent)
> Smoking (teen)
> Getting up in the morning (parent)
> . . .

THINK AHEAD

Anticipate a certain amount of resistance from your teen. Even if things have been going more smoothly, most teens have little patience for command performances that resemble being in school, which is how your teen may view family meetings for problem-solving training. It's not necessarily going to be easy, but in a very real sense you're substituting for a therapist here, so you'll have to take the high road and gently correct any uncooperative, inappropriate contributions from your teen, as well as modeling the right way to conduct yourselves. One thing you can do ahead of time is remind each other that the goal isn't to coerce the teen into defining the problem the same way you do (to "see it my way")—and then say this to the teen in no uncertain terms before the session begins. Also come to agreement with your teen's other parent on the criteria for deciding to call a time-out if things get heated.

Intensity 1: Mild (may irritate others)
Turning off lights (teen)
Putting feet on the furniture (parent, teen)
Using the computer (parent, teen)
Cleanliness (parent)
Which clothes to wear (parent, teen)

Save your list; you'll be working on it in the next two steps as well as this one.

Picking One or Two Low-Priority or Low-Intensity Issues to Work On with Problem Solving

1. *Now choose an issue of moderately low intensity to target for problem solving.* Ideally you might pick one that is ranked similarly by both you and the teen, in the category of 1–3. It should be significant to all of you, but not too likely to be incendiary. Let's say you pick time for going to bed. To test out your impression that the issue is low intensity, try this exercise. Close your eyes and imagine that you just discovered your teen was faking going to sleep at 10:00, waiting till you were asleep, and then getting up and playing computer games until 3:00 A.M. On the 1–5 scale, how angry would you be? If your rating is still 3 or less, the issue is mild to moderate in intensity. If your rating is 4 or 5, pick another issue.

2. *Schedule a family meeting to fill out the Problem-Solving Worksheet for this problem and agree on a solution.*

Defining the Problem

Having trouble defining the problem? Try the Problem-Solving Exercise on pages 268–269. You can do this together at a family meeting—especially if you can make it fun—or have everyone fill it out separately and then compare notes at the next meeting. Photocopy the form or download it from *www.guilford.com/ barkley16-forms.*

Problem-Solving Exercise: Defining the Problem

Name: _____   Date: _____

A good definition of the problem explains what it is that the other person is doing or saying that bothers you and why it bothers you. The definition is short, neutral, and does not blame the other person. Below are several definitions. Read each one, then say whether it is good or bad. If it is bad, write down a better definition.

A. **Mother:**   My problem is that I don't like to see your room dirty; all the clothes are on the bed and the dust is 2 inches thick. I'm upset when my friends come to visit and see the room looking that way.

  1. Is this a good definition of a room-cleaning problem?

    ____ Yes   ____ No
  2. If you said "No," write a better definition: _____
    _____
    _____
    _____

B. **Daughter:** I hate you, Mom. You just are a real pain. I'm missing out on all the fun because you make me come home by 9:00 P.M. on weekends.

  1. Is this a good definition of a coming-home-on-time problem?

    ____ Yes   ____ No
  2. If you said "No," write a better definition: _____
    _____
    _____
    _____

C. **Father:** Son, the real problem with you is that you don't respect your elders. Kids just don't know the meaning of respect today. When I was your age I would never talk to my father the way you talk to me.

  1. Is this a good definition of a talking-back problem?

    ____ Yes   ____ No

(cont.)

2. If you said No, write a better definition: _____

_____

_____

_____

D. **Son:** I get angry when you bug me 10 times a day about taking out the trash and feeding the dogs. I'm old enough to do these things without being reminded.

1. Is this a good definition of a chores problem?

____ Yes ____ No

2. If you said No, write a better definition: _____

_____

_____

_____

E. Below, a mother and a daughter define their problem about playing the stereo too loud. Notice how each accuses and blames the other; this is a poor way to define the problem. Read their definitions, then write a better definition for each person.

Mother: You are ruining your ears with that loud stereo. You just don't have good taste in music. How can you stand all that loud noise? I can't, and what's more I *won't* stand for it.

Daughter: Don't talk to me about taste in music. You sit around all day listening to 1940 junk music. No one listens to that stuff anymore. And get off my back about the loud stereo. I'll play it as loud as I like so I can enjoy my music.

Better definitions:

Mother: _____

_____

_____

_____

Daughter: _____

_____

_____

_____

Generating, Evaluating, and Choosing Solutions

Brainstorming solutions doesn't come naturally to all families, especially if you aren't all garrulous and used to free-flowing conversations (the kind that *aren't* arguments). If a mental block keeps the ideas from starting to flow, try keeping the solutions very simple; they don't have to be as complex as some of the ones in the therapist-assisted solutions shown for Scenarios A–C. Ones like these, proposed to solve a chores problem, are fine:

1. Do chores the first time asked
2. Don't have any chores
3. Grounded for 1 month if not done
4. Hire a maid
5. Earn allowance for chores
6. Room cleaned once—by 8 P.M.
7. Parents clean the room

WARNING: *Watch out for solution lists made up of nothing but the same positions that you and your teen started out with.* Remember what we said is the essence of negotiation: The goal is to reach a decision that everyone can live with and with which everyone will have to give up something to get something. If the issue is chores, and all of your teen's solutions are some variation on the "Don't expect me to do them" theme ("Hire a maid," "Let Mom do them," "Let the dust pile up," "Get Billy to do it") and all of yours are of the see-it-my-way variety ("Do the chores when told to," "Lose screen time when you don't do chores as told," "Do the chores as instructed or get more chores to do next time"), no one is showing willingness to compromise, so of course you're at an impasse. If you notice this has happened when trying to pick an idea from the list generated, go back to the brainstorming step and say, "OK, now let's switch viewpoints and list solutions that would work for the other person." This is a good place to inject humor to get things rolling. For example, if you're trying to resolve a curfew issue, you could say, on behalf of your teen, "You could just come and go as you please and never tell us where you're going or when you'll be back and we could just like it or lump it," and then back off to more reasonable solutions that illustrate compromise, while still representing your teen's point of view.

8. Close the door to room
9. Better timing when asking teen
10. One reminder to do chores

Q. *We just can't seem to come up with even six solutions, which keeps leaving us with too few to choose from, and then we can't reach an agreement. What should we do?*

A. Remind yourselves, repeatedly if necessary during brainstorming—this should be something of a mantra for most families—that saying it doesn't mean you have to do it. Both parents and teens can be afraid that if they utter the words of a solution that they're not sold on, it will be taken as some sort of promise to fulfill it. This is usually a trust issue, based on negative expectations of each other. If you think such assumptions are really keeping you stuck, consider going to Step 9 and then returning to this step.

Q. *Our son is so antsy and acts so impatient and aggravated by the whole process that we never get any solutions out of him. What do we do now?*

A. Some teens, especially those who have ADHD, really do have trouble sitting still and concentrating on this process. In that case, try brainstorming on your own and then evaluating your ideas to present two or three possible solutions to your teen to consider.

Q. *We often can't close the gap between our teen's and our favored solutions. Where does this leave us?*

A. If you still can't reach an agreement, reconsider the issue you chose. Maybe it was too high in intensity. Try again in the next day or two with something that's less of a hot button.

3. *Spend the next week trying to implement the solution.* If unsuccessful, look more closely at the solution you picked. Was it unrealistic after all? Maybe you can review the list again and pick another solution if there's another on which you were close to agreement.

Did you not define the problem along its most salient dimension? In Scenario C earlier in this chapter, Bettina and her parents were debating her curfew. But as they tried to implement the chosen solution, it became increasingly clear that the problem for her parents wasn't really the time by which she was required to return home at night; it was her spending most of her time with older teens. They were trying to stay in control of that matter, possibly even hoping secretly that having an earlier curfew would make it harder for her to socialize with these kids, through a restriction on their daughter's time away from home. That this wasn't really the parents' main concern became clear when neither Mom nor Dad could stick to their part of the bargain: Mom did try to sabotage Bettina by not reminding her of the curfew and gave praise only grudgingly, if at all. Dad didn't lecture his daughter about the curfew, but he started finding other things to pick at regarding her social life. When they went back to the drawing board at another family meeting, all this came to light. They realized that they had mixed up two problems that needed to be addressed separately: (1) Bettina's choice of friends and (2) curfew. First, they needed to problem-solve the choice of friends, then they could return to the curfew issue. They reached an agreement that when Bettina met a new, older friend (either boy or girl) with whom she wanted to socialize on weekend nights, her parents would find an unobtrusive way to meet and get to know the new friend—for example, by inviting the friend for dinner or

WARNING: *If there's ADHD in the family, especially in the teen and at least one parent, you'll have to take extra steps to remind one another of what the agreement requires of everyone.* The goal is to empower each other to fulfill this agreement, not to catch each other being noncompliant. So if you or your teen's other parent has ADHD, try to compensate by using timers and personal organizers that give audible reminders, Post-it notes, verbal reminders, and calendars with assignments written on them to give yourselves and your teen the greatest possible chance of succeeding.

to come over and hang out at Bettina's house. Her parents would then discuss with her their level of comfort with her going out at night with this friend. After this solution was implemented, they were able to return to the original curfew solution and implement it effectively. Bettina even volunteered to call her parents while she was out with her friends; her friends knew her parents and could now better understand the situation.

4. *Choose another issue to work on for the second week of this step.* But if you haven't succeeded the first time around or the process was so painful that you dread doing it again, get a therapist's help.

5. *Plan to incorporate problem solving into your daily lives from now on.* First schedule time: Establish a regular family meeting time to review and resolve problem-solving issues. Second, be sure to plan for practice: Can you practice in the car on the way to do regular errands? Early morning? Late evening? At mealtime? Using a private chat room online?

Get used to being principle-centered. Whenever you approach your teen from now on, think "How do I actively involve my teen in this issue, and how do I apply problem solving to it?" Use problem-definition statements whenever something bothers you about a family member's behavior. Start suggesting at least two alternatives when approaching someone about such an issue or prompt each other by asking "What are our choices?" For example, "Megan, I need you to help me with the dishes. We can do it now, or we can find another choice."

This strategy can be especially helpful when an issue comes up spontaneously, needs to be resolved right away, and immediately begins to spark an argument. In Chapter 12, Bruce Noonan and his parents came up with a spontaneous behavior contract when Bruce wanted his curfew extended so that he could go out that night with a girl he'd been pursuing. If they had found that they couldn't arrive at such a contract quickly, the Noonans could have used an abbreviated version of the problem-solving process to arrive at an agreement, whether it involved a behavior contract at the end or not.

Help your teen think this way too, using private cues for engaging in problem-solving behavior. To help Will evaluate ideas before acting on impulse, for example, his mother would say "What would happen if . . . ?" whenever she felt he needed to think before acting.

Plan ahead for problem situations. Don't just wait for "emergencies" to arise to put problem solving into effect. Instead of dreading a predictable problem, approach it with preventive problem solving. This will head off an awful lot of potential arguments between you and your teen.

If your family lifestyle is very hectic and you don't see where you would find time for problem-solving discussions, try to be creative. Family members can discuss a problem and complete a worksheet by e-mail or Skype, touching base in person when they've completed it. In this way, a parent who is away on a business trip could participate in a problem-solving discussion. Using technology will help you work at getting along better.

So will learning to eliminate negative communication patterns from the way you talk to each other during problem-solving sessions and at other times too. That's what we'll address next.

Step 8.
Learning and Practicing
Communication Skills

"He said I don't do the dumb chores when he tries to make me."

That's how 15-year-old Kevin rephrased his father's definition of a chores issue at a recent problem-solving session.

You may be able to guess what happened next. Dad blew up. First he railed against his son for labeling his "fair share of the household responsibilities" dumb. Then he switched to chiding his son for being "ridiculously childish" in describing the important lesson Dad was trying to teach as "making him" do anything.

Kevin seethed throughout his father's tirade and finally exploded himself, yelling "Why should I listen to anything *you* say when you treat *me* like such a kid?!" and then storming out of the house.

End of problem solving.

If this sounds like some of your problem-solving experiences, especially early attempts, this will be an important chapter for you. In fact, you may have decided wisely to do this step in the midst of your problem-solving training before returning to finish Step 7. That's the kind of resourceful flexibility that effective parents tap every day.

But even if you did pretty well with the problem-solving training, hot buttons like the ones Kevin pushed with his father are always lying in wait, ready to be activated. If any of you tend to act impulsively, perhaps due to ADHD or other temperament traits, those buttons are even more likely to get pushed on a regular basis. You have to find ways to steer clear.

You're probably pretty tired of hearing this by now, but there's really no way around it: It's up to you to learn and model the communication skills that will help you fade those hot buttons into the background of your interactions.

What we didn't show you in the little story about Kevin is that this is how his father defined the chores problem when they started the family meeting: "Kevin, you are *so* irresponsible. You *never* take the garbage out or mow the lawn when I ask you."

No wonder his son reacted defensively. That way of stating the problem broke a lot of the rules we laid out in Chapter 14. In this chapter you'll learn more about the negative communication styles that this kind of speaking reflects and how to catch them in your own communication patterns. Fortunately, we'll also show you that there are very straightforward alternatives. You can learn to substitute a different way of talking to your teen that will be much less likely to trigger a defensive response.

Understand, though, that straightforward doesn't mean easy, and certainly not foolproof. Communication is dynamic and reciprocal, a fairly unpredictable two-way street. You can control what *you* say and how you say it, but you can't control what your teen says or precisely how any exchange will unfold. You can only take the high road yourself, hoping that eventually your son or daughter will follow your lead.

And, of course, your teen may tend to express himself the way Kevin did even without provocation. That's the nature of the beast—and of the inherent traits that contribute to the development of defiance. Your teen's negative communication style may be a deeply etched habit by now, and even if it isn't, by nature he may be impulsive, hotheaded, or otherwise prone to shooting from the hip. You can discourage the use of poor communication styles by not feeding into them, but don't expect them to disappear entirely (any more than you should expect yourself never to be testy, have a bad day, get exasperated, or just forget to think before you speak). When your teen does say something that makes you see red, follow these two guidelines; they're the foundation of your work during this step:

1. *Count to 10 or take a hike.* Remember that we all revert to our worst communication habits when we are angry. Your best-laid plans may involve using a measured, dispassionate, nonaccusatory tone and being unflappable in the face of digs and taunts, but such noble intentions quickly turn to ashes when tempers ignite. The key is to cut off the chain of automatic reactions. Many anger management specialists recommend that you disrupt this sequence by learning to mentally shout "*Stop!*" when you feel the first signs of growing anger. This takes practice. Before you can do it you have to train yourself to recognize the physical signs of arousal, such as increased heart rate and flushed face. We've listed a few anger management resources at the back of the book if you're interested in learning more about these techniques. Whether you train yourself this way or not, the goal is to stop for long enough to let the mounting anger subside so you can think clearly about what to do or say next. Count to 10 or, if you find it hard to do that with the defiant teen present, say to your teen "I'll get back to you on this later" and then take a hike, a time-out, or whatever you want to call it: leave the room for a few minutes or however long it takes to calm down. When out of your teen's presence, do whatever calms you down: relaxation techniques, meditation, exercise, or the like. Above all, remember that you are the parent and "sticks and stones can break my bones but words can never hurt me."

2. *Keep a disability perspective and practice forgiveness.* OK, your teen may not have a disability per se, unless she does have ADHD or some other disorder that impairs her functioning. But you can view defiance as a behavioral disability that she has acquired—it certainly has interfered with her functioning and yours—and that may take a while to eradicate (or may never be eliminated entirely). For now she remains somewhat disabled by defiance and should be treated with a certain measure of

empathy and compassion. At the very least you can view the personality characteristics that have contributed to the development of defiance as a limitation that your teen never asked for. Naturally, we're not suggesting that you suddenly relieve your teenager of responsibility for her actions, including the way she speaks to you. What we *are* suggesting is that you avoid focusing on blame and personalizing your teen's problems. Remember that there is often an element of "can't" along with the "won't" in the way your teen behaves toward you. So, yes, tell her in a businesslike manner when the way she's talking to you is really inappropriate—using the terms that you'll learn in this chapter to help her understand *specifically* what she's doing wrong—but severely curtail the number of battles you wage over this issue and keep character assassination out of it. Character assassination is based on negative expectations and beliefs, which we'll address in Step 9. Indulging in character assassination tends to ignite anger in the assassin as well as in the victim. (How often have you found yourself on a righteously indignant roll, building your own ire with every accusation you make?) So taking a disability perspective and practicing forgiveness may be doubly potent, encouraging both you and your teen to exercise respect in the way you speak to each other.

GOALS FOR STEP 8

- Learn general principles of good communication.
- Recognize negative communication styles.
- Integrate a positive communication style into problem-solving sessions and other interactions with your teen.

Before you begin working on the goals for this chapter, remind yourselves of the fact that you're really not starting from scratch here. You already know plenty about good and bad communication styles and have had some practice in what to do and what not to do. In praising your teen you've learned to acknowledge the concrete positives you observe in your teen's attitude and behavior and to express your love and goodwill, always a beneficial foundation for communication. In giving effective commands, you've learned to be very specific, nonblaming, and businesslike when your interactions have a practical goal. And, of course, in problem-solving training you've started to hone your ability to negotiate without triggering arguments or blame-fests and to communicate with the mutual respect accorded by one adult to another. So think of this as Communication Skills 201, not the beginner's course, and call into play all the skills you've already acquired.

Learning General Principles of Good Communication

Like many good rules of thumb, these are easy to understand, harder to follow. Make them second nature by spending the first week of this step on the following actions.

1. *Memorize the following principles and start training yourself to act on them.*

- **Listen when your teen is in the mood to talk, but don't try to force the teen to open up to you.** Boy, is this hard for parents to do with their kids, no matter what the kids' ages! We're dying to know what's going on with our kids and may even feel we have a right to know. Where our teens' safety is concerned, we probably do have this right to a certain extent. That, however, doesn't mean our teens will tell us everything we want to know. Teenagers tend to clam up for days, even weeks, on end, communicating only the most essential, instrumental information, and then only in monosyllables and grunts. (This may be particularly, but not exclusively, true of boys; for more on the communication differences between boys and girls, see the Resources.) Their friends are more likely to be their sounding boards than their parents, as you undoubtedly already know. But this doesn't mean they don't need your empathic support and experienced advice. It just means you need to offer it judiciously, and *always try to remember*

THINK AHEAD

Follow the 10-words-or-fewer rule. This is a corollary of the principle emphasizing listening. In learning behavior management, you learned to stop using long tirades in which you badger and berate your teen to do what you want, replacing them with swift, fair, targeted consequences. But the same principle should be applied in general to communicating with your teen: *Don't lecture or nag; say it in 10 words or fewer, because your teen is tuning you out from the 11th word on.* Teens may hate being lectured more than just about any other parental transgression. It offends their sense of growing self-determination and demeans their feeling of competence. It can also make them avoid you like the proverbial plague. If you indulge in saying too much, stating the obvious, and restating your position (over and over), your teen may fear that you'll take the most innocuous conversation as an opportunity to lecture. It's an easy trap to fall into when we parents feel like our teens aren't hearing us—which is often the case with a defiant teen. Make a big effort to stay out of it. When you're talking to your teen, break your points down into several phrases of 10 words or fewer, asking for a response between phrases. He may very well ask what you were thinking, and he'll appreciate the fact that you waited to hear that he was interested before "going on and on." Or he may not. At least you tried not to lecture. Over time this could make him much more likely to approach you when he wants to talk because he won't feel like you're always in control of when the encounter begins—and when it ends. Remember, a discussion is the opposite of a lecture, and a discussion means you and your teen are communicating with each other.

to listen first. As Steven Covey said in his best-selling book *The 7 Habits of Highly Effective People,* "First seek to understand, then to be understood." This is good advice for all of us.

Your defiant teen may be even more likely than other adolescents to be circumspect with you. Experience has taught him that discussions with you are fraught with peril (here come those negative expectations again; if you feel they're interfering in all your communication with your teen, consider jumping ahead to Chapter 16 or combining your work on Steps 8 and 9 for the next few weeks), so he may not talk to you unless the need is pretty compelling. This is a good reason for you to be alert to the signs that your teen wants to talk—or at least be heard. Different teenagers give different signals that they need to talk and want to open up, so you'll have to get to know the ones favored by your son or daughter. When you spot them, make yourself available. Don't push, but stick around and be patient. It may take your teen a little time to get going.

WARNING: Silence is golden. You might think of this as a corollary to the "Follow the 10-words-or-fewer rule." Not only should you suppress the urge to lecture or nag—or to expound on anything, really—but you should consider just saying nothing at times when you'd ordinarily think your teen should be willing to make pleasant conversation. Maybe you're driving your son to school and think since you're sparing him the bus ride he should be willing to talk with you on the way. Or you believe a proper start to a good day includes pleasant small talk over breakfast—or that the day should be capped by a nice family chat over dinner. These are reasonable expectations ... as long as your teenager is really a 40-year-old in disguise. Fully formed adults usually have more control over their moods and the actions that flow from them than adolescents, and we might reasonably expect a peer to converse at these times. But your teen may not be a morning person or may be making a big mental effort to soothe his nerves over an upcoming test at breakfast. In the car she may be wondering whether the girls who excluded her from their gossip the day before are going to shut her out again. At dinner your teen may be plain old tired and just not interested in what you want to talk about. Cut your son or daughter some slack as long as he or she is not being outwardly rude or defiant and let silence reign. As you know, teens can be moody and irritable. They're also going through so many changes that they need a lot of time to think through a million different aspects of their lives; let them do it. Demanding that they talk almost never pays off and may just make them avoid being around you altogether so they're not forced to speak when they don't want to (or really can't)—which will mean you won't be on hand when the mood to confide in you or ask your advice *does* strike.

• **Use active listening to encourage your teen to express opinions and feelings and make your teen feel understood.** You're already doing this in problem solving, when you repeat back one another's definitions of the problem at hand. But it's just as important when there's no problem to tackle. One of the best ways to encourage a taciturn teen to open up without forcing it is to show actively that you're listening, hearing, and understanding. If your teen starts complaining about those chores you problem-solved, resist the urge to criticize him for whining about a conflict that's already been negotiated and just show you understand what he's saying: "You're saying you hate taking the garbage out because the bags leak and always seem to mess up your gym shoes?" If he answers "Yes," that's what he's saying, respond with "Yeah, that must be a real pain to clean up" or something along those lines. Like the positive attention and praise that felt stilted when you first began to issue them, this technique may feel a little artificial at first, but look for opportunities throughout the day to do active listening in all settings and you just may find your teen much more eager to talk to you about the things you do want to hear as well as those you don't. Note that active listening involves paraphrasing or reflecting back the content or feeling tone of your teen's statement, *without adding any of your own opinions*. Parents often fall prey to the temptation to add something to the reflection, which undoes its effectiveness. Take the following example:

> *Teen:* Why do I have to do algebra anyway? It's totally useless to my future.
>
> *Parent:* So you think algebra won't help you in *whatever* future you do have?

There was a sarcastic implication in the parent's remark that the way this teen is going, including not doing well in algebra, the future looks dismal. An appropriate active listening statement would be "Seems like algebra is a waste of time because it has nothing to do with your future."

- **Honestly express how you feel, good or bad, in language that gets the point across without hurting the teen.** When we get angry or frustrated, looking for something or someone to blame for our discomfort or dissatisfaction is an unfortunate instinctual reaction. It's particularly easy to yield to this instinct when our anger or frustration seems caused by the other person. So Kevin's dad called him irresponsible and exaggerated the frequency with which his son shirked his chores. Naturally, Kevin balked at being demeaned in this way. When he started following this principle, Kevin's father learned to say something more like "I get mad when Mom or I have to take out the garbage or mow the lawn because you don't do your chores when we ask." But again, it's not just in problem-solving meetings that you should apply this principle. Try to use "I" statements anytime you feel aggravated by something your teen does or doesn't do: "I need quiet when I get home from work and am really bothered by your stereo when it's above a certain volume." "Finding clothes and books strewn around the living room when I get home makes me feel like I can't relax after a long day at the office." "Language like that hurts my feelings and makes me feel like you don't respect me or my wishes." "When you're not home by your curfew, I worry about whether you're safe and can't sleep." And don't forget to apply the same rule of thumb to positive statements: "I really appreciate your thinking of me and cleaning up the kitchen so I

WARNING: *If your teen has ADHD, learn to distinguish between truly negative communication and ADHD communication, dealing with the former and ignoring or working around the latter.* Making the distinction will take some practice (and a cool head on your part). If you have a lot of trouble with this problem, you should consider enlisting the aid of a therapist. But it boils down to this: Truly negative communication is intentional, premeditated, proactive, critical, and demeaning, aimed at manipulating and skewering your weaknesses. ADHD communication can hurt just as much but is reactive, spontaneous, impulsive, nonsensical, poorly timed, and rarely efficacious in getting the teen what he wants from you. You may be able to anticipate the latter when your teen's medication is wearing off. Don't take such communication personally; try to divert the conversation or take a hike.

don't have to deal with it." "I feel so proud of you when you work so hard." Even "Hearing you laugh really makes me feel good."

Q. *The only time my daughter seems to want to talk to me is when I'm running out the door to work, on the phone, or in the midst of paying our bills. When I try to talk to her later, she clams up again. How are we ever going to find the right time to talk?*

A. Many teens complain that their parents don't listen when they do want to talk; their parents complain that the kids always pick the worst time to get garrulous. Again, it's all up to you. You may not be able to delay going to work—or can you?—but it's important to stop and take the time to hear your teen out whenever you can. Ask the person on the phone if you can call back; put off paying the bills or ask your spouse (if available) to take over the bill paying while you talk with your daughter. Showing that you're there to listen when your teen needs to talk expresses not only your caring but also your respect. Nonetheless, there's no doubt that it's frustrating to feel like you're on call all the time and that you're always called at the *wrong* time. An antidote may be to set up situations that regularly provide other, more natural settings for the teen to open up. Many teens will open up if they realize Mom or Dad is always around and unoccupied for a few minutes at a predictable time and place—in the kitchen after school, at the breakfast table, over coffee after dinner. These are not opportunities to pump your teen but just to be there, receptive, if she feels like talking. And then there's always the time-honored method of taking advantage of chauffeuring. Some of the most important confidences end up offered in the car, probably because it's socially acceptable for your teen to look out the window in the car where not making eye contact anyplace else would seem rude, and because your eyes are on the road instead of trained on the teen, as if she's on the witness stand.

2. *Introduce the positive communication principles to your teen and practice them in a dialogue where you switch roles.* At one of your family meetings, introduce the principles to your teen. Say that you want to start using them in your interactions with your teen because it's important to you to reach your goals (such as problem solving) and to talk to each other generally in a way that reflects the love and respect you feel for your teen. Make sure your teen understands the principles by giving some of the examples of positive communication provided above. Stimulate discussion, if it seems like a good idea, about these skills by asking what everyone thinks are your family's good communication habits. Then talk about the idea that most conversations have some goal or another and discuss how these principles can facilitate reaching them. This would be a good time to bring in an interaction that didn't go well if you've had one recently, eliciting everyone's comments about how the principles of positive communication could have improved the encounter and permitted goals to be reached.

Now try practicing a dialogue using the principles of positive communication. Since you and your teen's other parent (if there is one) have reviewed the principles before this meeting, you can start out by modeling a positive dialogue. After you model the dialogue, have one parent and the teen do the practice, then the other parent and the teen.

Assign one person to start out as speaker and one as listener. The first speaker's job is to express his feelings and ideas to the listener without blaming, accusing, or criticizing. The listener's job is to pay attention, understand what the speaker is saying, and then paraphrase or repeat it without adding her own opinions.

Pick an innocuous topic to discuss between parents—even a funny one—to keep this exchange light. Here's an example:

Mom: I'm really tired of this car. It's boring. I looked at a red Ferrari the other day, and I really think we should buy it.

Dad: You're tired of the Ford and want something a little racier?

Mom: Yes, I think it's time for a change. I want something fun to drive.

Dad: So, you think a sports car would be more fun than the van?

Mom: Definitely. Let's go look at it now.

Dad: You're pretty eager to make a change in what we drive, I guess.

Mom: Yeah, I'm really excited about this.

Dad: I can see that. I haven't seen a grin that big on your face in a while.

In your model dialogue, be sure that the speaker makes several statements and the listener paraphrases them, then switch roles and do the same thing, like this:

Dad: I do have one question about this idea: Where are we going to fit the five kids?

Mom: Oh, you're worried about how we're going to drive the kids around in a two-seater?

Dad: Yeah, and I don't think we can afford to keep the van *and* buy a Ferrari.

Mom: So you think this purchase might be a little extravagant too?

Dad: Probably. Especially since I hear those Ferraris are always in the shop.

Mom: So then we'd be without transportation altogether?

Dad: Yeah, and little Tina is pretty young to be taking the city bus to preschool.

Mom: So you think the kids' needs have to come first?

Dad: Well, probably . . . or we could buy the Ferrari, take off for Malibu, and let the kids fend for themselves. . . .

Now try it with each parent and the teen.

If you spot places where all of you tend to ignore a particular principle of positive communication, this is a good time to point it out, but avoid the urge to zero in on any one family member's communication "flaws," especially the teen's. If you or your teen's other parent is willing and able to identify your own slips, on the other hand, go ahead and point them out to model the self-assessment and monitoring that you want all of you to start doing to become more aware of your own communication patterns. Some parents find that they are more likely to have a successful problem-solving discussion that stays positive if they discuss a problem in a public setting, such as over coffee or hot chocolate at Starbucks or at a favorite fast-food restaurant. The presence of other people often prompts people to stay more positive even if they are bothered by what someone in the family has said. So think about trying to have your first few positive communication practice sessions out somewhere public. Others have found that a good initial way to motivate adolescents to practice communication is for the parent and teenager to text each other from separate rooms in the house; this slows down the communication process and causes them to think before responding.

3. *Agree to keep track of and reward yourselves for your use of positive communication principles over the next week.* Don't turn this into a complicated contest, but agree that someone in each exchange (between parents as well as between a parent and the teen) will try when it's over to ask, "Did we use positive communication here?" If the two of you agree that you did, award yourselves a point. For an agreed-on total number of points after the week (say 15), give yourselves a reward you've designated at the beginning of the week (such as having pizza from your favorite pizzeria delivered on Friday night, renting a favorite movie, getting a favorite and somewhat expensive bottle of wine, or a manicure/pedicure).

Consider giving yourselves credit not just for adhering to the principles above but also for the following actions:

- Stating the other's opinion
- Making suggestions
- Asking what the other would like or wants
- Praising, complimenting
- Joking (good-naturedly)
- Listening
- Compromising

Recognizing Negative Communication Styles

It's not hard to spot most kinds of negative communication: accusations, denials, threats, commands, excessive interruptions, sarcasm, poor eye contact, and a host of other habits impede effective expression of feelings and listening to others. Family members can get so enraged by negative communication that you all get sidetracked from problem solving and stuck in reciprocally negative communication loops: "No, I didn't." "Yes, you did." Ad nauseam. As you know by now, this kind of poisonous behavior can infect even the most mundane of encounters ("What's for breakfast?" "Why should *I* get *your* breakfast?!") in addition to more formal negotiations.

Sometimes the only way to eliminate these entrenched ways of talking to each other is to look closely at the negative components that make up the pattern.

1. *Review our list of negative communication habits with your teen and identify those that apply to your family, then agree to spend a few days at the beginning of the second week of this step monitoring your own and one another's negatives.* At a family meeting at the beginning of the week, introduce the Negative Communication Habits list below, talking about them as much as necessary to be sure everyone understands what these behaviors look like. Keeping the mood light, pinpoint which of these bad habits the family exhibits (keep this nonaccusatory by not naming names but saying "We" as much as possible) and how it impacts family relations.

Have a copy of the list for everyone (photocopy the form or download it from *www.guilford.com/barkley16-forms*), and keep one posted on the refrigerator, bulletin board, or someplace else where everyone will see it often. To increase your awareness of negative communication, agree with your teen that for the next 4 days, anyone who notices a negative communication occurring can point it out in a neutral way, without any repercussions. Family members can comment about their own statement or another family member's statement. For example, "That's a lecture," "That's a defensive comment," "I just was accusing," "You're bringing up the past," "I'm not making eye contact," and the like. Family members are not yet required to change their communication, just to listen to one another's feedback. Some families may prefer to check off in writing on our list which of the negative communication habits they caught themselves using. Either the verbal or written approach will work; do what fits your own style best. And if your teen balks at participating, say that you (and the teen's other parent, if there is one) are going to monitor yourself anyway because you're convinced that this will improve

Negative Communication Habits

Name: _____

	Day 1	Day 2	Day 3	Day 4
Insults				
Interrupts				
Criticizes				
Gets defensive				
Lectures				
Looks away				
Slouches				
Uses sarcasm				
Goes silent				
Denies				
Commands, orders				
Yells				
Swears				
Throws a tantrum				
Nags				
Dredges up the past				

family communication. Your teen may jump into the exercise after seeing you monitoring yourselves for a few days. But if he doesn't and you really want him involved, consider offering an incentive, à la behavior contracts.

2. *Now consider the positive alternatives.* If you kept a written record, at the end of the 4 days (you can use a different number of days if more or fewer seems likely to work better for your family), take a look at your form and simply make a mental note of which habits seem to crop up most often. If you and your teen gave each other verbal feedback about negative communication habits, try to recall which ones cropped up most often. Now look at the alternatives on the list below and consider how you could adopt those instead.

Alternatives to Negative Communication Habits

Negative	Positive
Insults	States the issue
Interrupts	Takes turns
Criticizes	Notes good and bad
Gets defensive	Calmly disagrees
Lectures	Keeps it short and straight
Looks away	Makes eye contact
Slouches	Sits up straight
Uses sarcasm	Talks in normal tone
Goes silent	Says what he/she feels
Denies	Accepts responsibility
Commands, orders	Asks nicely
Yells	Uses normal tone of voice
Swears	Uses emphatic but respectful language
Throws a tantrum/loses temper	Cools it, counts to 10, takes a hike
Nags	Asks once or twice
Dredges up the past	Focuses on the present

Together with your teen or spouse or partner, pick one interaction from the last week where your goals were thwarted by poor communication habits. Identify the negative habits that took hold. Discuss them, talking over the positive communication habits you could have used in place of the negative ones. Make a commitment to try to work on implementing these positive communication habits over the next week. If you prefer, rewrite the negative encounter, substituting the positive communication habits you could have used in place of the negative. If you have time, write out the full dialogue, as in a script. Now reread your new script and ask yourself whether it led to the goal you originally set. If not, try revising it until it does. Or reexamine the goal; maybe it was one you couldn't realistically expect to achieve in a single interaction or under those particular circumstances. If that seems likely, what would you do differently next time? Break the goal down into individual objectives and tackle them one at a time? Wait until a different time or place to broach the subject? Now take one last review of the whole scenario and ask yourself whether you could picture yourself putting it into effect. Is it realistic? If it's overly ambitious or unrealistic in any way, see if you can extract a couple of lessons that *are* realistic that you can apply to future encounters.

Integrating Positive Communication Styles into Problem-Solving Sessions and Daily Interactions

Here's the payoff: applying what you've learned about positive and negative communication patterns to real interactions with your teen. Naturally this will be an ongoing process and what you'll do during this week is just a start. The structured problem-solving sessions offer a good place to test your new communication methods; then you can try to incorporate positives into spontaneous interactions. First, try the following little test:

1. *See how well you can identify positive and negative communication habits.* Together with your teen, review the underlined

statements below. Just read the statements aloud and then ask everyone to identify which negative communication habit they illustrate. Finally, see if you can all suggest a more positive way to make the statement. The negative communication habits and a positive alternative statement follow each underlined statement, but don't read those aloud until you're all finished trying this on your own.

Mother: "Your room is a pigsty." This mother is making an accusatory, critical remark. It would be better to say, "I'm very upset with the mess in your room."

Teen: "You're always telling me 'You don't respect your parents.' I can't stand that stupid talk." This teen is sarcastically criticizing his parents in an exaggerated fashion. It would be better to say, "I don't like it when I'm falsely accused of being disrespectful."

Dad: "We've discussed your delinquent friends a hundred times. I've told you not to hang out with that crowd. They're a bad influence on you. You'll end up dropping out of school and going to jail." This is a putdown and a lecture. It would be better to say, "I'm concerned that your friends might have a bad influence on you."

Dad: "It's been 3 years now that you've failed to do your chores. Today it was your room, last month the lawn, last year the trash—it's always something." This father is dredging up the past. It would be better to stick to the present: "I'm disappointed that the chores are not done on time."

Teen: "Some dad you are! You don't understand me." This teen is putting down his father. It would be better to say, "I don't feel that you understand what I'm saying; let me explain this again."

Teen: "I didn't do it; John left the dishes out." This teen is denying responsibility. It would be better to say, "I honestly am not sure if I left the dishes out, but I'll put them away."

2. *Conduct a regular problem-solving session, paying attention to communication habits and how they do or don't help you reach your goal of compromise.* At this point you should be equipped to spot various communication habits that interfere with the negotiating process. The trick will be to bring them to the surface without turning the session into an argument over who said what in what way, diverting yourselves from the problem at hand and creating another one to boot. Don't hesitate to use the "Count to 10 or take a hike" strategy if communication gets heated and you can't think of a nonconfrontational way to get the person who is communicating inappropriately to change tack. But first try simply holding your ground and modeling the appropriate alternative. If your teen yells, speak in your normal tone of voice (don't lower your voice to a whisper, which will only seem condescending). If your partner becomes bitterly sarcastic, interject some benign, good-natured humor. If someone makes a demand in a bullying tone, in return make your own request, very nicely. When someone makes an insulting accusation, try rephrasing it to state the issue impartially, as if the person had expressed it that way to begin with. When one person repeatedly interrupts, keep asking the other person in the room if he or she would like to say something. Doggedly make eye contact, sit up straight, and use all your body language to express respect, no matter how disrespectful others act. Remember, take the high road and your teen may follow.

3. *Take your new positive communication habits into your everyday interactions.* You'll get the hang of this, especially if you start with yourselves (not with monitoring and correcting your teen) and concentrate at first on the innocuous exchanges of mundane life. Low-stakes subjects, where there's really no negotiation to do, afford you the luxury of focusing on how you put your requests and comments. Make a point of spotting and avoiding sarcasm, harshness, putdowns, and other negatives—even of the least aggressive kind—in the way you talk to your partner, especially within earshot of your teen. Quickly apologize when you slip into old bad habits. It may seem artificial, even quaint, at first, but the goodwill that accrues from respectful, empathic communication styles will feel so beneficial that you'll find yourselves channeling the concepts into your own language before long.

Q. *All this communication stuff is well and good, but my teen goes into tirades of profanity that just go on and on. He uses more four-letter words in a minute than you would hear in a week in a bar. What should I do about this?*

A. Communication training is not what you need first. Your teen is violating a basic rule for living in a civilized household: Treat others with respect. Remember your nonnegotiable rules. You need to come up with consequences to enforce the nonnegotiable rule "No profanity." Treat each burst of profanity as one episode, even if it goes on for several minutes, and administer a consequence for the episode. Consequences will vary from teen to teen but typically involve grounding or loss of significant privileges such as electronics for a young teen and driving for an older teen. After putting the consequences into effect, you've laid the groundwork for communication training. Invite your teen to earn positive incentives by participating in practice sessions where he role-plays the use of appropriate language to express his extreme anger. You might also problem-solve with your teen other ways such as physical exercise that he can release his anger when he feels the urge to use profanity. If you try these suggestions and they fail, consult a therapist.

Coping with Communication Problems: One Family's Experience

In 14-year-old Lauren's family, weeks sometimes went by with no mother–daughter communication in between hostile silence and bitter barbs. Lauren's father, Mac, had grown weary of playing interpreter at some times and peacemaker at others and dove enthusiastically into working on communication skills.

Maybe too enthusiastically; during the second week of this step, Mac got so involved in pointing out his wife's and daughter's slips into negative communication habits that at one point Lauren reeled around and said, "Dad, stop following me around just to catch me saying something wrong! I *get* it!" Mac was shocked. The family had gotten so dependent on his mediation that he assumed his "impartial" comments would be helpful. He backed off, vowing to himself to pick his communication battles more judiciously.

Meanwhile, Lauren and Jan worked especially on active listening and nonaccusatory expressions of their feelings. At first Jan found herself invoking the "Count to 10 or take a hike" rule so often that she wondered if she and her daughter would ever finish a conversation. She just hadn't realized how vulnerable to escalation even their briefest talks had become, about seemingly benign topics like the fact that it was time to get in the car to go to school. Of course those subjects took on a tone that wasn't so innocuous when the exchange started with "Will you *please* get going so you don't make us late *again*?!" from Jan or "Come *on*, Mom! You're *so* slow that I'm standing here waiting for *you*" from Lauren.

When Mac was on hand to point out that Jan's tone was accusing and critical of a "crime" her daughter hadn't yet committed, or that Lauren was being quite sarcastic, even switching their attention to Mac gave the two enough breathing room to calm down. They weren't always able to laugh off their transgressions, but the truce they had called often lasted all the way to school.

Over the week, a pattern began to emerge. Jan started to notice her tendency to go on the defensive when her daughter either glared at her and stalked off or launched a character attack as a diversionary tactic to avoid doing something her mother wanted. First she simply noticed mentally that she was blaming and being overly critical. Then she started noting it out loud— "I just criticized you really harshly"—and rephrasing what she wanted to say in a direct, nonaccusatory way or stating her feeling about Lauren's reaction: "I get very frustrated when you just ignore me as if what I say doesn't matter."

Toward the end of the week, Jan was shocked when Lauren bit off a sarcastic retort and said, "Wow, that was pretty sarcastic" with a sheepish laugh and said, "What I meant was. . . ." The next morning, when Mac started to issue a correction after hovering over them in the kitchen, they both looked up quickly, said "OK, we get it!" and grinned at each other.

When it came time for the family's weekend meeting, Mac started by defining the problem at hand: "Mom and I have tried to give you plenty of phone time, but we think you're starting to abuse the privilege. You're texting constantly, and you're putting off chores and homework because of it. I'm not even sure you're ever getting the homework done since lots of times you're still texting when I go to bed. And you're also really disrespectful when I remind you that you have other things to do. Having the door slammed in my face is just *not* acceptable, and I—"

"Dad, remember the 10-word rule!"

"Yes, Mac," Jan interrupted. "Stop lecturing. I think we need to simplify this—"

"Yeah, Dad, you don't need to go on and on and *on*."

"Lauren, your reminder about the 10-word rule was enough. Please let me finish," Jan said, turning to her daughter and husband. "I think we need to pick one problem with the phone and try to resolve that. Mac, I would appreciate it if you could briefly define the cellphone problem."

Mac: "I'm upset you're texting, not doing chores or homework—nine words, how's that?"

Jan and Lauren together: "Wow!"

Jan and Mac agreed that their top priority was to find a way to ensure that Lauren's phone use didn't interfere with the tasks she needed to get done that day. At first Lauren defined the problem this way: "You just want me to stop texting so you can nag me about my math and cleaning my room and finishing the dishes, and all the other millions of jobs you have for me every night."

Jan interjected with "Now listen, young lady," leaning in close to stare her daughter down.

"I *am* listening," Lauren snapped. "How could I *not* listen? Dad never *stops* talking, and you just keep yelling at me!"

"Lauren, you are supposed to start talking to us like you're an adult, *so keep your voice down!*" commanded Mom.

"*Fine*," Lauren said and turned away from her mother.

"Lauren," said Mac in a conciliatory tone, "please define this problem in your own words, and try to say it calmly."

Lauren, her arms crossed over her chest, refused to look at either of her parents. Jan, lips clamped tightly together, picked up a magazine and began flipping through it angrily. Mac sighed.

"Can we please start over?" Mac pleaded. "Look at you two. Even when you're not saying a thing, you're fighting. I found this article," he said, reaching for the photocopied pages sitting on the table next to him, "and it says—"

Lauren glanced up to see her mother's shoulders shaking silently.

Laughing quietly, Jan looked at her husband with affection as he went on to explain that somewhere between 60 and 90% of all communication is thought to be nonverbal.

It turned out to be a long meeting. The three found themselves having to start over a few more times, when either mother or daughter blurted out some incendiary comment, a fight began, and then both clammed up, having to be coaxed out of silence by Dad. But ultimately it was fruitful. At one point Lauren came to her father's defense when Jan's good-natured jabs at her husband's talkativeness took on a sharper edge: "Mom, Dad's just trying to help. That was pretty critical." Jan cut off the retort that came to her lips and suggested they try to list the family's communication strengths—and after that their weaknesses.

They all agreed that Mac was often good at dispassionate expression and always there to listen. Jan had become skilled at active listening, especially after taking necessary time-outs when she felt her anger rising, and could quickly lighten up a heated discussion with humor. Lauren had started to use a lot more "I" statements than "you" statements with her mother and had her mother's wit.

Once they agreed on these strengths, the missing positives were pretty obvious, and they were each able to list their own weaknesses. Mac agreed he had to pay a lot more attention to the "10 words or less" rule and to monitor himself assiduously for lecturing, as well as to stop pushing everyone to talk about everything all the time. Jan decided she needed to watch her tendency to turn requests into criticisms and pay more attention to her tone of voice. Lauren agreed to try to make her "I" statements about her feelings less strident and more matter-of-fact and to stop locking her mother out with sullen silence: "But only if you'll try to *listen* to me, Mom."

Jan's surprise at that comment put her on the defensive, but after taking a deep breath she said, a little tersely, "You feel I don't listen to you?" Lauren replied, "Yeah, sometimes I come home from school and want to talk to you about something, and you just have this long list of chores for me." It was a sobering moment for Jan. Privately she resolved to invite her daughter to talk when she got home before giving her any "assignments" and to just be quiet at other times when they were alone together and watch for signals that her daughter might want to talk.

All three felt good about what they had accomplished, in goodwill alone, so they made sure to incorporate the intent to keep polishing their communication skills into the solution they arrived at about the phone.

After taking time for a quick "How was your day?" conversation when Lauren got home from school, Jan would ask Lauren what homework she had, and the two would review how much time it seemed likely to take. Lauren would then ask Jan what help she needed around the house. The two would negotiate when everything would be done—the homework might have to get done first, but maybe chores could wait till later in the evening, after Lauren had had an hour's phone time. Each day Jan would tell Lauren how much time she could have on the phone and when, and her daughter would have to stick to that. But, before setting the time, Jan was to ask whether there was anything special or urgent she needed to talk to her friends about. Lauren could say she really needed to talk to so-and-so right away, and Jan would invite her but not press her to explain and then allow her to negotiate to have part of her phone time earlier.

When she started texting, Lauren would tell her dad she was getting on the phone, he would set a timer, and then she would tell him when she was off. If she was still using her smartphone after the timer went off, he would wait 5 minutes and then remind her to get off. If she asked for just a little longer, he would grant her another 5 minutes *if* in his judgment she had asked appropriately, but then she had to be off. If she violated this rule, she would lose phone time the next day.

The solution wasn't foolproof. Mac caved at first and kept letting Lauren extend her phone time in a string of 5-minute increments. This angered Jan, and the two bickered about it while Lauren chatted away and postponed her responsibilities. Jan then tried to clamp down and cut her daughter's phone time way back, which led to a brief screaming match from which the two were able to pull back long enough to begin to talk civilly. This led to a candid conversation in which Jan learned that Lauren felt her mother (and even her father—though he was more indulgent, he was still, well, paternal) never asked her why phone time was important to her, didn't let her participate in decisions about how she spent her own time, and showed little empathy for the trials and tribulations of her social life. It was going to take time, but gradually Lauren and Jan were finding that middle ground between hostile silence and bitter barbs.

You and your teen can do the same.

Step 9.
Dealing with Unreasonable Beliefs and Expectations

"Sticks and stones can break my bones, but words can never hurt me."

How many times did you say this to your child when she was younger and came running to you upset about what another child had said about her? Now it's time to heed your own advice. By the end of this step, this famous proverb will become your mantra for dealing with your beliefs, expectations, and attributions about your teen's behavior.

We parents so often interpret our teen's words in extreme ways. Our interpretations then rile us up to the point of losing control and acting rashly. We act on emotion, not reason. Yet effective use of the skills you've been learning in this program requires acting on reason, not emotion. This can be quite a challenge, as even the simplest interaction can demonstrate:

Mrs. Raphael: Hilary, clean your room.

Hilary: You can't make me. I'm out of here.

Mrs. Raphael: You're grounded, young lady!

What might Mrs. Raphael have been thinking when Hilary defied her? Quite possibly her thoughts might have gone like this: "This terribly disobedient child! She should clean her room when I tell her to. And she should never talk to me like this. I never would have talked to *my* mother that way! She isn't going to amount to anything when she grows up if she keeps this up." And how might Mrs. Raphael feel as a result of having these thoughts? Probably very angry and frustrated. How easily might she handle the situation with calm and objectivity? Not very easily. The point is that her negative thoughts about her daughter's defiance elicited anger, which made it hard to objectively use the skills learned in this program.

What might Hilary have been thinking when her mother asked her to clean her room? Quite possibly something like this: "There she goes again, loading on the chores. If I clean my room, she'll have 10 more chores for me to do and I'll never get to the party with my friends. My mom's so unfair! She always ruins everything for me!" How is Hilary likely to feel? Very angry. And she's likely to storm out of the room and try to escape. As with her mother, Hilary's extremely negative interpretations of her mother's request make her feel furious, impeding rational resolution of the problem.

Over time, as Hilary and her mother have thousands of such interchanges, they each start to form extremely negative and distorted beliefs and expectations about each other and their relationship. Eventually, even what seem like extremely minor comments trigger those negative beliefs, which lead in turn to highly charged reactions and fuel conflict and arguments. This mother and daughter illustrated the cognitive component of our model of parent–teen conflict. It's our *interpretations of events* in our interactions with our teens, as much as the *events themselves*, that fuel our extreme thoughts and emotions, preventing use of rational skills for resolving problems.

Event → Extreme Thought → Anger → Conflict

We let the words rather than the sticks and stones break our bones.

The purpose of this step is to help you examine extreme beliefs and expectations that often operate under the surface of parent–teen (and other) relationships, pulling the strings of our communication and behavior in ways that make it hard to make enduring change.

GOALS FOR STEP 9

- Try to identify the negative beliefs and expectations that you and your teen hold.

- Collect evidence for and against a closely held unreasonable belief to see if you can replace it with a more reasonable alternative.
- Incorporate more reasonable, realistic, positive beliefs and expectations into your communication and problem solving with your teen.

Unreasonable beliefs and expectations can make fruitful communication and negotiation impossible. If you firmly believe that your daughter will start an argument anytime you two disagree, you're not likely to get anywhere in problem solving. If you expect your son to behave exactly the way he did at the age of 9, you're going to be at loggerheads every single day. Fifteen-year-olds who think they have the right to make all their own decisions are going to have a hard time meeting you halfway on the negotiables.

The trouble is, it's hard to get these irrational ideas to loosen their tenacious grip because we're often not conscious of the role they play in the choices we make regarding our teenagers. That's why it's important to take a systematic approach. The process laid out in this chapter is based on *cognitive restructuring,* a process found to be very effective in cognitive-behavioral therapy, a contemporary form of psychotherapy whose effectiveness is backed up by a wealth of research data. In cognitive restructuring you test the validity of unreasonable beliefs (what psychologists call *cognitive distortions*) and then replace any that prove unsound with ones that are more reasonable, the same way you'd rebuild a crumbling chimney by replacing its weak bricks. The steps look like this:

1. Identify the extreme thought.
2. Provide a logical challenge to the extreme thought.
3. Identify an alternative and more realistic thought.
4. Collect evidence to disconfirm the extreme thought and confirm the more reasonable thought.

Since we'd all like to think we're pretty rational, at least most of the time, admitting to having irrational beliefs can be a bitter pill. This series of steps makes us act like scientists, putting a little distance between us and the object of the "experiment," our deep-seated attitudes.

Identifying Your Negative Beliefs and Expectations

Close your eyes and imagine you're opening the mail. You find a progress report from your teen's school. The report says he's failing English and math and has 15 late assignments in history. Suddenly you can feel your blood begin to boil and the tension mount throughout your body. Your son lied to you again! He said he was up to date on homework and passing all his courses. This is one more example of irresponsible behavior. He is *always* irresponsible. You told him to keep an assignment book and get help from the teachers. He *never* does what he's told. He is *so* disobedient. If he keeps on going this way, he's going to fail. He will never graduate, never go to college, never get a good job. You'll be supporting him until the day you die. And the thought of confronting him is not appealing at all. He'll deny everything at first, then blame it all on the teachers, showing you total disrespect.

He's just doing all of this to make you mad and upset. He has no consideration for your feelings.

Now open your eyes. How do you feel? What are you thinking?

Most people would feel full of anger and indignation in this situation. Their heads would usually be filled with resentful accusations.

Now think about this: How would you react if your son walked through the door at this very moment?

Yell? Scream? Instantly ground him (for life)? Shun him? Take away every privilege he has? Threaten? Get in his face and demand an explanation?

You'd almost have to be superhuman not to have some of those reactions.

Unless, that is, you could stop yourself from the kinds of extreme thinking that we saw triggered in that imaginary letter-reading incident and in the simple exchange between Hilary and her mother—which is the goal of this step.

Extreme thinking evokes extreme emotions, which makes it hard to deal with your teen rationally. Negative expectations and beliefs can either eat away at your goodwill toward your teenager or ambush you like a marauding platoon. You need to protect yourself from them.

There are two ways to do this:

- Examine them now, during the next 2 weeks, and do everything in your power to replace irrational beliefs with more rational ones, while at least becoming aware that the negative beliefs you can't seem to get rid of entirely are waiting to rear their ugly heads.
- Be prepared with a crisis plan for those occasions when these beliefs come roaring back to life to wreak havoc in your interactions with your teen. We'll help you develop such a plan in the final step of this program.

1. *Start by resolving not to personalize your teen's problem behavior.* That means simply don't always take everything your teen does as being personal, as if your teen is intentionally out to anger you. Remember, a certain amount of conflict between parents and teens, especially younger teens, is inevitable and even healthy. Review Chapter 3 if you need a reminder that all kinds of seemingly malicious behavior is just pretty normal developmentally. In fact, one of the authors (Barkley) conducted a longitudinal study in which he followed several hundred children to the ages of 24–32 years, taking measures of their behavior and family interactions throughout adolescence. He found that when the parents reported oppositional behavior in their teenagers—defiance, argumentativeness, and resistance toward the parents—without antisocial or delinquent behavior, these teens were more likely to graduate from high school, to receive further education, and to use drugs less than teens who were not oppositional in these comparatively benign ways. This essentially says that a little defiance and arguing, challenging, or debating by teens who are otherwise not delinquent or antisocial is healthy and positively associated with several good outcomes.

If, despite such compelling evidence that a little benign oppositionality is a good thing, you're still expecting Utopia at home, imagine a nation establishing its independence, going from a dictatorship to a democracy. What often happens? There may be a bloody revolution; at the very least, there's a lot of verbal rhetoric and power plays. Why should you expect your family to make it through the independence seeking of your adolescent without a disturbance of the peace?

You've acquired a lot of behavior management strategies for keeping the independence seeking of your teen largely constructive throughout his or her maturation, but don't expect an uninterrupted peace. We worry more about adolescents who never do anything rebellious than about those who do rebel.

While you're taking development into account, also consider any limitations your teenager has (see Chapter 4). If your teen has ADHD, bipolar disorder, another diagnosis, or personality characteristics that you know affect his or her capacity to behave appropriately or to achieve, be sure your expectations don't exceed your teen's capabilities—a sure recipe for blame from you, resentment from your teen, and conflict between you.

Remember Gina, the 13-year-old with ADHD introduced at the beginning of this book? Gina's parents were completely thrown by her recent refusal to take the medications that had been helpful to her in the past. Weren't teens supposed to *mature* as they got older, not *regress*? Gina's parents—and you too, if your teen has ADHD—need to keep in mind that ADHD is a *developmental* disorder; teens with ADHD lag in maturity 3–5 years behind their peers without ADHD. So expecting age-appropriate behavior from a teen with ADHD flies in the face of biology. Also, because teens need to act as if they are infallible, they often can't admit to having a disorder or disability and may reject ADHD and its treatment. This problem needs to be tackled via open, mutually respectful problem solving, not by laying down the law—which is sure to be broken. Gina's parents gave some thought to extra privileges—some extra allowance, more time with friends, and the like—that they could offer in exchange for Gina's accepting her medication more calmly, and then took the options to their daughter for her to choose an incentive, which they then incorporated into a very effective behavior contract.

At the same time, Gina's parents had started fading out their reward system for motivating Gina to do her homework, thinking that they no longer needed these incentives to urge Gina to remember to bring her books home, to hand in her completed homework, and to study for tests. When she didn't, they started imposing punishments. And the war was on.

Gina's parents forgot the cardinal rule of positives first. They never should have returned to punishments without trying to reinstitute rewards first. But they're also forgetting that Gina has a disorder that places limits on what she can accomplish and internalize. This is not to say that they should lower the academic bar for their daughter. She's bright and capable of achieving, but coming down hard on her for occasionally forgetting a book, failing to turn homework in to the teacher, or not being able to concentrate long enough to study after finishing regular assignments is acting on unreasonable expectations and will feed defiance.

For teens who have any kind of limitation or disability, we encourage parents to memorize and repeat this mantra to themselves with great regularity: *We will encourage our teen to go for the stars, to do her best, but we will accept that it is not a catastrophe when she fails to achieve perfection, and it doesn't mean that she is headed for certain ruination or that she is purposely trying to anger us.*

In fact, this is not a bad motto to adopt for *any* teen.

Q. *I can't believe I've raised such an insensitive kid. I think John is just trying to hurt me. How can he behave the way he does?*

A. Is your son really insensitive? Do you have evidence that he's purposely trying to hurt you? Is that the only reason he could possibly have for doing what he does? Could it be that there is a delay in his development of the cognitive ability to take another's perspective, which is central to empathy? We'll help you look more closely at these questions further along in this chapter. For now, though, consider the possibility that John really does want to please you but just doesn't know how to do it. We're not asking you to believe that right now; just consider it. And remember that sometimes what looks like a "won't" from a teen is really a "can't."

2. *Identify which unreasonable beliefs you hold with regard to your teenager.* As mentioned in Chapter 6, both parents and teenagers are prone to unreasonable beliefs. In fact, we've noticed that parents typically fall prey to one set of irrational beliefs and expectations and adolescents another.

Distorted, extreme beliefs often held by parents fall into these categories:

Ruination: Giving teens too much freedom will end in disaster.

Perfectionism: Teens should behave flawlessly all the time.

Malicious intent: Teens misbehave intentionally to anger parents or get even.

Blind obedience: Teens should do everything parents tell them to do.

Constant appreciation: Teens should express gratitude for everything their parents do for them.

Distorted, extreme beliefs often held by teenagers fall into these categories:

Ruination: Parental restrictions on freedom will ruin teens' lives.

Unfairness: Restrictions from parents are unfair, especially any that are more stringent than those imposed on peers or siblings or what parents require of themselves.

Autonomy: Teens should have as much freedom as they want and can handle it effectively.

Blind obedience: Parents should do whatever teens ask of them—that's what they're for, isn't it?

Constant appreciation: Parents should be openly grateful for every crumb of compliance that teens manifest or any work they do around the home—and if they really loved their children, they'd give their teens more freedom.

All parents and teens believe these things to some degree, but it's blind, rigid adherence in the face of clearly conflicting evidence that impedes effective problem solving and conflict resolution. *Research has found that families with oppositional teens adhere to these beliefs more than other families.*

So, at the beginning of the 2 weeks you'll spend on this step, review the chart on pages 309–312 and see if you can identify any beliefs and expectations you hold, particularly in the categories of ruination, perfectionism, and malicious intent. These are just examples within the categories we've listed; you can probably identify others you subscribe to (e.g., under "Driving," maybe you believe your teen should always leave the family car washed and the gas tank full). Check off any unreasonable beliefs you think you hold.

Typical Unreasonable Beliefs
and Expectations Held by Parents

Unreasonable beliefs	Reasonable beliefs
☐ **I. Perfectionism/obedience:** Teens with ADHD should behave perfectly and obey their parents all the time without question.	It's unrealistic to expect any teen to behave perfectly or to obey all the time; we strive for high standards but accept imperfections and remember the teen's need to strive for independence from parents.

☐ *A. School*

☐ 1. He should always complete homework on time.	1. I'll encourage him to complete homework all the time but recognize this won't always happen.
☐ 2. She should study for 2 hours every night, even when she has no homework.	2. Many teens need a break from their numerous obligations today and can be encouraged to study but should not be expected to put in this much time every night.
☐ 3. He should always get A's and B's.	3. If my teen has always been a good student, maybe this is reasonable to expect *most* of the time. But I need to make sure I know what the teen really is capable of.
☐ 4. She should do papers for the love of learning.	4. Many teens still need salient external reinforcers to stick to the work they need to do in high school. They're maturing, but not yet adults.

☐ *B. Driving*

☐ 1. She should never get any speeding tickets.	1. Many teens get a speeding ticket. They should be responsible for paying it and accept any legal consequences (such as suspension of license).

(cont.)

☐ 2. Teens shouldn't adjust the radio, change CDs, or talk or text on their cellphone while driving.

2. Teens should understand the risks of being distracted while driving, but most will indulge sometimes. I could make it my teen's responsibility to pay for hands-free equipment.

☐ 3. She will always stop completely for stop signs.

3. I should always stop completely at stop signs to model good behavior when my teen is in my car and only expect my teen to do as well as I do.

☐ *C. Conduct*

☐ 1. He should never treat us disrespectfully.

1. Teens can't become their own person without some rebellion. Some back talk is natural. He shouldn't curse or ridicule severely, and he might be expected to apologize occasionally.

☐ 2. She will impress all the relatives with her love for family gatherings.

2. I'll give her space. Teens just don't want to be with their families that much. This is normal. She should attend some family functions, but that is all I can reasonably expect.

☐ 3. He should get out of a bad mood when we tell him to change his attitude.

3. Teenagers are moody and can't always help it. He should let us know when he is in a bad mood and keep to himself. We should not make a lot of demands on him at such times.

☐ *D. Chores*

☐ 1. She should put away the dishes the first time I ask.

1. It won't always happen the first time, but after several reminders I should act, not yak (e.g., apply consequences).

☐ 2. He should always get his room spotless.

2. He should get it generally neat. "Spotless" isn't realistic.

(cont.)

☐ **II. Ruination:** If I give my teen too much freedom, he/she will mess up, make bad judgments, get in big trouble, and ruin his/her life.

He/she will sometimes mess up with too much freedom, but this is how teenagers learn responsibility—a bit of freedom and a bit of responsibility. If they backslide, no big deal. I just pull back on the freedom for a while, and then give my teen another chance.

☐ A. Room incompletely cleaned: he will grow up to be a slovenly, unemployed, aimless welfare case.

A. The state of his room has little to do with how he turns out when he grows up.

☐ B. Home late: She will have unprotected sex, get pregnant, dump the baby on us, take drugs, and drink alcohol.

B. I have no evidence that she would do all these things. She is just self-centered and focused on having fun. So she will be punished as we agreed for coming home late.

☐ C. Fighting with siblings: He will never learn to get along with others, have friends, have close relationships, or get married. He will end up a loser and be severely depressed or commit suicide.

C. There is no scientific evidence that sibling fighting predicts later satisfaction in relationships. Siblings always fight. They will probably be closer when they grow up.

☐ **III. Malicious intent:** My adolescent misbehaves on purpose to annoy me, hurt me, or get even with me for restricting him/her.

Most teens are driven more by self-centeredness and independence seeking.

☐ A. Talking disrespectfully: She's mouthing off on purpose to get even with me for _____.

A. Impulsive teens just mouth off when frustrated. I'll try not to take it to heart.

(cont.)

☐ B. Doesn't follow directions: He doesn't finish mowing the lawn just to bug me.

B. Teens are often allergic to effort. They don't take the time to plan to upset you by not doing things; they just have an agenda more pressing to them.

☐ C. Spending money impulsively: She bought $100 worth of CDs just to waste our money.

C. She probably just saw the CDs and had to have them. Teens often don't think ahead and therefore don't budget well. She won't get any extra money for lunch or gas.

☐ **IV. Love/appreciation:** My teen should show love and appreciation for all the great sacrifices I make. If he/she really loved me, he/she would confide in me more.

Teens do sometimes take their parents for granted. C'est la vie.

☐ A. Money: What do you mean you want more allowance? You should be grateful for all the money I spend on you now. Some kids are not so lucky!

A. My teen will have to earn more allowance. I'd appreciate a thank you even though I understand the teen doesn't really think about what I do for him/her.

☐ B. Communication: She never tells me anything anymore; she must not love me.

B. It's natural as teens individuate to keep more to themselves. As long as I am available when she wants to talk, that's all I can expect.

☐ C. Spending time: If he really loved us, he wouldn't spend so much time alone in his room.

C. Spending time alone has nothing to do with love. It has to do with wanting privacy as he becomes more independent.

You can start examining your own irrational beliefs by just checking off the categories you think you subscribe to, including any specific examples that ring true for you. But if you believe you really don't hold any such negative beliefs, review how your problem-solving and communication training has gone over the last few weeks. Try to remember times when you said something impulsively that you wished you could have taken back or times when a problem-solving session fell apart. If you look at these incidents as honestly as possible, can you say that they were fueled by some negative or extreme belief, particularly about your teen? Maybe you attacked your teen verbally to preempt the assault you're sure your teen will take every opportunity to make against you? Or you were beginning to squirm under your teen's logical counterargument to a "Because I said so!" kind of dictate by you, showing that you might just believe your teen should still be seen and not heard or should do what you say unquestioningly at all times? Do your best to write down a belief that *could* undergird what you said or did during these encounters.

Now think about other times when you've had conflicts with your teen over the last couple of weeks. You might want to write down a brief description of these incidents just so you can look at them collectively. Doing that might spark recognition of a theme. Any common threads you can find may lead you to a belief that underlies your part of the conflicts.

If there's another parent in residence, you might try sharing your discoveries and ask each other some reality-check questions: "Do you think these are extreme beliefs that I demonstrate, especially when talking with our son [daughter]? Do you think there are others I've missed?" Try not to be defensive in having this conversation; humor will go far here.

Keep in mind what you've learned. If you find it useful, record the extreme or unreasonable beliefs or expectations you think you may have demonstrated in recent weeks. You'll be using the list again, so it won't be wasted time (or paper).

3. *Help your teen identify which unreasonable beliefs he or she holds with regard to you.* This is a trickier investigation to undertake. We don't have to tell you that teens don't like to be told what they think and believe. But you may have to help them here because at this developmental age they simply don't have the ability for a great deal of introspection. And we already know where they stand on humility. Try some of our suggestions, but if all you end up getting is anger and resentment, back off and focus for now on your own beliefs. Remember our four-factor model from Chapter 2; sometimes you can only change your own parenting style and beliefs.

So you may want to tackle this exploration from a couple of angles. First review the following list yourself (with your teen's other parent if there is one) and draw your own conclusions about which expectations and beliefs your teen holds. Be prepared to support your conclusions with evidence from recent behavior by the teen. Then, taking a tongue-in-cheek approach, work the extreme beliefs you feel are relevant to your teen into an imagined exercise. At a family meeting or at any free moment, say to your teen:

> "Close your eyes and imagine you just walked in from school. I immediately start in on you: 'Show me your planner! Do you have any homework? I need to see it right now! Your math teacher e-mailed that three assignments are missing. And your room is a real pigsty—clothes and games all over, dirty plates, old food, and much more! You have not cleaned it up. That's totally irresponsible. So I have completely reorganized it while you were at school. While cleaning, I found your password and checked your blog on your computer. What were you thinking when you said those awful things about Dad and me? And who is this boy [girl] whom you think is so hot that you want to kiss and do more? You're grounded indefinitely. And no computer or cellphone either!'
>
> "Now open your eyes and tell me how you'd feel if this actually happened."

Your teen will probably tell you that she would be ready to kill you. Ask your teen what she was thinking during your diatribe. She'll probably bring up themes of unfairness, ruination, and autonomy. Help her see the connection between her thoughts and feelings and how her feelings might be different if her thoughts were different. Do this in an informal way; don't make a big deal out of it.

Be sure to make the point that extreme beliefs lead to extreme emotions and behavior. In fact, that's how you know an irrational or extreme belief is likely to be operating: you find yourself overtaken by a rather extreme emotion. That's when you should take hold of yourself and ask what you're thinking that's leading to that extreme feeling. Invite your teen to review the list of unreasonable beliefs in the table on pages 316–317 and consider more reasonable ways of thinking about such situations. Are there any that your teen would check off as her own right now? Ask your teen to try to note informally any extreme beliefs that she experiences over the next few days. Share your own list of extreme beliefs with the teen.

If your teen doesn't agree that she holds any of the beliefs in the table, you can try asking leading questions, like "So you believe our rules are fair and just all the time and you're fine with them staying just as they are?" Say it with a smile and keep the conversation light. If you can bring up examples of statements the teen has made that illustrate a particular belief without making it sound like an accusation, do so. The goal is simply to figure out which types of beliefs your teen holds that enter into the greatest number of conflicts between you.

Sometimes what comes out of this will lead to some interesting insights. Mark started out trying to turn the focus on his parents rather than himself: "You think you can control me, and you can't. I'm 17 and very close to being out of here anyway." His parents were about to rise to the bait and respond with something along the lines of "You're damn right we can control you!" But they paused when they realized how quickly this discussion could heat up and rephrased Mark's statement as "So you believe we can't control you at all?" They said this without any emotion, giving a convincing impression of just wanting to clarify and make sure they understood (active listening). They did not address the belief's validity at all but just wrote it down.

Typical Unreasonable Beliefs
and Expectations Held by Teens

Unreasonable beliefs	Reasonable beliefs
☐ I. **Unfairness/ruination:** My parents' rules are totally unfair. I'll never have a good time or any friends. My parents are ruining my life with their unfair rules. They just don't understand me.	Yes, I don't like my parents' rules and maybe they are sometimes unfair. But who said life is supposed to be fair? And how many other teenagers have gone through the same thing? They turned out OK. So will I. I'll just have to put up with it the best I can.
☐ A. Curfew: Why should I have to come home earlier than my friends? They will think I'm a baby. I'll lose all my friends.	A. My friends are loyal. They will understand that my parents are creeps about curfew. I won't lose any friends.
☐ B. Chores: Why do I get stuck doing all the work? Sam [brother] doesn't have to do anything. That's unfair!	B. Sam has some chores too. I'll count them up, and if I have more, I'll talk nicely to my parents about it.
☐ C. School: My teacher is unfair. She picks on me all the time. I always get stuck doing extra homework. I'll never have time for fun. Life is one big homework assignment.	C. Maybe she does pick on me. There could be a reason. I never am with the class or know the answer when she calls on me. Maybe if I kept up with the work she wouldn't call on me so much.
☐ II. **Autonomy:** I ought to have complete and total freedom. My parents shouldn't boss me around or tell me what to do. I'm old enough for freedom now.	No teen has complete freedom. No adult really does either. Sometimes I need my parents, like for money or, God forbid, even to talk to in times of trouble. I want a lot of freedom, but not total freedom.
☐ A. Chores: I don't need any reminders. I can do it totally on my own.	A. I have not been getting them done on my own. I need to stop being a jerk and accept a little help.

(cont.)

☐ B. Smoking: It's my body. I can do whatever I want with it. You have no right to tell me not to smoke.

B. It is my body. But do I really want to mess it up? My friends have gotten hooked on smoking. It costs a lot. And it tastes terrible when you kiss someone.

☐ **III. Appreciation and entitlement:** My parents should be very grateful for any little thing I do around the house. If they really loved me, they would get me all the stuff I want.

Parents are pleased when I do things, but within reason. In addition, material things don't tell you whether someone really cares about you. It's how you are inside that makes the difference.

☐ A. Chores: My parents should be very overjoyed and happy that I cleaned the bathroom and should kiss my feet.

A. Chores: They should be happy I cleaned the bathroom, but within reason.

☐ B. Concert: If my parents really loved me, they would let me go to the rock concert with my friends.

B. If they really love me and think it is dangerous to go to the concert, they would try to stop me. I won't use this to judge how they feel.

☐ C. Clothes: If my parents really cared about me, they would buy me these designer clothes.

C. Clothes: I would like designer clothes, but that's not how I tell whether my parents love me. I can tell from how they act toward me and the affection they show.

☐ D. Electronics: My friends all have the latest smartphones and laptops, and so do my parents. I deserve them too.

D. Electronics: Mom and Dad need up-to-date computers for work. I can wait for the next model as long as my current ones are working.

☐ E. Personal space: I should be able to use the basement family room as my bedroom so I can have more privacy and more space to have friends over.

E. Personal space: I should be able to use the family room when friends come over as long as it's not imposing on anyone else. But it's fair for my parents to expect me to sleep in my bedroom so they know when my friends have gone home and I've gone to bed.

Q. *We tried to come up with a list of our beliefs, but none of us felt like these were really ideas we operate on. What does that mean?*

A. It may mean you know you hold some version of one or more of these beliefs and you know they are exaggerated, overgeneralized, or illogical. In that case, your embarrassment at admitting to them indicates you're already primed to replace them with more reasonable ideas. We've found that individuals who can clearly articulate their unrealistic ideas may have a harder time changing them because they don't see a thing wrong with them. If you're hesitating, be forgiving of yourself (and your family members) and treat the entire subject with humor.

But if you really feel stumped, there are two ways to spot the likely presence of an underlying extreme belief:

1. Anyone who is staunchly unwilling to compromise on an issue may be harboring unreasonable beliefs about it. Dig a little deeper.
2. As we said earlier, wherever an extreme emotional reaction comes up, it's probably being fueled by an extreme belief.

Starting to Replace Unreasonable Beliefs with Reasonable Alternatives

During the first week of this step, see if each of you can pick one unreasonable belief to test out in the real world and replace it with something more realistic.

1. *You (and your teen's other parent if there is one) should pick a belief that enters into a lot of conflicts and test that one.* Look at your list of unreasonable beliefs if you wrote them down; otherwise just pick one that seems to keep entering into problem encounters with your teen. If it resembles or matches one in the table on pages 309–312, look at the reasonable alternative. Does it make sense to you? Even if you're not sure it's more valid than your original belief, can you consider the possibility that it might be? If so, this is a good one to test.

There are a number of ways to test the rationality of a belief, depending on its content. First, check the norms for your teen's behavior by talking to parents of other teens in your community. It may also help to ask yourself how you felt when you were your teen's age. Say you believe that your teen should never get a speeding ticket and therefore imposed a severe penalty when she did, with the threat of an even worse consequence for even a minor driving infraction in the future. You can test whether your belief is reasonable by asking yourself whether other teens get speeding tickets. Did you? If not, how about your friends and siblings when they were teenagers? You can also go online and check the statistics on teen speeding. All of this will at least show you that expecting a teen *never* to get a ticket is unrealistic. It may be desirable, but it's an expectation that's unlikely to be met. You can also remind yourself of why teens get speeding tickets in the first place: First, they're less experienced behind the wheel and sometimes just don't realize how fast they're going. Second, they love excitement and are prone to push this envelope just like all the others in their lives. Third, they may be showing off for their friends. And fourth, they think they won't get caught. You may not consider any of these "good" reasons, but they do show you how many different factors may lead your teen to speed—other than that she's on the path to a life of crime, that she's trying to ruin *your* life, or that she has absolutely no common sense.

What about beliefs about the freedom that teens should have? As you clearly know, this is a bottomless pit of potential conflict with independence-seeking teenagers. Let's say you believe that if you let your 16-year-old daughter stay out till 1:00 A.M., she'll get into all kinds of trouble and ruin her life. You can test this belief similarly by looking at other kids who stay out that late. But it's data that's tricky to gather. Of course you can't be sure of whether your teen's friends or any other 16-year-olds you know are getting in trouble when they stay out late. But if you have close friends or siblings with teens, you can at least ask about their track record with late curfews. Or consult normally responsible youngish adults and see if you can find some who had late curfews.

Second, test your belief by actually granting your teen some additional freedom and observing what happens. If your teen handles his or her new freedom responsibly, perhaps your belief was exaggerated; if your teen does not handle it responsibly, perhaps your belief was realistic and you should pull back on that freedom for now. We're not suggesting, obviously, that you yield to your teen's desire for absolute autonomy and throw her into the water in the hope that she'll learn how to swim. But you can negotiate a gradual increase in freedom, making the next step toward independence contingent on your teen's handling each increment responsibly. It will take time to prove to yourself that your belief was unreasonable, but then many deeply held core beliefs took a long time to develop and will take a long time to shed.

Third, ask yourself whether your belief is serving some important function or purpose in helping your family function and keep it all together. If so, should your teen be involved in this function, or is there a better way to handle it, permitting your teen to do the normal developmental task of becoming more independent? Maria and Joe, introduced in Chapter 6, were brought up to believe that the oldest child in the family has to be available to take care of the younger ones. To them, that 14-year-old Mike has to take care of his 7- and 8-year-old siblings after school is a nonnegotiable. Because of their belief, Mike was serving a babysitting function for his siblings. But is their belief that he should give up recreation and socializing after school every day to do this job reasonable? Maybe not. Does this interfere with his developmental task of becoming more independent by spending time with peers? Their son is 14. He's not an adult and his siblings are not his kids. None of his friends have to babysit every single weekday, all afternoon. Mike is in the thick of his biggest surge toward independence and biologically *needs* to spend time with his friends and away from his parents. So maybe what's nonnegotiable—and a reasonable expectation—is that Mike help out as much as possible while his parents find other ways to supervise the kids at least part of the time so that Mike is allowed the freedom that he needs—and that he has earned by his largely responsible behavior in taking care of Tina and Tommy. Maria and Joe need a babysitter since they both work, and they can't afford to pay one privately all week. They found other solutions: The little kids go to their church's free afterschool program 2 days a week and one other day they go to the home of a neighbor, who sends her kids over to Maria and Joe's on Saturday mornings while the parents shop. Mike babysits the other 2 days. If something important to him comes up that would interfere with that schedule, he's allowed to ask his parents to hire a sitter in exchange for doing extra chores that he would have been paid for that week.

You met Cal and Jackson in Chapter 6 too. Cal's ruination belief about his son Jackson was harder to disprove. He had seen too many kids "go wrong" who, in his eyes, clearly loafed around and acted like total slackers. The only way he could test his belief was to try his best to answer questions like these candidly:

Is your view of your teen absolute, black-or-white, all-or-nothing?

Could it be exaggerated?

What's the logical basis for this belief?

Can you find examples of others who disprove your belief?

What is the worst that could happen if Jackson didn't do his chores on time?

Cal had to admit when pressed to consider his son's performance in all arenas of his life that Jackson was a model team member—always on time for practices and games and willing to play any role assigned by the coach—a student who turned in most of his homework, and a person who was well liked by classmates. This didn't sound much like a kid destined for destitution. Then he remembered a story he'd read in the paper about hugely successful adults who had had very checkered childhoods filled with lawbreaking and even violence. Logically, if these people could rise above much more serious misdeeds, Jackson wasn't necessarily doomed by not being stellar at getting his chores done.

2. *Now it's your teen's turn to test a belief.* Once you've tested a problematic belief or expectation and replaced it with a more reasonable alternative, get together with your teen and share your experience. Showing your teenager that you possess the humility to identify and correct your own extreme thoughts will go a long way toward urging him to do the same. You have two options here: Have your teen pick a belief to test or pick one for him. Take the former tack if your teen's pride really seemed to be at stake when you tried to identify unreasonable beliefs together. This way he'll be able to pick one that isn't that important to him and avoid the humiliation he may be anticipating from having to admit to being "irrational." The latter approach may be preferable if you don't think your teen is capable of choosing a belief that won't start a fight right now. Kevin's parents picked his smoking belief, guessing that their competitive son might enjoy the intellectual challenge of trying to confirm the belief that "You have no right to tell me not to smoke." In fact they decided to turn the belief-testing process into a friendly contest. Each (parents and Kevin) would research the statement and come back in a week with a number of well-supported points making their case, as for a debate. They enlisted Kevin's aunt, a college professor whom Kevin respected and loved debating with, as the judge. In the end, Kevin agreed with her conclusion that the parents had prevailed—that they did, in fact, have the right to tell him not to smoke—though he didn't agree that he would necessarily obey any dictatorial command never to smoke. More important, in his parents' opinion, was that they had shown Kevin that they respected his intelligence and that discussions between them would be based on a sincere effort to be logical and avoid exaggeration. He was much more willing to continue the discussion of beliefs and expectations in the future as a result.

Some families, like Kevin's, do best when they examine their beliefs through the lens of logic. Others do better by looking at the local norms. We're not suggesting that you compromise your individual and family values by conforming to the average, but it really never hurts to ask yourself "What would most people think in this situation?" Frankly, you may be forced to answer that question because it so often forms the core of a teen's argument for her own stance.

Let's say your teenage daughter wants a 1:00 A.M. curfew, but you started out believing that if she stays out that late she'll get in huge trouble and her life will be ruined. Your teenager claims that no one else her age has a curfew at all. To test this claim, check out the local norm—or, better yet, make it your teen's responsibility to test this belief, presenting you with data on who among her friends has what curfew (with the agreement that you can and will call parents to confirm). You may easily be able to ascertain that almost all the kids her age have a curfew. You could leave it at that and consider yourself the victor since you've already disproven your teen's principal argument. But then the issue would remain unresolved and lead to increasing disputes in the future.

So let's assume that your teen's curfew has been 10:00 (you were pretty determined to protect her, after all), and this research has revealed that your teen does have an earlier curfew than the majority of kids her age. Maybe, in fact, the other kids do almost all have a 1:00 A.M. curfew. And none of them is in jail or has been expelled from school or is in other big trouble that you can discover. But you still feel that 1:00 is too late, and you have concrete reasons, such as that your daughter won't get enough sleep and—since you intend to wait up for her to ensure her safety—neither will you. Where can you compromise? Can you extend the curfew to something in between the old time and 1:00? Can you allow a 1:00 A.M. curfew with certain restrictions, such as when your daughter is at the home of a family you know and trust and you can ascertain that the parents are home? The point is that, if you have begun to see that your original belief was exaggerated, and if your teen can see that her argument was extreme, you can start to meet in the middle. In fact, that's another question it never hurts to ask yourselves: "What's a middle-of-the-road position on this issue?"

Q. *My daughter is ridiculously stubborn and just won't budge from her original position in any discussion. How can we get her to admit that her beliefs aren't reasonable and there are alternatives to consider?*

A. Again, to a teenager, backing down from her original position is a defeat and means demonstrating weakness. With your daughter—and many other teens—it's probably best to stay away from any approach that smacks of "You're wrong." Instead, to get her to consider more reasonable beliefs, always stress tangible contingencies: that if she tries to reach a middle-of-the-road position, she might end up with a later curfew, she might be able to stop you from nagging her about her homework, she might be allowed to wear whatever she wants to school, and so on. Of course this means *you* have to enter the discussion prepared to compromise. If you go in seeking a TKO (technical knockout), you might as well both just stay in your corners.

Incorporating More Reasonable Beliefs and Expectations into Communication and Problem Solving with Your Teen

Whenever you challenge and replace extreme thoughts, the door opens to negotiating a compromise on an issue that has bogged you down or led to blowups in the past.

1. *During the second week of this step, meet with your teenager and negotiate (or renegotiate) a compromise where you haven't been able to do so before.* We've given you a glimpse into how this might work in the illustrations above. So we're not going to go into a lot more detail here except to give you a more complete example of one family's efforts at the end of this chapter. For whatever belief or beliefs you've challenged and replaced during this step so far, sit down with your teen and see if you can come up with a happier ending now that you've eliminated extreme thinking that got in the way in the past.

2. *Start trying to catch yourself in unrealistic beliefs and expectations as you go about your day.* A red flag to watch for, of course, is the instinct to answer "Because I said so!" when your teen demands an explanation for a restriction or other dictate you've imposed. If you can't think of at least one good reason for your command, there's a chance that it's based on a belief that doesn't hold water. When that happens, do your best to back off and reconsider. There's no shame in catching yourself being wrong and backing up a little. Seeing that you're capable of doing this— and even that you can apologize—will cement, not undermine, your authority with your teen.

If you find, as many of us do, that a certain belief keeps popping up to make trouble even when you've already determined that it's not entirely reasonable, try a type of rehearsing that we call *rational restructuring.* Let's say that your son has a history of lying, especially about whether he's done what he's supposed to do, whether it's homework, chores, or even personal hygiene. You've taken lots of behavior management measures to discourage this behavior, and you know that he doesn't do it very often anymore. But you can't quite shed the suspicion that he's lying if he hesitates at all when you ask him if he's done what he was supposed to do. Sometimes you immediately snap at him to show you the completed work; other times you hold back but then let your suspicion creep into later encounters ("Well, if you're *sure* you finished that math, I *guess* you can go out. . . ."). Either way, an argument ensues at some point.

To avoid letting yourself be carried away by your old expectations, write a list of cues that typically trigger your suspicion that your son is lying. Then imagine yourself in each of those situations and imagine your worst fears about the situation ("He's not answering my question about his math. . . ." "Oh no, he hasn't done *any* of his homework and he's going to fail!"). Tune in to exactly how you feel as you're having the extreme thoughts. Now challenge the validity of that thought ("He was at his desk without any music or the computer on for over an hour. . . ." "He must have gotten *something* done") and rehearse an alternative reaction

("I'll give him a minute to gather his answer—he's not always that articulate—and if he doesn't sound certain to me, I'll tell him that he doesn't sound very sure of his response and so I'd like to see the homework"). Tune in to how you feel as you substitute a reasonable reaction for an extreme belief. Repeat this imaginary exercise daily to make it your new fallback reaction in the real situation. Remind yourself of your mantra, "Sticks and stones can break my bones, but words can never hurt me," as you engage in rational restructuring exercises.

Coping with Unreasonable Beliefs and Expectations: One Family's Experience

Talk about an uneasy peace! It's taken Mark and his parents months to establish a relationship that's not conducted 100% of the time at the top of everyone's lungs. With the help of a therapist, Sandy and Doug gradually took back control over their household, using points plus behavior contracts to get their 17-year-old to adhere to a short but critical list of nonnegotiables: Go to school, don't curse at your parents, do a prescribed set of chores every week, tell us when you'll be home when you go out, and call if you're going to be late.

Because of Mark's age and the fact that he had been roaming free for a long time, they minimized the limitations on his freedom. In fact, because what he seemed to want most was to get away from home, they used money and the use of one of their cars as primary incentives for following the rules. The biggest rewards were given for school attendance and performance. After all, their main priority at this point was to make sure their son graduated from high school and had a chance at attending college.

Things were much calmer at home. But Mark was hardly ever there, and an uncomfortable, distant coolness seemed to have replaced the histrionics. Sandy started to wonder if she should have been more careful about what she wished for as she pictured her only son leaving home and maybe never looking back. This wasn't the way they had imagined things when they had encouraged their spirited little boy to explore the world with a certain amount of abandon. Sandy and Doug both started to try to have friendly conversations with Mark when he was around, but they usually ended in an awkward silence that made everyone feel like fleeing the room. And the more they pushed their son to talk to them, the more he started to snap at them again. Occasionally he'd blurt out a string of obscenities and then storm out of the house. Sandy began to wonder if they were right back where they started.

Sandy and Doug took their concern to their therapist in a meeting without Mark. The therapist helped them recognize that fear was standing in the way of their taking that extra step toward a mutually respectful adult relationship with their son. They were afraid that relaxing their vigilance with Mark would undo all the control they'd regained. They were even still a little bit afraid of their 6-foot-2-inch son. The therapist suggested that they were probably conveying that reticence to Mark and asked them if they knew how he was interpreting it. They had no idea.

Over a couple of additional sessions, Sandy and Doug figured out that their main fear was that their son would never succeed on his own, and they knew he'd leave home as soon as he graduated, whether he was going to college or not. Their therapist gently pointed out to them, after a certain amount of probing and also meeting with Mark separately, that the parents were subtly conveying this lack of confidence to their son. Mark, in turn, was convinced that his parents didn't care about him at all— that they were just treating him like some kind of necessary evil. He also resented the fact that they were now making him "pay" for what they had led him to believe were his rights as a family member in the past.

One of the problems, it turned out, was that Sandy and Doug hadn't changed the "deal" between them and their son for months. As we said, they were afraid if they gave Mark an inch, he'd take the proverbial mile. But they needed to show their son their appreciation and their confidence that he could succeed by granting him additional privileges and especially independence over time. They shouldn't wait until a problem arose that forced them to change the system; change needs to be built into the system, to reflect the natural developmental changes that teens, even older teens, are going through.

Mark hadn't been able to respond openheartedly to his parents' overtures to him because he didn't believe they were sincere. Doug and Sandy made a point of stepping up the positive attention and praise before expecting their son to reciprocate. Meanwhile, they talked to Mark's teachers and college counselor about his prospects and were pleasantly surprised to hear that he had gone to the counselor's office himself to ask about engineering programs and admission standards and that his math teacher thought he had a real affinity for the subject. Sandy and Doug used this news to offer Mark another step toward the independence he craved: his own car if he prepared all his college applications by December 1 of his senior year. They created a timeline for completion of each step, including visits to campuses he was really interested in, and checked in with him as each one was completed. Sandy did a little rational restructuring to rehearse resisting the urge to nag about revisions of essays and calls to schedule interviews.

Sandy and Doug realized they had been acting on two extreme beliefs: (1) ruination—if they relaxed their vigilance with Mark, he would act out, never graduate, and fail to go to college; and (2) perfectionism—Mark should engage in "cozy" conversation with them because, after all, they are his parents. With their therapist's help, they challenged these beliefs and creatively used their new behavior contract to spur Mark to get his college applications done on time. As they demonstrated, cognitive restructuring can be combined with some of the other techniques taught in this program.

When December rolled around, with a dramatic flourish Mark showed his parents his applications, all ready to send in. A week later Sandy and Doug left a set of keys and an owner's manual on Mark's bed. When he came whooping downstairs, Sandy started to say "Hey, have fun—and drive carefully!" but her son interrupted: "What's the matter? Afraid to ride with me? Come on, let's go out for a test drive."

17
Step 10.
Keeping It Together

You've been on quite a journey. Before setting out, you probably felt frustrated and helpless, with no idea where to turn to resolve the defiance that was ruling your lives. We hope you feel differently now that you've spent a few months working so hard at forging new paths around that dead end. You now understand the nature of defiance and how four factors—your teen's characteristics, your characteristics, the environmental situation you find yourself in, and your parenting practices—have interacted and contributed to the development of defiant behavior in your teenager. You've retraced your steps to see how endless repetitions of the coercion cycle have resulted in a pattern of defiant behavior and negativity between you and your teen. These insights opened a window to change, helping you grasp what a big difference you could make just by changing what *you* do in your roles as parents.

Your first step toward rebuilding a positive relationship with your teen involved adopting principles for parenting the defiant teen. You then made turning your teen's behavior around a manageable task by dividing the world of issues between you and your adolescent into the nonnegotiable bottom-line rules for living in a civilized household and the negotiable issues—everything else.

You learned to use consequences wisely to enforce the inviolable rules. As for the rest, you've become a pretty skilled negotiator, providing the right incentives to guide your teen toward behavior that will serve him—and you—well and coaching your teen in problem-solving skills that will serve him well in the adult world he's poised to enter. Along the road, you've all learned to communicate in a more positive manner and to replace negative beliefs and unrealistic or unreasonable expectations. You're well on your way to the desirable destination of less conflict, greater mutual respect, and a positive future for your son or daughter.

Broken down this way, you can see that you've accomplished quite a lot by working through the program in this book. Now we want you to take a step back, look at the big picture, consider these techniques tools in your toolbox, and think about when you'll use each tool in the future. We also want you to take stock of where you started, how far you've come in this journey, and what you need to do next.

GOALS FOR STEP 10

- Know when to use which tools, skills, and strategies.
- Agree on a plan for defusing crises.
- Review the outcomes of your efforts and decide what to do next.

Knowing When to Use Which Tools and Skills

Your goal is to make knowing when to select and implement the skills and tools that you've learned second nature. One way to ingrain them is to make sure you can reel off the list of skills mentally so that they're there to be called up when needed. It may sound silly, but memorizing the list of skills can make them easier to access when the heat of a crisis fogs your mind.

1. *Consider writing the following list on a card you can keep in your wallet or someplace else accessible or post it somewhere private* *where you'll see it often, like on the inside of your medicine cabinet door.* Or program it into your smartphone or computer. Review it regularly—when a crisis comes up if you need a mental distraction, if you find yourself brooding about your teen and what he is—or might be—up to, when you worry about his future or worry whether you've made any real progress:

- One-on-one time
- Respect, approval, recognition, and praise
- Ignoring attention-getting bids from your teen
- Effective commands
- Point systems
- Behavior contracts
- Response cost (penalties)
- Grounding
- Problem solving
- Communication training
- Replacing negative beliefs and unrealistic expectations

2. *Analyze a problem situation and select the tool or skills to resolve it.* Whenever a conflict threatens or a problem blossoms, review your list of tools and ask yourself which fits best. Let's say your 15-year-old daughter comes home distraught because her best friend is trying to steal her boyfriend; she insists on a 1:00 A.M. curfew next Saturday so she can stay until the end of the party and make sure her boyfriend sticks with her. Although you recognize a potential curfew conflict brewing, your daughter's upset about her boyfriend is paramount. You could select active listening, a communication tool, and let your daughter tell you exactly how she's feeling. Later on you can deal with the curfew issue by using problem solving.

What if your 16-year-old son's school calls to tell you he has skipped his afternoon classes three times in the past week? School attendance is a nonnegotiable issue. This infraction calls for implementing consequences for violating a nonnegotiable issue. You ground him for the next 2 weekends and require him to do homework during the grounding.

Imagine your spouse is "freaking out" because you signed up your 15-year-old son, who has ADHD, for driver's ed. Your spouse believes this is a setup for catastrophe—after all, your son can't get his homework done, can't keep his room clean, and is very disorganized. Half the time he doesn't even have his head screwed on right. How is he ever going to handle a car? You've analyzed the situation carefully and feel he has responsibly pulled his grades up and deserves this opportunity. You probably should have consulted your spouse before signing him up; now you need to go back and talk it over with your spouse and develop a consistent approach. You may need to help your spouse with unreasonable beliefs about ruination, using cognitive restructuring as outlined in Step 9.

Over time and with practice, you'll become adept at recognizing when a new problem demands, for example, that you immediately focus on giving effective commands and then, if your teen doesn't respond appropriately, writing up a behavior contract. This might be the way to go if some old habit of your teen's you had hoped to extinguish—such as swearing—rears its ugly head again. You'll come to know when it's smart to go right to problem solving—such as when unexpected events bring up the question of whether a rule can be waived or bent or permanently amended. Sometimes a crisis might call for grounding but should be followed up immediately with problem solving. There might be a reason, for example, why your son took your car without asking, so even though it's strictly against the rules and grounding is justified by your previous experience with similar behavior, you recognize the signs that your son really needs more freedom and see the wisdom in moving directly to seeking a compromise.

There are a million ways to combine these tools and techniques to allow your teen to keep moving forward toward autonomy as she must. As you use your tools and skills, you'll get a better and better feel for which to apply first in various types of situations. You can even review the Issues Checklist in Chapter 14 and ask yourself how you'll handle typical conflicts over each issue, creating an informal sort of "playbook" or "script" to follow in different circumstances. Be creative in using the tools we've given you. If you're angry and upset and really can't figure out what to do, stare at the list of tools and think through the consequences of applying each strategy to your present situation. Even if you don't come up with a good idea, the time you take to review the list will cool your emotions so you can approach the situation rationally.

3. *Know whether certain conditions in your family demand that you favor certain skills over others.* Beyond the types of individual situations just discussed, there are certain inherent conditions in families that might call for a different order as a matter of course:

• Families that have a lot of problems with negative beliefs and unrealistic expectations, unearthed during Step 9, should go directly from one-on-one time, praise/ignoring, and effective commands to challenging and replacing these thoughts (the skills in Step 9). As you learned in Chapter 16, these beliefs and expectations can cause such stubborn problems you won't get anywhere until you address them. When problems came up between Lauren and her mother, they would start sparring sarcastically as quickly as if the bell had rung to signal the start of Round 1. In fact, when Mac once used this metaphor to describe his wife and daughter's interactions, Lauren and Jan thought it was so apt that the next time a fight started Lauren interjected "Ding!" This stopped her mother in her tracks. After Lauren explained that she had just realized they had started "boxing," mother and daughter agreed that from then on when either of them noticed they were coming out swinging, they'd say "Ding!" and then try to figure out what negative beliefs were behind the sudden explosion.

In Step 9 you had a chance to identify the cognitive distortions operating behind the scenes with your teen, but you may not have been entirely aware of how big a problem these are for you. Distorted thinking may be a major problem for your family if there's lots of quickly triggered anger (as for Lauren and Jan), if you often catch yourself brooding about your teen's behavior, if your teen immediately stops fulfilling her part of behavioral agreements at the merest sign of you slipping on your part of the bargain, if any of you tend toward fairly rigid or stubborn thinking, and, in general, if defiance has been going on for a long time, meaning you've all had a long time to form negative expectations.

• Certain characteristics of your teen (Factor 1 in the four-factor model) dictate the use of some tools more than others. For example, families with teens who have ADHD and who are very immature need to stick to contingency management more than problem solving. Problem-solving and communication training won't work well. Gina, who is only 13, needs the immediacy of points and contracts to keep her on track. Her parents know she needs the positive attention of praise, ignoring minor infractions, and one-on-one time more than most kids and dole it out generously. At this point they model problem solving for Gina by doing it between the two of them when discussing a behavioral issue and how to fit it into their existing contingency management plans. Gradually they intend to draw Gina into these discussions, but they won't make her an equal participant until she shows the ability to make a meaningful contribution to negotiations and an ability to compromise.

Families with older, more mature teens might have to skip contingency management after applying the basics and go right to problem-solving and communication training. If your teen is pretty independent and has been earning increasing autonomy by showing that he can handle the responsibility, unilateral control through point systems and contracts will be less and less motivating. At 15, Kevin is still a pretty loose cannon—by nature and developmental stage—but he's very intelligent and much more motivated by exercising his debate skills than earning points, which he laughs at. So his parents problem-solve virtually everything with him. Seventeen-year-old Mark is close to leaving the nest. His parents didn't find behavior contracts very effective with him when they started this program—except for a few select contracts that they worked out with his therapist. As mentioned earlier in this book, they worked out a point (dollar) system with him where he would get paid for attending and performing well at school, which got its potency from Mark's drive to, well, drive—an expensive privilege.

Agreeing on a Plan for Defusing Crises

At times you'll be ambushed by life and find that some situation or issue you hadn't anticipated creates a major disagreement between you and your teen. Suddenly, without warning, an emotional riot has broken out. What can you do to minimize these ambushes, and how can you quell the riot once it's been incited?

   1. *Review the types of crisis situations you've encountered throughout this program.* What types of situations have caught you off guard? Which issues remain hot despite your best efforts to keep things cool? Think about where you tend to get sabotaged despite your best efforts and then review how emotions escalated during those encounters. What triggered loss of control for you, your teen's other parent (if there is one), and the teen?

   If you have trouble finding any common threads between crises that have come up over the last few months, try looking back at your Issues Checklist. Crises are most likely to occur around the most intense and conflicted issues on your list. These issues can be hard to resolve fully. (Note, by the way, that by "resolve" we don't mean getting your teen to see the issue your way but rather arriving at a compromise that everyone can live with for dealing with the issue.) If you find, in fact, that past crises and the issues of highest intensity on your checklist don't coincide, something must have shifted. See Action Step 4 below.

   2. *Problem-solve alternative responses to prevent loss of control.* Once you've pinpointed the types of situations or issues that often lead to an argument or an explosion of defiance from your teen, do some problem solving together to see what you could do differently to prevent loss of control for each person. Most of the time you're going to need to calm down first and then solve the problem at the core of the crisis later. There are two groups of responses you can consider as ways to head off loss of control:

- **"Stop" responses:** You've already done this every time you've called a time-out from escalating emotions. There are all sorts of variations on this theme: counting to 10, leaving the scene, using calming language, and so forth. During a family meeting, talk about these possibilities and have each family member commit to using at least one of these "stop" responses when a crisis comes up.
- **Emotion-calming responses:** There are also ways to take the edge off anger during a crisis: relaxation training, meditation, mental distraction, physical exercise, punching a pillow, and so on. You'll find sources of information on methods like relaxation training, meditation, and mental distraction in the Resources at the back of the book, but you need to know that these methods take time and practice to learn. You may find that they have benefits that extend to your whole life and are therefore very good uses of your time, but while you're learning them, you can simply take the physical approach—pace around the room, toss a ball between your hands, give yourself a time-out by going to another room so as to interrupt the conflict and give yourself (and your teen) time to think and recover your normal emotional demeanor. Each family member should agree to use one of these methods as well as the "stop" responses.

3. *Role-play a mock crisis of the type you've identified and use these new alternative responses to see if they seem likely to help.* If not, go back to the problem-solving drawing board.

4. *Play detective to analyze any new problems that come up.* If your review of recent crises reveals that new issues may have come up between you and your teen, try completing the checklist again. The evolution of your teen's priorities is rarely announced, and your response can be unconscious and visceral (often thanks to the deep-rooted beliefs and expectations you started to address in Step 9). But if you don't bring new issues to light, they'll continue to catch you unaware.

Sometimes you may find yourself blindsided: Maybe an entirely new development in your teen's life brings up a new issue—your son has his first girlfriend and starts violating curfew in an attempt to appear "cool" or your daughter gets her driver's license and immediately starts to get parking tickets. Or the teen balks at a rule that he used to accept. Maybe an issue you thought you had learned to address suddenly starts causing problems out of the blue. In that case, consider keeping a journal about the problem, writing down what provokes conflicts around it and what consequences you imposed for defiance on the part of your teen. Look back at Part I of this book to see if you can figure out an explanation for the problem's occurrence in the first place, whether it's related to your teen's personality, a developmental transition, a problem like ADHD, or stresses occurring in *your* life that could be changing your behavior unknown to you (e.g., you're becoming inconsistent or letting negative beliefs about your teen take control of your interactions). If you don't find any answers there, try a quick review of the steps of the program and the skills listed under the following goal: Has your parenting style and use of these skills fallen by the wayside? Finally, can you do some contingency management or schedule a family meeting to do concerted problem solving so that this problem no longer creates spontaneous eruptions?

Reviewing Your Efforts and Deciding What to Do Next

Working with defiant teens is very challenging—we're not implying that it's a snap now that you have all the tools and techniques from the 10-step program. Nonetheless, we'd like you to take stock of your experience with the various tools and skills that we've shared with you in this book.

Using the checklist below, rate whether you implemented each skill, and if so, how effective it proved to be. We'll help you use your answers to these questions to plan your next step in working with your teenager.

If you answered Yes to five or more (50% or more) of the tools, then you have really made a huge effort to use evidence-based

Defiant Teen Intervention Outcome Checklist

Please review each of the interventions listed below. Circle Yes or No depending on whether you implemented each intervention. For those interventions that you implemented, rate the effectiveness of the outcome. "Effectiveness" means "Did it improve things for you and your teen?" Rate effectiveness on a 1–5 scale as follows:

1 = not at all effective; 2 = a little effective; 3 = moderately effective; 4 = effective; 5 = very effective

Intervention	Did you use it?		If Yes, how effective was it?				
One-on-one time	Yes	No	1	2	3	4	5
Praise, etc.	Yes	No	1	2	3	4	5
Ignoring bids for attention	Yes	No	1	2	3	4	5
Effective commands	Yes	No	1	2	3	4	5
Point systems	Yes	No	1	2	3	4	5
Behavior contracts	Yes	No	1	2	3	4	5
Response cost	Yes	No	1	2	3	4	5
Grounding	Yes	No	1	2	3	4	5
Problem solving	Yes	No	1	2	3	4	5
Communication training	Yes	No	1	2	3	4	5
Replacing negative beliefs and unrealistic expectations	Yes	No	1	2	3	4	5

interventions to improve your relationship with your teen, whatever your effectiveness ratings. Congratulations on a great effort! Examine your effectiveness ratings carefully. Depending on your teen's level of defiance, your personal characteristics, and your life situation (remember the four-factor model), your efforts may have been more or less effective. If you rated the applicable tools as 3 or higher on effectiveness, continue to use them, refine your efforts, and you may well find that a self-help approach is sufficient for coping with your teen's defiant behavior at the present time. If you rated the applicable tools 1 (not at all effective) or 2 (a little effective), you may want to consider seeking the help of a mental health professional to see if you can get better results.

If you answered Yes to fewer than five (50%) of the tools, ask yourself what interfered with trying them out. Were you so discouraged by your teen's extremely intense defiance that you didn't even try to change your parenting style? Were you too busy with other things to commit the time to working on these skills? Do the skills seem irrelevant to your situation? Did an unsupportive spouse sabotage you? Are you experiencing mental health problems such as depression, anxiety, or substance abuse that interfered? As you search for the answers to these questions, we urge you to consider seeking mental health assistance so that you can address these factors and get help with parenting your challenging adolescent.

Even if you cannot detect any changes using our checklist and don't feel like you got much out of our program, you need to consider whether that is a rational belief. Can you honestly say you've made no strides, that your relationship is every bit as difficult as it was before you started this program? Take a moment to review the little improvements you've noticed over the last few months. Maybe your son is as ornery as ever; you're still constantly bracing yourself for an argumentative response to everything you say. But he's stopped swearing in the house. Or your daughter still treats you like a necessary evil and tries to spend every minute possible with her friends instead of family—but she at least asks if anyone needs to use the family's iPad before she monopolizes it and volunteers information about her ETA (estimated time of arrival) back home when she goes out.

These may be small successes, but they're successes nonetheless, and you can build on them. Keep expressing appreciation for the respectful communication from your son and the consideration of your daughter. Show your compassionate, reasonable attitude by ignoring minor relapses in these areas when they occur. Your teen will get the message, however subtle it is, that you are an empathetic parent of a maturing individual who deserves respect for acting more and more like an adult.

And while you're examining your belief for rationality, ask yourself how long you'd been having problems with your teenager before seeking out this book. If you go all the way back to when defiance first appeared, you'll probably remind yourself that the seeds were sown long before you started addressing the problem with this program—maybe years ago. In that case it's not very realistic to expect the biggest problems to disappear within a few months, is it?

So keep at it. There are three ways to continue the good work you've already started and make the benefits grow: You can come up with an "emergency plan" of emotion-dampening techniques that you and your teen agree to use when discussions get heated. You can figure out the best order in which to use your skills in different situations and practice applying them that way until you do it automatically. Finally, you can practice problem solving with your teen so that this skill so critical to successful management of adult life is ingrained before you pass the baton.

This is training you don't "finish"; they are techniques to apply for the rest of your lives together. If you're discouraged by minimal change, these strategies will keep you going for whatever time it takes to see noticeable improvement in conflict levels. If you're seeing a significant improvement already, they'll keep you from getting overconfident and "relapsing" into the coercive patterns that got you in trouble in the first place. Above all, think of these strategies as a way to keep you "honest"—that is, consistent in your reclaimed role as an authoritative, compassionate, proactive parent of a teenager you can be proud of. And if you ever find your resolve wavering and old, inconsistent parenting styles creeping back in, remember that you can always call a therapist and get some extra help.

Ultimately, this book's goal has been to help you develop a better relationship with your teen. That is a relationship that will continue for the rest of your life. Keep asking yourself what you want this relationship to be like. Years from now, what would you like your son or daughter to say about you and how you raised him or her, especially during adolescence? Keeping this image in mind can help you make better choices when you try to manage your teen's misbehavior, engage the teen in problem solving, work to improve your communication, and reevaluate your own beliefs about what teens and parents should do when interacting with each other, especially around problem issues.

In a sense, we've tried here to encourage you to remember—always—that you're the adult, and so it naturally falls to you to maintain your maturity, composure, and sense of what matters in the long run whenever you're dealing with your teen, rather than reacting in a tit-for-tat fashion in response to whatever emotional flak your teen may be exploding at you at the moment. You can be the emotionally reactive, demanding, dictatorial parent your teen seems to be unconsciously pressing you to be, or you can be the best possible parent, the parent that you know you can be, no matter how your teen may behave. In the end, the choice is always up to you.

Appendix A

Problem-Solving Worksheets

Problem-Solving Worksheet
for Tony Santo and Parents (Scenario A)

Date: _8/08/13_

Problem: _Parents (Tony's parents were in agreement on problem definition): "I don't want you to have a party without an adult present because I'm worried that your friends might make poor choices and get themselves or you in trouble or mess up the house." Tony: "I'm embarrassed when you're around during a party, so I don't want you to be there."_

Proposed solutions	Teen + −	Mother + −	Father + −
1. _Tony's parents "bite the bullet" and let him have the party his way._	+	−	−
2. _Tony doesn't have any parties until he turns 18._	−	+	−

[Notice that the first two solutions are the original extreme positions for this family. You'll find this is often the case in your own problem solving.]

	Teen	Mother	Father
3. _Tony has a party for 10 friends that Mom and Dad approve of and they leave the house during the party._	−	+	+
4. _Tony has a small party at a public place where there's supervision other than parents (like at a sports club)._	−	−	−
5. _Tony has a party for 100 kids but his young uncle supervises instead of his parents._	+	−	+
6. _Tony has the party with his parents home, but they stay on the third floor of the house the whole night, coming downstairs only if Tony calls them._	−	+	−
7. _Mom and Dad spy on the party through closed-circuit video cameras set up in every room and relayed by satellite to another location._	−	−	−
8. _Tony hires the linebackers on his school football team to serve as bouncers in case anyone gets out of line._	+	−	−
9. _Tony has a party for 100 kids and his parents stay away, but it's an afternoon pool party and everyone has to be gone by 5:00 P.M._	−	−	−

(cont.)

344

10. *Tony's parents agree to go to a neighbor's house down*   –   +   +
    the street for the evening but will "drop in" unannounced
    a couple of times, pretending they need to pick something
    up, and if anything doesn't look OK, they'll stay.

Agreement: *Tony has a party for no more than 40 friends; his 25-year-old uncle is on*
hand but "doesn't act like he's a chaperone" and agrees to call Tony's parents if there's any
sign of drinking or drugs, or if the party gets too loud or rowdy. If any alcohol is
discovered at the party, it will be shut down immediately, with police involvement if
participants defy the order to shut it down. Tony agrees to let his parents review the guest
list in advance and discuss with him anybody about whom they have concerns.

Implementation Plan

A. Teen will do: *Tony will give Mom and Dad the guest list before the party and tell all*
   guests that if the noise isn't kept down, the party will be over immediately.

B. Mom will do: *Mom will contact the uncle, her brother, and enlist his cooperation*
   and assistance.

C. Dad will do: *Dad will review the guest list and talk to Tony about it.*

D. Plan for monitoring whether this happens: *Tony's uncle, Dan, will go outside*
   periodically during the party. If the party sounds too loud from the street, Dan will
   discreetly tell Tony to turn the music down. If Tony doesn't obey within 5 minutes, Uncle
   Dan will give him another warning. If he still doesn't do it, Dan agrees to call Mom and
   Dad, who will come home and kick everyone out.

E. Any reminders that will be given. By whom? When? *See D, about Uncle*
   Dan's warnings regarding the music volume.

F. Consequences for compliance and noncompliance: *If Mom and Dad resist*
   the urge to interfere and do not come home during the party, Tony will thank them and
   make sure that the house is spotless by noon the next day. If they do interfere, Tony will
   get to have another party 1 week later, during which they can't interfere. If Tony sticks to
   the agreement, his parents agree to let him have a 2-hour party for six people next
   month without any adult supervision. If he doesn't comply, he'll be grounded for the
   following weekend, during which he'll have to clean the whole house, and will not be
   able to have any party, supervised or unsupervised, for 3 months.

Problem-Solving Worksheet
for Bettina James and Parents (Scenario C)

Date: _11/10/13_

Problem: _Mother: "I don't want you to have as late a curfew as your friends because I'm worried that you won't be safe being out as late as kids 2 years older than you." Father: "I don't think you should have a later curfew because you haven't shown that you can obey the one you have, so you haven't earned any additional freedom." Bettina: "If I had a later curfew, I wouldn't feel like I had to break it. When I have to go home before all my friends, I feel embarrassed."_

			Evaluations			
Proposed solutions	Teen		Mother		Father	
	+	−	+	−	+	−
1. _Bettina has no curfew and comes home when she feels like it._	+			−		−
2. _Bettina's curfew is changed to half an hour EARLIER until she obeys it for 2 weeks straight, then moved back to the current time and kept there for the foreseeable future._		−	+		+	
3. _Bettina keeps this curfew but MAY be allowed to stay out later IF she calls her parents half an hour before curfew and asks permission._		−	+		+	
4. _Bettina's curfew stays the same, but she now gets grounded for the rest of the weekend, with work duty, if she's even 5 minutes late._		−	+			−
5. _Mom and Dad hire a babysitter to accompany Bettina wherever she goes._		−		−		−
6. _Bettina has no curfew but has to check in by phone with her parents every half hour._	+			−		−
7. _Bettina's curfew stays the same, but she can ask for an extension BEFORE she goes out, which her parents may or may not grant._		−	+		+	
8. _Bettina's curfew remains the same until she has obeyed it for 3 weeks. Then it's extended by half an hour._	+		+		+	

(cont.)

9   *Bettina earns $25 for each weekend that she comes*   +   +   +

    home by curfew.

10.   *Bettina loses 15 minutes of curfew for every weekend*   +   +   +

    that she comes home late.

Agreement: *Everyone agreed on solutions 8, 9, and 10. So they combined these three.*

Implementation Plan

A. Teen will do: *Bettina will be home by 10:30, with no grace period and no extensions,*
for 3 weeks. Then she'll come home by 11:00, with no grace period, for 3 weeks. If she
comes home on time, she'll get to choose a store where her parents will buy her a gift
card. If she doesn't come home on time, she will lose 15 minutes of curfew time starting
the next day. If she then meets the curfew for 3 weeks, she will get back the 15 minutes.

B. Mom will do: *Mom will remind Bettina of the curfew before she goes out, remind her*
that there's no grace period, and praise her for coming in on time. She'll buy the gift
card of Bettina's choosing if she earns it and drive her to the store at Bettina's request
(with a day's notice).

C. Dad will do: *Dad, who starts his workday later than Mom, will be the one to wait up for*
Bettina. When she comes in on time, he'll praise her. If she doesn't come home on time,
he'll tell her about the change in curfew in a businesslike way, with no lecture.

D. Plan for monitoring whether this happens: *Dad will wait up to be sure he*
knows when Bettina gets home. They'll keep a chart and check off the days to keep track
of when the two 3-week periods are up, along with any changes in curfew.

E. Any reminders that will be given. By whom? When?   *See "Mom will do."*

F. Consequences for compliance and noncompliance: *For Bettina, as noted*
above. If Mom doesn't remind Bettina of the curfew or fails to praise her the next day for
obeying it, $1 is added to the total she can earn for 3 weeks of obedience of the new
curfew. If Dad lectures Bettina, another $1 is added.

Appendix B

How to Find a Therapist

A therapist trained in behavioral family therapy, behavioral parent training, or cognitive-behavioral therapy (CBT) is most likely to be able to help you to work with your defiant teenager using the techniques described in this book. Ideally, the therapist should be familiar with the manual for professionals that accompanies this book: *Defiant Teens: A Clinician's Manual for Family Intervention* by Russell A. Barkley, Gwenyth H. Edwards, & Arthur L. Robin (New York: Guilford Press, 1999).

There are several ways to locate such a therapist. First, contact the psychology department of a major university, medical school, or teaching hospital in your area. Ask whether there are any faculty in these settings who are familiar with the *Defiant Teens* approach to family intervention; often faculty in such settings are trained in the latest evidence-based approaches to family intervention and may also have private practices. If they don't practice this approach, they are likely to know mental health professionals in your community who do use it.

Second, go to the websites of one of the major national organizations to which cognitive-behavioral therapists belong: the Association for Behavioral and Cognitive Therapies (*www.abct.org*) or the Academy of Cognitive Therapy (*www.academyofct.org*). Also go to the websites of support organizations for parents of children with ADHD and related conditions and look in their listings of professionals: Children and Adults with Attention-Deficit/Hyperactivity Disorder (*www.chadd.org*) or the Attention Deficit Disorder Association (*www.add.org*).

Third, contact your state psychiatric and psychological associations or go to the website of the American Psychological Association (*www.apa.org*). Click on "Find a psychologist," type in your ZIP code, and you will get a list of psychologists in your area.

When you have located one or more mental health professionals, call or e-mail them to inquire whether they work with families with defiant teens using the approach outlined in this book. Here is a suggested e-mail or phone request:

Dear Dr. [therapist's name],

I am the parent of a teenager with a great deal of defiant behavior, and I am looking for a therapist to work with my spouse, my teenager, and me. I recently read Your Defiant Teen *by Dr. Russell Barkley, Dr. Arthur Robin, and Christine Benton and wish to find a therapist who uses this approach. I found your name through [website or organization]. If you are available, I wish to set up an initial appointment to discuss my situation. My phone number is [insert phone number].*

Thank you,
[your name]

Don't expect most therapists to discuss matters in detail over the phone. Instead, it's wise to go to an initial appointment to see if the therapist is a good match for your needs. Look at this appointment as a "test run" to determine whether the therapist uses the approach you need and whether you "click" interpersonally with the therapist. Do not take your teenager along to this appointment, but do take a list of questions, such as:

1. What experiences have you had working with parents and teenagers using the *Defiant Teens* approach or other cognitive behavioral methods?
2. How do you approach parent–teen conflict and defiant behavior in teenagers?
3. How many sessions and how long does therapy typically last?
4. What are your fees and do you take our insurance?

You want to be confident that the therapist is a good match for your family. It's worth paying for several initial interviews with different therapists to find the right one. After an interview with a therapist, ask yourself the following questions: Did you feel comfortable with this therapist? How do you think your teenager will react to this therapist? Did the therapist seem to have the experience and background necessary to help your family?

If you still cannot find a therapist trained in the *Defiant Teens* approach, try to find a therapist with whom you are comfortable and ask whether that person is willing to learn to use this approach. Therapists can learn to use the approach by attending workshops of the major national organizations mentioned earlier in this appendix.

Resources

Websites

The following websites provide a variety of information and resources, some specific to defiant behavior and some broader sources of information on a range of behavioral, emotional, and cognitive problems in teenagers.

U.S. Organizations

American Academy of Child & Adolescent Psychiatry (AACAP)
www.aacap.org
   A wealth of information, resources, and referrals on teenage psychiatric problems. Check the Facts for Families webpage on ODD; also refer to the Books section below.

American Academy of Pediatrics (AAP)
www.aap.org
   Lots of educational materials available on a variety of childhood and adolescent disorders.

Attention Deficit Disorder Association (ADDA)
www.add.org
   Referrals to professionals and support groups, an e-newsletter, and many articles on specific ADHD-related subjects and other resources.

Children and Adults with Attention-Deficit/Hyperactivity Disorder (CHADD)
www.chadd.org
   Referrals to physicians and local support groups, plus extensive information on ADHD in all age groups.

ConductDisorders.com
www.conductdisorders.com
   A parent forum/message board that also offers resources and useful links on ODD, ADHD, conduct disorders, and other defiance-related problems.

emedicine (WebMD)
www.emedicine.medscape.com/article/918095-overview for information on ODD.

Focus Adolescent Services
www.focusas.com
   A wealth of resources, links, and referrals to organizations, books, residential programs for teens, and more. Lots of information on parenting style and methods, teen behavior problems and other adolescent issues, and adolescent development.

Internet Special Education Resources (ISER)
www.iser.com
   Resources for parents of children with learning disabilities, autism, and ADHD assessment and education.

Mental Health America (formerly the National Mental Health Association)
www.mentalhealthamerica.net
   Referrals to professionals who treat specific disorders and local support groups. Offers a wealth of information and resources on psychological and psychiatric issues in various age groups.

National Alliance on Mental Illness (NAMI)
www.nami.org
   Support groups and advocacy. In particular, check the Child & Adolescent Action Center.

National Institute of Mental Health (NIMH)
www.nimh.nih.gov
   Part of the U.S. Public Health Service, involved in research into juvenile emotional, cognitive, and behavioral disorders.

Society for Adolescent Medicine (SAM)
www.adolescenthealth.org
   Referral service to adolescent health professionals by discipline (including psychologists) for both the United States and abroad.

Students Against Destructive Decisions (SADD)
www.sadd.org
   Founded to fight teenage drunk driving, this grassroots organization has expanded to include in its mission drugs, violence, depression, and suicide. Helpful support and information for struggling teens and parents, including a monthly "Teens Today" article reporting on research in adolescent development and related issues and links to other articles.

U.S. Department of Education
www.ed.gov
   Under "parents," you'll find detailed information about your teen's rights if he or she has a disability, as well as the individualized education program (IEP) process.

Organizations Outside the United States

Australian Clearinghouse for Youth Studies (ACYS)
www.acys.info
   A clearinghouse funded by the Australian government that offers links to a wide variety of resources on adolescent issues.

Canadian Mental Health Association (CMHA)
www.cmha.ca
   A nationwide charitable organization promoting education and offering resources on mental health issues.

Canadian Psychiatric Association
www.cpa-apc.org
   Good source of information on psychiatric issues from the Canadian Academy of Child and Adolescent Psychiatry.

Canadian Psychological Association
www.cpa.ca
   Mainly for professionals, but includes information on many psychological and psychiatric problems.

Headspace
www.headspace.org.au
   Australia's new national youth mental health foundation, which promotes early and effective treatment for young Australians affected by mental illness. Has links to sources of help, including hotlines.

MIND
www.mind.org.uk
   A leading mental health charity in England whose mission is mainly advocacy and education; offers links to articles on youth mental health in the United Kingdom.

Richmond Services Ltd.
www.richmondnz.org
   Leads to mental health services for New Zealand and Australia (and also to some extent for England and Scotland).

Royal College of Psychiatrists
www.rcpsych.ac.uk
   With headquarters in London and branches in Ireland, Northern Ireland, Scotland, and Wales, this organization has information on a range of psychological issues, problems, and age groups.

SANE
www.sane.org
   A charitable organization based in Melbourne dedicated to advocacy, research, and education for and about mental health.

SANE

www.sane.org.uk

A charitable organization based in London with the goals of raising awareness and respect for those with mental health issues, undertaking research into the causes of these problems, and offering support to individuals and families struggling with these difficulties.

Young Minds

www.youngminds.org.uk

The national charity dedicated to improving the mental health of children and adolescents. Besides a Parents' Information Service, it provides readings and resources, information for young people, and links to extensive information on behavior problems (among other mental health issues).

Books

American Academy of Child and Adolescent Psychiatry & Pruitt, D. (2000). *Your adolescent: Emotional, behavioral, and cognitive development from early adolescence through the teen years.* New York: Harper-Collins.

Andrews, L. A. (2004). *Meditation.* London: Franklin Watts.—This slim volume, part of the Scholastic Books LifeBalance series, offers a good introduction to meditation and other forms of relaxation for teens.

Bradley, M. J. (2002). *Yes, your teen is crazy: Loving your kid without losing your mind.* Gig Harbor, WA: Harbor Press.

Cohen, C. (2000). *Raise your child's social IQ.* Silver Spring, MD: Advantage Press.—This is an excellent book for parents on teaching social skills.

Covey, S. (1998). *The 7 habits of highly effective teens.* New York: Fireside.—This book is written by the son of Steven Covey, author of *The 7 Habits of Highly Effective People.* It includes a section called "The 7 Habits of Highly Defective Teens" that humorously warns teens against counterproductive practices like not cooperating.

Cox, A. J. (2006). *Boys of few words: Raising our sons to communicate and connect.* New York: Guilford Press.

Dendy, C. A. (2006). *Teenagers with ADD and ADHD: A guide for parents and professionals* (2nd ed.). Bethesda, MD: Woodbine House.—This is the best parent guide on raising a teen with ADHD.

Edwards, C. D. (1999). *How to handle a hard-to-handle kid: A parent's guide to understanding and changing problem behaviors.* Minneapolis, MN: Free Spirit.

Faraone, S. (2003). *Straight talk about your child's mental health: What to do when something seems wrong.* New York: Guilford Press.

Forgatch, M., & Patterson, G. (2005). *Parents and adolescents living together: Part 2. Family problem solving* (2nd ed.). Champaign, IL: Research Press.

Glasser, H., & Easley, J. (1999). *Transforming the difficult child: The nurtured heart approach.* Tucson, AZ: Nurtured Heart.—This is an outstanding book for parents of children with ODD. DVD, VHS, CD, and cassette are also available. See also Glasser's website: *www.difficultchild.com.*

Goldstein, S., Brooks, R., & Weiss, S. (2004). *Angry children, worried parents: Seven steps to help families manage anger.* Chicago: Specialty Press/A.D.D. Warehouse.

Greene, R. (2005). *The explosive child* (3rd ed.). New York: HarperCollins.—See also Greene's website: *www.explosivechild.com.*

Kindlon, D., & Thompson, M. (1999). *Raising Cain: Protecting the emotional life of boys.* New York: Ballantine.

Last, C. G. (2006). *Help for worried kids: How your child can conquer anxiety and fear.* New York: Guilford Press.—Last describes a variety of relaxation methods for young people.

Miklowitz, D. J., & George, E. L. (2008). *The bipolar teen: What you can do to help your child and your family.* New York: Guilford Press.

Murphy, T., & Oberlin, L. H. (2002). *The angry child: Regaining control when your child is out of control.* New York: Three Rivers Press.

Papalos, D., & Papalos, J. (2006). *The bipolar child: The definitive and reassuring guide to childhood's most misunderstood disorder* (3rd ed.). New York: Broadway Books.

Parrott, L., III. (2000). *Helping your struggling teenager: A parenting handbook on thirty-six common problems.* Grand Rapids, MI: Zondervan.—This book includes relaxation training for teens.

Patterson, G. R., & Forgatch, M. (2005). *Parents and adolescent living together: Part 1. The basics* (2nd ed.). Champaign, IL: Research Press.

Phelan, T. W. (1996). *Self-esteem revolutions in children: Understanding and managing the critical transitions in your child's life.* Glen Ellyn, IL: ParentMagic.

Phelan, T. W. (1998). *Surviving your adolescents: How to manage and let go of your 13–18 year olds* (2nd ed.). Glen Ellyn, IL: ParentMagic.— Video and DVD are also available. See also Phelan's website: *www.parentmagic.com.*

Pipher, M. (1994). *Reviving Ophelia: Saving the selves of adolescent girls.* New York: Ballantine.

Videos

Robin, A. L., & Weiss, S. (1997). *Managing oppositional youth.* Plantation, FL: Specialty Press.

See also book listings above.

Index

About the Authors

Russell A. Barkley, PhD, ABPP, ABCN, is Clinical Professor of Psychiatry and Pediatrics at the Medical University of South Carolina in Charleston. The author of numerous bestselling books for professionals and the public, including *Taking Charge of ADHD* and *Your Defiant Child*, Dr. Barkley has worked with children, adolescents, and families for over 35 years. His website is *www.russellbarkley.org*.

Arthur L. Robin, PhD, is Director of Psychology Training at Children's Hospital of Michigan and Professor of Psychiatry and Behavioral Neurosciences at Wayne State University. Dr. Robin is a practicing psychologist with more than 40 years of clinical experience.

Christine M. Benton is a Chicago-based writer and editor.